BONO ON BONO

BONO ON BONO

CONVERSATIONS

WITH

MICHKA ASSAYAS

WITH

A FOREWORD

BY

BONO

HODDER &
STOUGHTON

Copyright © 2005 by Michka Assayas

First published in Great Britain in 2005 by Hodder and Stoughton
A division of Hodder Headline

A Hodder and Stoughton Book

1 3 5 7 9 10 8 6 4 2

A CIP catalogue record for this title is available from the British Library

Hardback ISBN 0 340 83276 2
Trade paperback ISBN 0 340 89747 3

Printed and bound by
Clays Ltd, St Ives plc

Hodder Headline's policy is to use papers that are natural, renewable and recyclable products and made from wood grown in sustainable forests. The logging and manufacturing processes are expected to conform to the environmental regulations of the country of origin.

Hodder and Stoughton Ltd
A division of Hodder Headline
338 Euston Road
London NW1 3BH

Picture Acknowledgements

©2004 Band Aid Trust/photo Dave Hogan/distributed by Getty Images on behalf of Band Aid Charitable Trust: page 4 bottom. ©Adrian Boot/urbanimage.tv: page 1. © Patrick Brocklebank: page 2 bottom. ©Bill Clark/Corbis Sygma: page 7 bottom. ©Anton Corbijn: page 3 bottom. © Colm Henry: page 2 top. ©Stephen Jaffe/AFP/Getty Images: page 8. © Sam Jones/Time Inc/Time&Life Pictures/Getty Images: page 6. © David McNew/Newsmakers/Getty Images: page 5 top. ©Neal Preston/Corbis: page 3 top. ©Brian Rasic/Rex Features: page 5 bottom. © John Reardon/The Observer/Getty Images: page 4 top. © Ian Waldie/Getty Images: page 7 top.

TO MY CHILDREN: ANTOINE AND EVA
AND TO HIS: JORDAN, EVE, ELIJAH, AND JOHN

ACKNOWLEDGMENTS

I'd like to thank Bono first. He certainly has confirmed his self-awarded reputation of being the world's most faithful *and* unreliable friend. Bono—thanks for your time, though I had to fight for it, and, above all, your invaluable trust and generosity. I doubt a thousand bottles of Chablis Premier Cru will repay that. But I can try small installments . . .

If it weren't for Catriona Garde, these conversations would not have happened. Catriona—you had the patience of an angel in the midst of chaos. I think this halo is getting bigger by the minute.

Paul McGuinness, Edge, Adam, and Larry—thanks for letting him do this. Hope you won't be pulling a face once you've read it.

Ali—thanks for your hospitality in Killiney and Nice. Hope you'll love your cameo.

I would also like to thank Sheila Roche and Dennis Sheehan for their help in Bologna; Susan Hunter, Nadine O'Flynn, and Candida Bottaci at Principle for helping me in Dublin; Christophe and Lorna Marécaut in Nice—you've been wonderful.

Ed Victor—you always said the right thing at the right moment. But your best advice materialized on four wheels. Not forgetting everyone at the agency: Maggie, Linda, Abi, Edina, Cristina, Hitesh, Gráinne.

Andrew Nurnberg—thanks for your encouragement.

Bill Flanagan—we had a great conversation too. Your advice was a rare thing.

Josh Behar—thanks for your enthusiasm.

Julie Grau, Katy Follain, Nick Davies, Olivier Nora, Jean-Paul Enthoven— thanks for your support.

Not least, Clara—thanks for helping me believe in what I've done here.

FOREWORD BY BONO

Michka,

I thought I should drop you a short note on our book project. I just read it back: verbose, pretentious, immodest—and revealing. I wish I didn't recognize myself, but I do. No full stops or commas; long answers to short questions—annoying questions sometimes, but always in the pursuit of truth.

I don't know why I agreed to this, but I did. It probably relates to your first chapter. To be serious for a second, I thought I had gotten away from my father's death. I thought I had escaped lightly into busyness and family. I've always considered myself as good at wailing—"keening," we call it in Ireland. But, as it turns out, I'm better at other people's tragedies. There's no obvious drama in the slow extinguishing of a well-lived life to a common scourge like cancer, but it had a dramatic effect on me and seems to have set off some kind of chain reaction. Maybe you're right, this is as close as I'll get to introspection.

Ali says I haven't been myself and should go on and talk to somebody about what must have been a complicated childhood. She says I'm angry about something, and for fear of her own wrath, I seriously thought about it, but concluded I was too busy.

You, Michka Assayas, became that opportunity to look back into the house of my various lives and tidy my room.

Your exhibitionist patient,

Bono

NICE, JANUARY 21, 2005

INTRODUCTION

What does it take to get Bono on the couch? As he confesses here, "I never talk at length with anybody who's writing or recording. They're usually drinking." It's hard for me to say exactly why I became Bono's talking, drinking, and writing pal, but I can try to explain how it happened.

I first came face-to-face with Bono and U2 in May 1980, in what appears to me as a different lifetime. I sported a kind of bowl haircut then and wore spectacles with thick gray plastic frames. I was trying for a "new wave" preppy look—wide-striped yellow and wine polo shirt and black baggy trousers, tightened over the ankles. It was my first week as a music reporter for a Paris-based magazine called *Le Monde de la musique.* I was not a fraud, but I felt like one. I mean, I was twenty-one, with a degree in French literature and an approximate grasp of the English language. *Le Monde de la musique* was a very serious and sad-looking mag—it was printed in black-and-white and was mainly devoted to covering opera, prestigious conductors, and jazz virtuosos. They viewed rock music as a *mouvement culturel,* which was their way of referring to the latest musical trends coming from London. For my first assignment, they sent me there to check out the scene and suss out the Zeitgeist. The *New Musical Express* was my bible then. Each week, its writers Paul

Morley and Ian Penman would champion some obscure band from Manchester whose first single (and choice of haircut and record sleeve) was supposed to set off an aesthetical and existential earthquake. I would write down the names of these bands and managed to meet most of them. Some were great—Young Marble Giants, especially, who made just one extraordinary album, *Colossal Youth*, before vanishing. Some were good—Psychedelic Furs, the Monochrome Set. Some were . . . well, interesting. U2—I didn't know them. I hadn't listened to a single note of their music before I set off to interview them.

The four members of U2 shared a Spartan two-room furnished flat in Collingham Gardens, near South Kensington. They struck me as incredibly warm and welcoming people. I found myself immediately under the spell of that voluble little guy from Dublin with the broad smile and funny name; I remember listening to him, dreading somehow that the music wouldn't be as good as the talk. Most musicians I'd interviewed were kind of nonplussed by my abstract questioning, probably wondering what the hell that French windbag was sputtering about. Not Bono. He looked as overexcited and insecure as I was, eager to dive into what I thought were deep subjects—the importance of youth cults in London, how U2 refused to fit into them, how the utterance of the soul had been tragically neglected in modern music, etc. To make his point, he'd try out different ideas, getting more and more heated in the process. His face would light up when he'd eventually hit upon the right one. The place was so small he'd walk and bump into walls while talking (now I remember that all of U2 would unfold their sleeping bags in the same room). I kept developing instant theories about practically everything that went through my head. What I didn't fully grasp myself, Bono would get anyway. (To quote Bob Dylan's words in *Chronicles*, "When Bono or me aren't exactly sure about somebody, we just make it up." So I have company.) I've kept other visual memories from that day: The Edge's jeans, covered with punk graffiti, his benevolent smile and measured speech; Adam's smile too, albeit of a more mischievous kind; and Larry, looking like a fifteen-year-old, hanging his head throughout the interview. At the end of it, they gave me a copy of their first single on Island Records, "11 O'Clock Tick Tock." It had a navy-blue sleeve, with black "new wave" streaks. To no immediate avail—I had no turntable while in London. So I had to see them play live in order to decide if the music measured up to the talk.

That very night, U2 performed in a pub called the Hope and Anchor. Or was it the Moonlight Club? I can't be sure. There weren't many of us there: about seventy, I would say. I felt excited and embarrassed at the same time. When a club is half full, it looks like everyone involved—band, audience, club owners—might have made the wrong decision. Thinking back on that night, I remember this tall guy with long hair who stood in the audience right in front of the low stage, totally pissed, ranting loudly and cryptically between numbers. I watched him, wondering if he was going to attack someone, on or off the stage. But the band didn't seem to care. A punk singer would have attacked the troublemaker, or encouraged the crowd to do so, would have fed on the tension anyway. Not Bono, not U2. They didn't seem to see or hear that tiresome chap. Bono probably climbed on the PA stacks, or something to that effect. In hindsight, I think he and U2 were sort of blind to the people there. We weren't a particular audience in a particular club in London, but rather a kind of makeshift template for the ideal audience, while U2 themselves were not this particular band from Dublin, but a makeshift template for the ideal band. Although they were quite aware there were only seventy of us there, they were busy focusing on something greater though invisible. I guess I was busy focusing on that too. Both band and audience felt the presence of an unborn beauty that night. We made a connection; it has been a strong one ever since.

During the first half of the eighties, I would champion U2 and steadfastly review their records and concerts in *Rock and Folk* (a monthly magazine) and *Libération* (a daily). When Bono and Edge first visited Paris, I took them to Notre-Dame; it was their idea, not mine. I still have the sight of Bono breaking through the traffic, limping across like the hunchback of Notre-Dame. That was *Jackass* while Steve-O was still in kindergarten. I couldn't swear to it, but I am almost certain that Bono had his first meal in a Parisian restaurant in my company. I'd go to see U2 backstage regularly. In that long-forgotten era, they didn't apply the concept of military security to music groups. Caked with sweat, Bono looked like a groggy boxer. What I loved about U2's music is that it had a sort of inspired clumsiness to it. They'd be daring in an unrealistic way—that was the utopian and retro part of it—but, at the same time, quite aware of their limits in a very realistic way, and determined to make the best of it by producing the biggest and most visceral noise—that was the punk and contemporary part of it. They were too unhip for the hip, and, for a while, too challenging for the unhip. They were entering a wide empty continent, still unpopulated—that long white frozen steppe you'd see them riding horses on in the "New Year's Day" video. Lots of people would eventually follow them and colonize that wide open space, but in those days it felt lonely and bleak; you weren't really sure you wouldn't be left stranded and forgotten about, stuck there with those clueless Irish people and feeling silly about yourself.

In 1987, *The Joshua Tree* was released and went to number one on nearly every list. Some people thought U2 were the new Rolling Stones. This was ironic because with each new record they made, the band thought it was committing commercial suicide. And each time, success came back with a vengeance, as if irritated by their contempt for it. It took the arrogance of their wanting to make a "pop" record about ten years later (*Pop*) to bring about (relative) commercial disappointment. Like most critics, I'd enjoyed being there and being part of it, but I'd rather push the "fast forward" button on their outright colonization of the music world. Even though I thought some of their songs were great, my heart simply didn't beat at the same pace. So I lost track of them. A sort of shyness overcame me too. These guys were becoming superstars, and that created a kind of awkwardness. The thing is, U2 didn't need people like me anymore. So it felt natural to take a back seat. Sure, I thought *Achtung Baby* was great, but nobody needed to hear that from me.

A few years later, I grew out of this shyness. That unbending suspicion I had about huge success was quietly loosening. So I took a kind of ex-boyfriend initiative. In 1997, I phoned the editor of the French weekly magazine *Les Inrockuptibles,* and asked him to send me on assignment to interview Bono and Edge, who were then promoting the *Pop* album. I guess I wanted to know whether the past was somehow still breathing inside of us. Because inasmuch as I had been irrelevant to U2's destiny for such a long time, I felt U2 had become irrelevant to my life for too many years. Unconsciously, something inside me rejected this notion and wanted to make it right. So I went back to Dublin for the first time in thirteen years. When he entered the hall of Hanover Quay studios and saw me waiting there, Bono looked flabbergasted, as though I had come back from the dead. Then he came up to me and gave me a long, silent hug. He kept on saying: "I had no idea it was you . . . I had *no idea* . . ." In the blink of an eye, thirteen years were reduced to a speck of dust. We walked down to a pub, and pretty soon I forgot about the Che Guevara cap and the cigarillo. I remember I confided my skepticism about the whole Zoo TV thing, and we had a bit of an argument about it. It felt we were simply resuming the ongoing conversation we had started out in Collingham Gardens. I realized that, in my mind, it had never broken off.

On my way back to Paris, I started searching for a reason to see more of Bono in the future. That's when I thought of collaborating on a book with him. I proposed to follow U2 during the PopMart tour, keeping a sort of diary. But Bill Flanagan had already written *U2: At the End of the World,* and done a fantastic job. Bono and I talked on the phone, and he said that the band would have agreed to it, except for Larry, who had apparently said: "I don't want to be in a book ever again." When the PopMart tour stopped in Paris a few months later, I was there. The following morning, when I came home, a message had been left on my answering machine. A sort of breathy voice came out: "This is an old Irish friend . . . I called out your name during the show, did you hear it? . . . I have a terrible hangover. . . . You can call me back, I am staying at the Royal Monceau, under the name Penny." I couldn't make it this time. We had to wait for four more years. Not such a long time, according to our standards.

In July 2001, U2 gave a most extraordinary performance at the Palais Omnisports de Bercy, in Paris. I went backstage and congratulated Bono. He looked at me with this intense gaze of his and, completely out of the blue, just said: *"We've got to make a book together."* Really? During the show, he'd shouted out my name from the stage (again), during the break in "I Will Follow," when he recited a list of all the places that U2 had played in Paris. So, that's it. The singer from the number-one rock 'n' roll band in the world calls out your name in front of twenty thousand people. Somehow, you've got to answer that call.

I wrote a letter to Bono after that night, saying:

Here we are in 2001. You give one of the best performances of your career, and everything seems utterly natural to me: talking to you, linking the past and the present, etc. So an idea crosses my mind. You know, there is this tradition of books made not about, but with painters, writers, or cinematographers: some interviewer stages a series of dialogues centered on one specific aspect of their life and work (let's say: childhood and beginnings, their relationship with a particular artist, their achievements and failures, etc.), and then it gets published as a dialogue, a conversation. I find these sort of books very enjoyable, because they are quite the opposite of typical "rock books." Of course, one could argue that you are still relatively young to do this. But you know better than I do that 23 years of experience in your field means very old and wise. If this is meant to be, it will be. But if it's not . . . well, you know it might still happen when we're 60.

So here we are. In August 2001, at the end of the Elevation Tour, Bono lost his father. Months later, he agreed to start working on these interviews. While we were talking, I often felt that Bono and I resembled two elderly people in a convalescent home, with all the time in the world. Well, that's not really true, because Bono would usually break it off with his usual phrase "I'm gonna have to run"—which he duly did. When it stopped, I always felt I was waking up from a dream, but those were deep dreams, and urgent ones. In the words Bono used to sum up my approach, "I went straight for the jugular." I gave each conversation everything I had. I kept thinking: this might be the last one, maybe I won't get to talk to him anymore . . . But at the same time, Bono's words seemed to spring from a very serene and deep part of himself. He spoke with a compelling quietness and uncanny focus. The conversations were marked by an odd combination of urgency and serenity. It's not so much a paradox as a state akin to being suspended in the eye of the hurricane. I guess some of the greatest music comes from that place. I'd love to believe that a book could come from there too.

MICHKA ASSAYAS, NOVEMBER 2004

1. STORIES TO TELL THAT ARE NOT SONGS

This first conversation (presented here in four installments, i.e. chapters 1, 2, 3, and 4) took place in late 2002 in Bono's house by the sea in Killiney, near Dublin.

On a gloomy November day, Bono picked me up at the Clarence Hotel (that he co-owns with Edge) in his Mercedes. I noticed that he'd apparently given up ignoring red lights and driving the wrong way down one-way streets. He owns a dentist's car, and drives it like a dentist.

We drove alongside a gray sea through heavy rain. Bono talked about his new role as an ambassador for DATA (Debt, AIDS, and Trade for Africa). He also mentioned that he had written a play in just one week for an American director. When we pulled up to his house, the electricity was down because of the heavy rain, and the security gate had collapsed. Bono helped the caretaker shove it open. During a quick lunch, we chatted with his wife, Ali, who was busy organizing a fashion show to benefit the families of victims of the Chernobyl catastrophe. Bono showed me around the house and took me to the pavilion where Mr. and Mrs. Hewson (Bono and Ali) put up distinguished visitors: the walls were covered with letters from Bill Clinton, Salman Rushdie, Quincy Jones, and others. Though I looked far, I could see nothing from the Pope. We came back to the main house. I followed Bono to a small room that faced the sea, as an extension of his study. He took off his shoes and tucked himself up on the couch. We would be visited at regular intervals by his elder daughter, Jordan, and his two little boys, Elijah and John. Sometimes, Bono would halt the conversation to make a phone call. I remember he'd been expecting one from Prince, but got one from Bruce Springsteen instead. He was trying to organize the writing of a song to be performed during halftime at the Super Bowl, so that Americans would consider it a "patriotic act" to help Africans ill with AIDS get the drugs they need. Unfortunately, I don't think it went anywhere. We finished the day watching the MTV awards and eating pizza: U2 did not win any of the awards they'd been nominated for. Each time, though, Bono guessed who the winner would be, while Jordan and her younger sister Eve, who had arrived in the meantime, lay on the couch and sent text messages. Elijah was fascinated by Christina Aguilera's performance. A few weeks before, enthralled by Kylie Minogue, he had suggested to his father that he invite her for dinner one of these days.

You have given plenty of interviews. Why is it that you want to reveal yourself in a book now? After all, you've had plenty of opportunities . . .

Well, I'm a person that actually doesn't like to look back in my work, in my day, or in general. But maybe this is the moment. There are stories to tell that are not songs.

There is one important thing you just said off the record, before we got started, about your father, whom you lost recently. You mentioned his sharp wit and sarcasm. I was wondering: how come it never came out in your songs?

Yeah, it's interesting. My father acted kind of jaded . . . nonplussed. It was an act, but the world just couldn't impress him. So as a kid I wanted to be the opposite. Especially as a teenager when for periods it felt like my father had become my enemy. It happens . . . And so you reject the enemy's weapons of choice, which was his wit, his sarcasm.

That's a pretty tough portrait . . . What was your father really like?

As I say, a very charming, very amusing, very likable man, but he was deeply cyn-ical about the world and the characters in it: affection for the few, a sort of scant praise on even them. As I was saying, I got to make peace with him, but never really to become his friend. My brother did, which is great. Nothing extraordi-nary here, just Irish macho male stuff. We never really could talk. Even in his last days, when I used to come and visit him in the hospital, all he could do was whis-per. He had Parkinson's. I would lie beside him at night on a roll-up bed. Being sick, he didn't have to converse. I could tell you he was happy about that. In the day I sometimes would sit there and just draw him. I did a whole series of draw-ings of his hospital room, all the wires and tubes. Occasionally I would read to him . . . *[pause]* Shakespeare. He loved Shakespeare. If I read the Bible, he would just scowl. *[laughs]* It was like: "Fuck off!" In fact, the last thing he said was "Fuck off." I was lying beside him in the middle of the night and I heard a shout. And of course it would have been days of whispers. So I called the nurse. The nurse came in. He was back to whispers, and we both put our ears to his mouth. "What are you saying? Are you OK? Do you need anything? Do you need any help?" And the nurse was saying: "Bob, are you OK? So what are you saying?" "What's that? What d'you need?" "*Fuck off!*" He said: "Would you ever fuck off and get me out of here? I wanna go home. This place is a prison cell." And they were his last words. Not romantic, but revealing. I really had a sense that he wanted out of not just the room, but out of his body and his skeleton. That's clas-sic him. He would always pour salt—and vinegar—onto the wound. He could meet the most beautiful girl in the world. In fact, Julia Roberts . . . I remember introducing her in a club, and he goes: "Pretty woman? My arse." *[laughs]*

You know what it reminds me of? Brian Wilson's father . . . Have you read about it?

A little bit, yeah.

Brian Wilson's father dreamed of making it in the music business, like your father who fancied being an opera singer. He was a very severe presence

when the Beach Boys rehearsed. Brian Wilson kept on coming up with those amazing songs, and his father would go: "This won't be a hit. Get some proper work done." He was abusive, both verbally and physically. So there is an interesting thread there: maybe the harsher your father is on you, the more creative you can become, sometimes.

Yeah. If you meet up with two of my best friends, Gavin and Guggi,* sometime, you'll find that their two fathers gave them a lot more abuse than mine. The three of us grew up on Cedarwood Road: Guggi's now a painter, Gavin's a great performer, writing songs for a kind of "nouveau cabaret" and score for movies. But what separated them, I guess, is that they ran from the scold of their respective fathers to the bosom of their mothers. And I probably would have too, but she wasn't around. So that created its own heat, and looking back on it now, some rage.

Rage at what?

Emptiness . . . an empty house . . . aloneness . . . realizing I needed people.

You mean you wanted friends to fill in for your mother, and that made you much angrier.

I think so. And I think something else as well. If you wake up in the morning with a melody in your head, as I do, it's all about how much you compromise that melody to take it out of your head and put it into music. I'm a lousy guitar player and an even lousier piano player. Had I not got Edge close by who was an extraordinarily gifted complex musician, I would be hopeless. Had I not got Larry and Adam, these melodies would not be grounded. But it's still very difficult for me to have to rely. Your weakness, the blessing of your weakness is it forces you into friendships. The things that you lack, you look for in others, but there're times when you just become angry when you think: if only I

---

* Fionan Hanvey (a.k.a. Gavin Friday) and Derek Rowen (a.k.a. Guggi) created in 1978 the Virgin Prunes, an avant-garde punk rock band where Dick Evans, The Edge's elder brother, started out as well.

could get to this place . . . These melodies I hear in my head, they're just so much more interesting than the one that I'm able to play. Rage, there's a rage in me that I have to rely on others, actually, even though I'm very good at relying on others. And we are, I should say, in our group, the best example I know of how to rely on others.

What's so special about that?

It's the thing Brian Eno always speaks about. He says: "They should study that in the Smithsonian, how the four of you get on, how the politics of it work, the accommodation of each other by each other, it's quite something." But at the same time, it's uncomfortable sometimes. Think about that. Isn't that a frightening thing? You rely on your lover, you rely on your friends, and finally you have to rely on God if you want to become whole. But we don't like it. We do resent our lovers, especially the idea of relying on your friends to be whole. That means that on your own, you're . . . *[pause]* that old Zen fucking idea. You're the one hand clapping. *[laughs]*

This need to be carried by a group . . . did you become aware of it after you lost your mother as a young teenager? Or is it something you had in mind before?

As a kid I was actually not that interested in other kids.

I'm feeling there's a contradiction there. I have to rely on my own experience in order to understand yours. Like you, I had an elder brother with whom I felt very close. I could rely on him, which gave me the freedom to be a solitary child and feel protected at the same time. Whereas, from what you're telling me, for you it was a matter of survival to rely on your friends.

Not early on, you're quite right. Early on, I had supreme confidence in myself, and I was probably arrogant with it. I was very able intellectually in a lot of ways. I was popular. As a child, I played chess; I was pretty good at it. I played an international competition when I was twelve. What a pain in the arse!

Did you win?

No, but I did OK. And people made a fuss over me being a kid playing against adults. But the fact that my father taught me the game meant I had to learn to beat him as soon as I could. Maybe he let me win. But it felt great, and I've been playing chess ever since with declining results. But . . . confidence? Yes, plenty of it. And then it cracked. Every teenager goes through an awkward phase, and that was just exacerbated, I suppose, by there not being anyone in the house. The death of my mother really affected my confidence. I would go back to my house after school, but it wasn't a home. She was gone. Our mother was gone, the beautiful Iris . . . I felt abandoned, afraid. I guess fear converts to anger pretty quickly. It's still with me.

What else does it convert to?

I like to be around people.

Where?

One of the things that I love to do is to go to lunch. And I like to drink. I eat well.

Yes, I've noticed that. And actually wondered about it.

I'll gravitate towards the best restaurant in the city. It's not very rock 'n' roll! I think I go because, when I was a kid, food had no love at all in it. I really resented it. I couldn't taste it because she . . . my mother wasn't there.

You mean you had to cook for yourself at a very early age.

I even went as far as robbing groceries from the shops, and giving the money I was given by my father for groceries to my friends. I hated mealtimes. Remember this thing called "Smash"? It was an awful idea. You would pour boiling water into these astronaut-type tablets and they would turn into potatoes, then put them in the same pot as baked beans or something, then eat out of the pot, not even on a plate, in front of the TV.

You are describing a French chef's idea of hell, there.

It was comic tragedy. My brother, who used to work in the computer division of the national airline, discovered that he could buy airline food at a cheap rate. So he used to bring these packaged meals home, and our fridge was full of it. So I used to come on home from school and I would eat the airline food. Then an amazing thing happened. Our high school was near the airport. They didn't do lunches then, but they decided they were gonna do school lunches. So they bought them at the airport. So, I used to eat airline food at lunch. I would go home, eat the same fucking airline food for dinner. What happens then? You join a rock 'n' roll band and spend the rest of your life eating airline food. *[laughs]* It's enough to drive a fellow to a posh restaurant and might explain my expanding waistline. By the way, I'm not ready for my fat Elvis period yet. Stick around for the opera . . . Oh, that's why you're here . . . OK, back to the couch.

Time for a hamburger, here, maybe.

Seriously, I think my whole creative life goes back to when my world collapsed, age fourteen. I don't wanna oversell this, a lot of people had much bigger hills to climb. Wasn't it the Dalai Lama who said: "If you want to meditate on life, start with death"? Not girls, not cars, not sex and drugs . . . The first thing I started writing about was death. What a bummer this boy is! Actually, *Boy*, our first album, is remarkably uplifting, considering the subject matter.

And what was that?

Oddly enough, it's similar to our new album, *How to Dismantle an Atomic Bomb*. It's something to do with the end of innocence. But in our first album, it was being savored, not remembered. In that period, everyone was knowing. We were celebrating our lack of knowledge of the world. I thought, No one's

13

written that story. No one would be raw enough. Rock 'n' roll is rarely raw in an emotional sense. It can be sexual. It can be violent and full of bile. Demons can appear to be exorcised, but they're not really, they're usually being exercised. The tenderness, the spirituality, the real questions that are on real people's minds are rarely covered. There was a lot of posturing and posing. With that first record, I thought I would just let myself be that child, write about innocence as it's about to spoil. Rock 'n' roll had never taken on the subject of innocence and loss of innocence before, outside of romance, that is.

What I'm interested in is how you had the idea to face this very subject you just talked about. It is interesting to go back to this part of your life, where you had only dreams, and you had no clue about how you were going to fulfill them. Specifically, I want to know if your relationship with your brother, who is seven years older than you, helped you gain confidence.

It did and it didn't. I mean, he taught me to play the guitar. I learned to play on his guitar the songs that he had learned. As an example, he had the Beatles' *Songbook*, the one with the psychedelic illustrations. That book blew my mind. In fact, that book still blows my mind.

What was the first Beatles song that you learned?

"Dear Prudence." All the things you could do with the C chord. Neil Diamond . . . that's another songbook he had. I loved the "Diamond." A song called "Play Me." *[sings it]* Genius . . .

So back to your brother. Did you get on with him?

Yes, but we used to fight—physically fight.

Most children fight. What was so special about this?

Because you would have this sixteen-year-old little Antichrist who resents the house that he's living in. As I say, I'm sure I was a pain in the arse to be around. My brother would come home from work, I'd be sitting there with my mates and be watching TV. I wouldn't have done the washing up or something I said I would do. He would say something or he'd slam the door; we'd end up in a row. *[laughs]* There was literally blood on our kitchen walls, years later. I mean, we could really go at it.

But when your mother died, I'm sure he supported you. He had turned twenty by then.

He's a great man. My brother couldn't tell a lie. Back then he was trying his best. I remember once we had a big fight, and I threw a knife at him. *[laughs]* I didn't throw it to kill him; I just threw it to scare him. And it stuck into the door: *boing* . . . And he looked down at it, and I looked at it. And I realized: I didn't mean to, but I could have killed him. And I think both of us wept, and both of us admitted that we were just angry at each other because we didn't know how to grieve, you see . . . Because my mother was never mentioned.

How do you mean: never?

After she died, my father didn't talk about her. So it never came up. So that's why I don't have any memories of my mother, which is strange.

It *is* strange, because you were fourteen. I read that she died after she came back from her own father's funeral. Is that so?

She collapsed at the funeral of her own father, picked up and carried away by mine. She never regained consciousness. Well, actually, we don't know if she did or she didn't. My father, at his most fetal, when he was losing it or we'd been having a big row, would say: "I promised your mother on her deathbed that . . ." Then, he never finished the sentence. These and other things, I would have liked him to have coughed up at the end.

Do you feel there are questions you wanted to ask your father that remain unanswered?

Yes.

But why didn't you ask them?

I tried to. He didn't want to answer them.

Like what?

I wanted to get into the conversation where I could actually ask him why he was the way he was. I have discovered some interesting family history since, which is extraordinary. It's not something I want to talk about now. But no, he would disappear into silence and wit.

What is it exactly that you wished you knew about his way?

So closed, I suppose . . . And so disinterested, in a certain sense. As I say, my father's advice to me, without ever speaking it, was: "Don't dream! To dream is to be disappointed," which would be a pity, wouldn't it, never to dream . . . And, of course, this is where megalomania must have begun. To never have a big idea was his thing. That's all I'm interested in.

But how was he trying to put you off?

"Why would you want to go to university?" I mean, he was confused, but in the end he said: "Yeah . . . go to college. Sure, I'll help you . . ." He'd eventually pay for guitar lessons, but it didn't come easily to him. And yet the thing he regretted the most in his life is that he hadn't become a musician and a singer. I mean, that's very hard to figure out. I am now the father of four children, and I cannot imagine thinking like that. But his way of guarding you from being disillusioned was by not letting you have illusions in the first place. At some point he stopped reaching outside of himself. I think he maybe had to cut off something, and he didn't want his kids to go through that. Either that or he was just perverse. I can't figure it out. I mean, what else? What other explanation is there?

So what did he think would become of you?

Hmm . . . I think . . . either join the civil service, like he did, which was a safe job, which you couldn't be fired from . . . or a traveling salesman. A lot of our family were traveling salesmen. And of course that is what I have become!

In a way, possibly.

Oh no, in more than just a way. I am sure of it. I am very much a traveling salesman. And that, if you really want to know, is how I see myself. I sell songs from door to door, from town to town. I sell melodies and words. And for me, in my political work, I sell ideas. In the commercial world that I'm entering into, I'm also selling ideas. So I see myself in a long line of family sales people. I really do. Thank God for my Uncle Jack!

So there were success stories in your family, on your mother's side.

One of her eldest brothers was very successful in the insurance business. He went away to London, and then all over the world. They all did very well, but he did extremely well. I think that was another thing they thought I could become—an insurance salesman. For a circus performer who never looked for a net, that's pretty funny, isn't it? Anyway, it's a wonderful thing—I have to tell you—to come out of an environment where you really didn't have to achieve anything, isn't it? It's usually the opposite from that. But, God bless them, I was a very unruly kid. And when my mother died, that turned into re-bellion. So I can't really blame my father for not seeing my future as being bright, because he saw me setting fire to myself. I wasn't interested in school, though I was pretty good at it. It's really funny, you know, my grades were at the top of the class, until this period. Also, most of the people I was hanging around with weren't interested in school. So I don't want to hold him to too much blame.

Because you were trouble.

Yeah, that was really it.

Eventually you went to university, though.

Yeah, I did. Because my school friends were going. I was even interested in ideas then—I've always been interested in ideas. I mean, I was in university for two weeks, doing an arts degree in English and history. I would have loved that.

How do you mean "two weeks"?

I had falsely matriculated, they told me. In the National University, you are supposed to speak the national language, and I didn't. I had flunked Irish, and they found that out. They threw me out of college, even though they had accepted me on my other results.

How did your relationship with your father evolve after your mother died? I guess you've gone through various stages until his recent death.

After my mother died, I think I tortured my brother and my father. There were three men living alone in a house. There were some awful times that we shared, really, about as low as you can get for three men. I remember, physically, my father trying to knock me out. I never returned fire, but it was hard. Mostly, they were comical moments. He worked out some of his own anxieties by so-called "worrying about me." I'd be seventeen, and I'd be going out to punk rock gigs, and coming back. He'd be waiting for me at the top of the stairs, with some heavy artillery. *[laughs]* It was like an obstacle course for me and my gang of friends: how to get back in the house without waking him up.

I guess you gave the poor man many a sleepless night. Do you remember a particular episode?

I used to climb up the two floors on the drainpipe, and then I would reach over to the bathroom window, cross to the window—quite a tricky maneuver—put my hand in the window, open and get in, and go down, and let my friends in, so we can hang out some more. I remember, like, four in the morning, just as I'm making the most difficult part of the maneuver, my father wakes up and goes *[impersonating]*: "Is that you? Is that you?" And I'm outside his bedroom window, hanging out over the housing estate. I'm going *[mutters, putting his hand over his mouth]*: "Mmmmh. Yeah, it's me, yeah."—"Hurry up! And go to bed"—"Mmmh. Yeah, OK . . ." And he doesn't know I'm actually hanging outside his window like, fuck, I'm about to fall off and break every bone of my body. *[laughs]*

You make it sound like he frightened you a lot.

Not really. I guess it was just a combative relationship. We were very unusual, our community. Not every father has two kids calling for their son, wearing Doc Martens, sporting a Mohawk and an occasional dress. Or sometimes Guggi would call to the door on a horse. Because we were surrealists from a very early age, we thought this was very funny. Once, when we fell out, in my twenties, my mates came to wrap my car in tissue paper—the entire car—with dozens and dozens of eggs, turned it into papier-mâché, to seal it like in a cocoon of tissue and eggs. And when I woke up, they were firing eggs at me. Only problem was my father woke up, and he slept with a weapon under his pillow.

You mean a gun?

No. It was like an iron bar. So the two of us, myself and my father, were running down the road after my mates, both of us armed to the teeth. I mean, it was comical! And he was *[impersonating his father running out of breath]*, "I'm having a heart attack . . . I'm having a heart attack . . . Those fucking bastards! I'll get them . . ."

Why did you keep living with him, then?

He gave me a year at home, bed and board, free of charge. He said: "You got one year. If at the end of this year, things aren't happening for your band, you gotta go and get a job." Pretty generous when you think about it. He started to mellow. There was one extraordinary moment I remember when he really helped me out. This big shot came over to see the band, and offered us a publishing deal. It was a big moment for us, because we were really flat broke. And with the money that he was offering, we booked a tour of the U.K. We still hadn't got a record deal. We said: "On that tour, we'll get a record deal." But, on the eve of that tour, the publisher rang up and halved the money, knowing that we had to take it, because we'd already hired the van, the lights, the whole thing. The stories you hear—right?—about the music business as full of bottom-feeders are of course true. But we told this man to shove it up his own arse. We went to our families, and asked them for five hundred pounds each. My father gave it, Edge's father gave it, and I think Larry's father gave it. So the mood of the relationship, as you're asking me about, starts to improve.

Did your father eventually tell you he was proud of your success?

Uh . . . Yeah, I think he was proud, in some ways. I took him to the United States for the first time in the mid-eighties. He'd never been there, and he came in to see a U2 show in Texas. And I thought this would be amazing for him to see this. I got Willie Williams, our lighting designer, to have a Super Trooper focused on the sound platform, and at the right moment, I told the audience: "You know, there's somebody here tonight that's never been to Texas"—they scream and hoot—"that's never been to the U.S."—more screaming—"that's never been to a U2 show in the U.S."—they're going bananas—"LADIES AND GENTLEMEN OF THE LONE STAR STATE, I WANT TO INTRODUCE YOU TO MY FATHER, BOB HEWSON. THAT'S HIM THERE!" The light comes on, and my dad stands up. What does he do? He starts waving his fist at me. It was a great moment, really. Then, after the show, after coming offstage, he came back. I'm usually a bit dizzy and walking into walls for ten minutes. Normally no one would talk to me—I just need some moments to climb down a few gears. I heard footsteps. I turned round. It was my father, and he looked . . . almost emotional. *[laughs]* I said to myself, "God, he's actually going to say something. This is the moment I've waited all my life for . . ." I think there's tears in his eyes. He's putting his hand out to me, I put my hand out to him, and he looked at me with those red eyes. He said: "Son . . . *[big pause]* you're very professional . . ." *[laughs]*

Professional?! That's not quite the impression you made on me then.

That's fantastic, isn't it? I mean, especially if you came from punk rock, the last thing that's on your mind is being professional. But no, he was proud. I think he always probably found me very pretentious, which is probably right. I think he still found me a little preposterous, which I think is probably right. I think, like a lot of fathers with their sons, like no one else they know where to finger you. And he had a very, very wicked sense of humor.

Are you implying that he taught you valuable lessons for your life as a rock star?

He took the Dublin position of "My son, the fucking idiot." That was the whole thing. So when he walked into that kitchen, you see, downstairs, where there were those presses [Irish and Scottish for *cupboards*]—they're still there—he went: *[shouting]* "Ha! *[claps hands]* Did they see you coming, or what? You big eejit! Antiques . . . Ha! They're rabbit hutches. You wouldn't keep animals in them. You probably paid a fortune for them, haven't you? You fool." Any risk you were taking, he'd just look at you with his eye raised and would just shake his head in disbelief at your stupidity. "Oh dear, oh dear . . . You really didn't see that one coming, did you?" So, after years and years of things not utterly falling apart as he was expecting, he became kind of bemused at his own bad weatherman. My brother was always very industrious, a very innovative kind of a fellow, very savvy in business, knew how to make a buck, and ambitious in that sense. But I never showed any of that interest in making money at all. So my father thought this was very funny that I started to accumulate some cash.

He was right, I would say.

He was right. He thought: "God must have a sense of humor; he has given my son who never had interest in cash far too much cash. Now let's all have a bit of a laugh watching him flitter it away, because this boy obviously is going to blow it on all the wrong things."

What was he like with your kids?

He loved kids, loved his grandchildren. His big thing, of course, was, when I would have children, I would find out what it was like to be a father. The pain, the torture, et cetera. So when I went and told him that Ali was pregnant, he burst out laughing. He couldn't stop laughing. I said: "What are you laughing at?" He said *[very low voice]*: "Revenge."

So was he right? Has your experience of fatherhood been as difficult as his?

No. There's rarely a raised voice in our house. Ali's mood prevails. It's kind of serene in comparison.

And how did your father get along with Ali?

Oh, very well. Women loved him. He was completely charming and he was great company. And as long as you didn't want to get too close, he was happy. I think he could reveal himself to women a lot easier than to men, which is something I probably have in common with him. I think he was a very great friend. He had a lot of woman friends. And I do too. So there must be something there.

Did he give you any advice on how to handle your money?

"Don't trust anyone."

Did you follow him on that?

I absolutely didn't. Trust is very important to me. Let me digress. You know, in the supermarkets, they have a way of pricing. It's a digital readout: price-coding. So now, when you bring your food, you put it up and they just read it. Edge was telling me about this guy who recently did a study in MIT: ten percent of all accounting through this system is erroneous. Except the ten percent works both ways, which is to say . . .

...that sometimes you win ...

Sometimes you win, sometimes you lose. And it's completely even. So no one has really bothered about the system's problems. Therein, in a way, is a lesson about trust. If you trust people, you are going to be burnt ten percent of the time. I'm quite a trusting person; however, ten percent of the time, you're going to find yourself in situations that you wouldn't have, had you been more cautious. I mean, you're gonna find yourself in very good situations that you wouldn't have, unless you took the risk. I think, that's the difference between myself and my father.

What are the things that you feel most guilty about now regarding your relationship with your father?

Mainly, I just think he was dealing with a precocious child. Can't have been easy, and especially when he found himself trying to do it all alone. I just feel . . . I'm angry about . . . there was a sort of father-son tension, that I probably just let go of in the last few weeks. Ali said to me that since his death, I haven't been myself, and that I have been a lot more aggressive, and quicker to anger, and showing some of my father's irascible side. The Italians take a long time to grieve. You see them wear black for a year. When my father died, I went on a short vacation, which turned into a euphemism for "drinks outing." I don't like to abuse alcohol—anything you abuse will abuse you back. But it's fair to say I went to Bali for a drink. With my friend Simon [Carmody, screenwriter], we just headed off. I wanted to blow it out a bit, get the monkey off my back. But when I returned, funnily enough, it was still there. I think it's been around with me a lot. And so just on Easter, I went up to the church in a little village where we live in France, and I just felt this was the moment that I had to let it go. An emotional volcano had gone off during the week before Easter, and I just wanted to find out. I wanted to deal with the source of whatever it was. In this little church, on Easter morning, I just got down on my knees, and I let go of whatever anger I had against my father. And I thanked God for him being my father, and for the gifts that I have been given through him. And I let go of that. I wept, and I felt rid of it.

Once and for all?

I think *How to Dismantle . . .* also allowed me to vent all that stuff. The atomic bomb, it's obviously him in me. Yeah, "Sometimes You Can't Make It On Your Own" is my swan song for him. I sang it at his funeral *[recites, but does not sing]*: *Tough, you think you got the stuff / You're telling me and everyone you're hard enough / Well, you don't have to put up a fight / You don't have to always be right / Let me take some of the punches for you tonight / Listen to me now: I need to let you know you don't have to go it alone / Sometimes you can't make it on your own.* It's like a Phil Spector kind of a deal, very fifties. There's a verse I left out of the recording: *When I was a young boy in the suburbs of Cedarwood / I wanted to be great because good would not be good enough / Now that I'm older, I don't see things any clearer / We're closer now but still a long way off / I need you to know you don't have to go it alone / Sometimes you can't make it on your own.* And then it goes into this middle eight which is amazing. I scream and it goes: *Sing, you're the reason I sing / You're the reason the opera is in me / Still I need you to know a house don't make a home / Don't leave me here alone / Sometimes you can't make it on your own.* So it turns around at the end. It's a sort of simple song, but it's, I hope, the last song I will be writing about him.

So what did your father really see in your work, do you think?

I'll tell you what I think. The spiritual journey was interesting to him. Because he wasn't a believer; he didn't believe in God towards the end. He was a Catholic, but he lost his faith along the way.

Was there a specific event that led him to lose his faith?

I don't know what it was. I think the Church wore him down, all the scandals, and all that stuff. I would give him a Bible, or I would offer up, if he was interested, any kind of insights I might have had to some of the Gospels, or the way they were written, or the context of a particular passage. But finally he didn't buy into it. Yet he seemed to think this was the most important thing I had to offer. In fact, it was what he liked best about the band: our faith. He didn't understand some of the work of the nineties, because he felt it was irreligious.

Some of your fans had a hard time with the records you made in the nineties as well.

That's right. They didn't see it. On *Pop*, I thought it was a tough relationship with God that was described there: *Looking for to save my, save my soul / Looking in the places where no flowers grow / Looking for to fill that God-shaped hole.* That's quite an interesting lyric, because that's the real blues—that comes from Robert Johnson, it happens through the machine age, through this techno din, but there it is: the same yearning. But he didn't see it. A lot of people didn't see it, because they wanted to feel it, not think it. That's the difference. That was a thing that he seemed to think was important. My father used to say to me: "Have you lost your way?" I said: "Who's asking? What about you? You didn't have a way to lose!" We used to go down to the pub on Sundays and we would drink together. We drank whiskey, Irish whiskey, of course. Occasionally, he would ask a real question, meaning I had to give him a real answer. It was always about my belief in God: "There's one thing I envy of you. I don't envy anything else," he said to me one time. But think about it: I was singing, doing all the things he would have loved to have done, had a creative life. He said: "You do seem to have a relationship with God." And I said: "Didn't you ever have one?" He said: "No." And I said: "But you have been a Catholic for most of your life."—"Yeah, lots of people are Catholic. It was a one-way conversation . . . You seem to hear something back from the silence!" I said: "That's true, I do." And he said: "How do you feel it?" I said: "I hear it in some sort of instinctive way, I feel a response to a prayer, or I feel led in a direction. Or if I'm studying the Scriptures, they become alive in an odd way, and they make sense to the moment I'm in, they're no longer a historical document." He was mind-blown by this.

So . . . did he find you pious?

I wish I could live the life of someone you could describe as pious. I couldn't preach because I couldn't practice. It's plain to see I'm not a good advertisement for God. Artists are selfish people.

2. NEVER TRUST A PERFORMER

It's hard to say that we saw the sun setting on that day, for the light had remained unchanged since my arrival. The mood had become so peaceful we might as well have started working on a jigsaw puzzle by the fireplace. If there is an overused word in music writing and writing about art in general, it is "inspiration." Since U2's music has spiritual overtones, it's often been called "inspired" or "inspirational." It's a myth I've often bought into myself, and I wondered what Bono makes of it after all these years. Was he still buying into it himself or was he ready to debunk that notion? Regardless, he was eager to puncture the myth of celebrity.

I never believed in channeling spirits, but I have always had this very naive idea that some musicians are actually able to hear voices.

Yeah, but you want to be careful who you're listening to. That's all I'd say. *[laughs]* But, you know, you're right, the world demands to be described, and so, painters, poets, journalists, pornographers, and sitcom writers, by accident or by design, are just following orders, whether from high or low, to describe the world they're in.

So you're suggesting that the ideas that come to you are often cheap ideas, not even thought out?

That's right. In fact, often, the music that's the most eloquent is the least serious. That's the thing that intellectuals don't like. Think of the music of the seventies. It's become a kind of folk music now. The music in the seventies that lasted was a lot of the pop and the dance and disco music. And the supposed serious music of the seventies, fusion, progressive rock, et cetera, played by so-called great musicians, has dated so badly. You are right, Michka. The soul will be described, but God might not use the people that you expect.

Where does it come from? Do you start hearing a melody?

Yeah, I would hear some melodies in my head. I have no idea where they come from.

With the words?

Sometimes melodies, and sometimes words . . . *[gets up and comes back with a tiny sheet of yellow paper from a Post-it pad on his desk]*

What's this? Is it something that you've just written down?

I'm trying to find a recent example. This is the middle of last night. Apropos of nothing. *[reads] If your heart was hard, that would be better / You could only break it once or twice / After that it would be rid of blood and you could let it turn to ice . . .* I don't know. *[makes a dubious face]*

Not bad . . .

Yes . . . Whether they're dreams or overheard conversations, I don't know. *[laughs]*

I know what you're saying.

You've had that.

Yes, I've had that experience, in a way. Sometimes I see pictures that are greater than any pictures I have ever seen.

But you can't get them out.

No, because I'm not a painter, and that makes me very frustrated.

That's how I feel with melodies.

But, melodies, you do hear them, and you do have the ability to reproduce them.

Yes, it's just that I can't get them out, you see? Words, you can write down, but melodies are difficult because you compromise them with chords.

Yes, but you have Edge, you have the band.

Yes, but by the time I get to the band, they might have gone. *[stirs his spoon inside his cup of tea]* Strange . . . I haven't done that for years.

What?

I've put sugar in my tea. I don't take sugar. We keep on talking about the past, next thing I'm back there. Where were we? Oh yeah . . . melodies, I do have an ear for them. It's like spotting a good idea, because a great idea has a lot in common with a great melody: certain inevitability, certain clarity, a kind of instant memorability. It can be philosophical or commercial, or a political idea, like Drop the Debt. As I told you before, I do think of myself as a salesman of melodies and ideas. I come from a long line of salespeople on my mother's side.

That's what my relatives did, going back a long way on my father's side. They sold clothes.

Funny. That's the rag trade, right? That's the Jewish side. Great salespeople, the Jews . . . Someone suggested to me that my mother's side of the family may have been Jewish. Rankin is a Jewish name. A member of the family came up with some interesting stuff researching the name.

I have to tell you this. I saw this one picture of you from when you were younger, and I was completely flabbergasted because you looked like my father.

All my mother's side of the family have that taxi-driver-from-Tel-Aviv look.

Yes, the dark hair, or something. The first time I saw you, there was something familiar about you, like: "I've met this person before . . ."

You must have taken one of our cabs.

Yeah, and someone in my family sold you a pair of boots. Do you believe there's such a thing as folk memory?

Maybe there is sort of a DNA pool. You inherit a cough or a bad back from your father or grandfather, maybe other cultural preferences, interests. Though I haven't found myself studying the Kabbalah just yet. That said, I can lose myself in the Scriptures . . . and have well-known messianic tendencies. *[laughs]* It's true I have an interest in most things Jewish. I would take it as a great compliment if I turned out to be Jewish. I'd be very flattered.

So that's a possibility.

I don't know, but romantically I hope it's true.

How far back can you trace your mother's ancestors?

They just sort of turned up at one point.

How did your parents meet?

Well, they grew up on the same street.

In the northern part of Dublin?

Yeah. A working-class area, a district called Cowtown. Cowper Street. That's where the cattle market was. The farmers would come up from the country and bring the cattle into the city. The Dubs, as they were known, the inner-city people, would sit there with their nose turned up at the smell of cow dung, slagging off the muckers, the culchies, as the farmers were known, they'd think they were better.

What was your father's first job?

He was taken out of school at fourteen. The Christian brothers who taught him begged my grandmother not to take him out, because he was the best student they had had in years, but he was put into civil service at fifteen, which was a safe, pensionable job. He stayed in that job until he retired. Fear was a big part of his life, fear of what might happen, what could go wrong, that was one of his dynamics. And fear, as you know, is the opposite to faith. And I'm sure he got that from his father, who had TB, or the Depression of the thirties, or whatever. TB was a source of shame years ago in Ireland. It was a poverty disease. And his father had it. Obviously a lot of people used to have it. They used to lose weight. And people wouldn't admit to TB. So they used to weigh them at work. And my father told me that his father used to put lead in his shoes, so that when he was weighed, he didn't give away the fact that he was dying of TB, so he could keep his job. It's just the most disgraceful picture of where I guess Dublin and a lot of other places around Europe were, back then. But I think his aversion to risk probably came from that sense of jeopardy he grew up in.

Was he from a big family?

He had an older brother, two younger brothers, and a sister. Tommy, Leslie, Charlie, and Evelyn: the greatest people you could ever meet. Played cricket, listened to the opera. Working-class people who all broke the mold.

Did he have to support his younger brothers and sister?

Yes. That's true, but he was a Catholic, my mother was a Protestant ... or a Jew. *[laughs]* That was a big deal back in those days, because they weren't really allowed to be married.

So they had to hide?

No, they didn't have to hide, but their marriage was disputed in some quarters and not recognized in others.

But, obviously, the area was Catholic. Why did a Protestant family like your mother's live there?

I don't know. There was a small Protestant community in the middle of this Catholic area. Both my mother and my father didn't take religion seriously, they saw the absurdity of the fuss made over their union, though my mother used to bring us to chapel on Sundays and my father would wait outside. I have to accept that one of the things that I picked up from my father and my mother was the sense that religion often gets in the way of God.

Do you still have aunts or uncles who are living on your mother's side?

Yes I do. All my mother's sisters and brothers are alive. And all three of my father's brothers.

Did they look after you when your mother died?

Yes. There were two in particular: my aunt Ruth was very close to my mother, and Barbara was very close with my father.

Did they give you the warmth and support of ...

[interrupting] No, I wasn't available to it; I wasn't really open to it. I was just an obnoxious teenager. Barbara was quite a romantic figure. She read books. She often interceded with my father on my behalf. And Ruth was a more practical character: the no-nonsense of the Rankins.

So they defended you if your father was too hard on you?

They all felt that my father was too hard on me: everyone agreed on that. I don't know if he was hard enough. *[laughs]* Because I do think people should be hard on themselves, don't you think? We're in a climate of self-love, really. We're in a climate of self-love and self-loathing.

I think you're right. It's the two sides of the same coin. People are obsessed with themselves: everything comes out of themselves and returns to themselves. I guess that's the dead end of narcissism.

A degree of narcissism is necessary, I suppose, to look in the pool to see your reflection. And if you're gonna write, that's the excuse of writers for being selfish bastards. What about you? I mean, you don't seem narcissistic or self-obsessed.

Sometimes not enough!

But you write. Why do you write?

Well, because I'm unable to express things in another way. I often believe that the words that come out of my mouth are not the ones I should be using. I can't let things loose unless I'm really sure about them.

It's maybe good.

Yes, it's good, but sometimes it's an excuse ...

Oh yeah.

. . . for not putting yourself on the job.

That's true. That's often an excuse. You have to dare to fail. I think that's the big one: fear of failure. I've never had fear of failure. Isn't that mad?

That's the maddest thing, but at the same time I think that's the secret. Because you've never been afraid of making a fool of yourself, you've never been afraid of looking ridiculous. You've never doubted that you would make it. I was reading through this book that your friend Niall Stokes wrote, *Into the Heart: The Stories Behind Every U2 Song*, and he quoted this song that I had no remembrance of, I must confess, that went like: *A picture in gray, Dorian Gray.

Oh yeah, that's fantastic!

I felt like a star . . .

I felt the world would go far if they listened to what I said. I mean, it's ironic, and it's got some wit, but it's the thought that you have something to say.

I wanted you to succeed, because it was a sort of bet I'd made, but I never thought you'd make it this big. I thought you'd remain a cult favorite, like these eighties bands that you used to read about in the *NME* who were so proud to have street credibility.

I never had much interest in that. The sound of getting out of a ghetto is very different to the sound of getting into one. *[laughs]* It's a very different sound, whether that ghetto is an intellectual one, or the place where you grew up.

But look, Bono, you came from Dublin, which was the most provincial of places. You had the English language, sure, but nobody had made it from Dublin.

* "The Ocean," from *Boy*.

Philip Lynott from Thin Lizzy. The only black man in Ireland . . . and he joins a rock band! *[laughs]* That's great.

He was a big figure in the seventies, that's true. But was he the only model you had?

Bob Geldof was an inspiration. He was from Dublin.

True, you had the Boomtown Rats. They were big. So was it because of these two figures that you thought it was possible?

You're right in the sense that they didn't live in Dublin, they moved. Both Phil Lynott and Bob Geldof moved to London and, in Bob's case, colonized it. And I learnt a lot from Bob. I learnt a lot of my lip from Bob; I had a sense that the impossible was possible from him. Oddly enough, I didn't learn about social activism from him. In fact we used to argue about it. He used to tell me that pop and rock 'n' roll should never stray from sex and fun. Leave revolution to politicians! Right up until he had his epiphany, it was like: "It's only rock 'n' roll and I like it." No, we had to find our own way. It's true, in the end we stayed in Dublin, and it was us against the world. We weren't gonna be part of any scene.

I had this vision of you as innocents, which you obviously weren't. Young and coming from an innocent place and bringing your candor to a cynical place, and winning over the cynicism. Maybe it was a romantic French idea, that the beauty is to make an elegant gesture and then disappear. *[Bono laughs]* But what I underestimated was your hunger.

Yeah, hungry in a way that couldn't be fed: that's the thing. You know, I remember Adam saying to me somewhere around *Rattle and Hum*: "Look, we're here now; we don't have to try so hard," and Ali and I were asking the same thing, actually: "Can we relax?" And I said: "Well, we can relax, but we're about to become irrelevant any second. To be relevant is a lot harder than to be successful." If you're judging where we are by the fact that we can afford to buy this house, it's a dangerous measure. I judge where we are by how close am I to the melody I'm hearing in my head, and how close are we to what we can do as a band to realizing our potential. That's a different thing. I was unhappy . . . because I felt we were far from where we could be. We're getting closer now. We always had the grasp, it was just the reach was the problem. It's like a boxer with about six inches missing off his right hook, that's what it felt like in U2 most of the time. Just occasionally, just because we were quick, our inner force would knock one of our goals out, but normally, the reach was less than the grasp.

Of course in the eighties, you thought that bands like Echo and the Bunnymen or the Teardrop Explodes were more fashionable, that the British press would praise them more than U2. Was there a time when you felt those bands were now behind you? Was it because of America?

These are great groups you're talking about, but they had the conflict of being celebrated in their countries of origin. We weren't a British band. We accepted the U.K.—they never fully accepted us. Because Irish people are very different to English people, actually. I love the English reserve, I love the rigor, but I think we were just kind of bleeding all over them a bit too much, too emotional, and just too in-your-face. We were hot when they were cool. We had a phrase to describe some of the bands of the time—not the Bunnymen or the Teardrop Explodes—but the ones you'd see walking down the King's Road in London, so looking the part with so little to say: "Everything but It." We, on the other hand, had "Nothing but It." And that was the difference. Some of the bands really could have been contenders, but the mood of the time and media didn't encourage thoughts of world domination like the Beatles, Stones, or even the Sex Pistols. They weren't allowed to own up to their ambition. It was like the cultural revolution, it was like Mao. The music press just wouldn't let you put your head above the parapet. You know, you'd have a custard pie. I thought: "Fuck, I don't mind. I'll be the clown, throw the pie." Because my definition of art started with: you put your hands in under your skin, you break your breastbone, you rip open your rib cage. If you really wanna write, that's what you ought to do. Are you ready to do that? Or is rock 'n' roll for you just a pair of shoes and a haircut, or a certain sour existentialism or a certain sweet decay? That was one of my first definitions of art. Blood. That comes from Irish literature, that comes from Oscar Wilde writing *De Profundis,* that comes from Brendan Behan walking on the stage while his own play is being put on in front of an audience, telling people to fuck off. In Ireland, that pain of opening your rib cage, it's in us.

That's not just Irish, you know. There is this famous quote from Louis-Ferdinand Céline, who wrote *Journey to the End of the Night*: "When you write, you should put your skin on the table."

Rock 'n' roll is often the opposite. Rather than putting your skin on the table, it's finding a second skin, a mask.

That's one of the big contradictions for an outsider like me. How do you reconcile your earnestness with the need for a showbiz facade?

Never trust a performer, performers are the best liars. They lie for a living. You're an actor, in a certain sense. But a writer is not a liar. There's a piece of Scripture: "Know the truth, and the truth will set you free." Even as a child, I remember sitting, listening to my teacher in school talking about the great Irish poet William Butler Yeats. He had a writer's block—there was a period where he couldn't write. I put my hand up and said: "Why didn't he write about that?"—"Don't be stupid. Put your hand down, don't be so cheeky." But I didn't mean it as a smart-arse. I have lived off that idea: Know the truth, the truth will set you free. If I've nothing to say, that's the first line of the song. In fact, even on our second album *[October]*, I was about having nothing to say: *I try to sing this song . . . I try to stand up but I can't find my feet / I try to speak up but only with you am I complete.* This has always been the trick for me. And maybe it is just that: a trick. But it tricks me out of myself. I am able to write, always, because as a writer, I am always unable not to be true. As a performer, it isn't always so. You know the thing that keeps me honest as a performer? The fucking high notes I have to sing. Because unless I am totally in that character, I actually can't sing—it's out of my range. That's what keeps me honest on a stage. If I could perform with one step removed, I probably would. It is very costly, by the way, to go on tour and have to step into those songs every night. I suppose I'd like to be a non-Method actor.

Well, you put yourself closer to the tradition of gospel, of the preacher possessed. I mean, when rock 'n' roll first appeared, it had evolved from mad preachers.

That's right.

Are you implying that you're not able to be a pure comedian, and that you've become this mad preacher?

Isn't that interesting that U2 is, in one sense, in exactly the same spot as so many rock 'n' roll people, right back to Elvis? That thing of the gospel and the blues: one hand on the positive terminal, one hand on the minus terminal. And Elvis's dance was really electrocution.

Coming back to the early eighties, is there some point when you said to yourself: maybe this won't work out, maybe this band will fail, and maybe I will have to go back to having a proper job, and earning a living and being a serious person?

Maybe before PopMart [the 1997–98 U2 tour]. Around that time.

That was late.

Yeah, because, well, we were risking bankruptcy. You see, Zoo TV cost so much, I mean, it cost a quarter of a million dollars a day to take that thing around. So, if ten percent less people had come to see us, we'd have gone bankrupt, and with those kinds of bills, you don't go bankrupt a little, you go bankrupt a lot. I can't think about it now. A quarter of a million dollars a day, that's a lot of money. We've since found good people who are prepared to take that risk for us, but anyway at the time it was scary. I remember speaking to Ali about the consequences of failure. She was fearless: "What's the worst, to sell the house, and get a smaller one to get rid of the other one we don't need, end up living like all our friends who lead a normal life? What's wrong with that? They're still our friends. It wasn't like we changed communities and we're like a great disgrace. They'd probably be relieved: 'Oh, thank God . . .' " *[laughs]* She didn't mind. I didn't mind. *Rolling Stone* described it as the *Sgt. Pepper* of live shows. It was groundbreaking. We had fun, and in the end it made a few quid. A few. But this is better; I don't want to be glib or churlish. It's better to be on top than at the bottom. But that's the only time I actually thought about failure. I never thought about it up to that.

Be honest. Are you really telling me that you'd never contemplated failure before?

I don't remember it. I would get angry, I would get upset that we weren't what we could be, I remember that. I don't remember thinking that we never would, I always thought we would. And as soon as we did, it would be clear, you know. *[laughs]* Doubt, self-doubt was about the material, the doubt was about our abilities, but the destination was never a doubt. If we weren't able, we had the faith, because we could still walk into a room, play together, and the hairs of everyone's neck would stand up, everyone. No matter if there was five people in the crowd, or five hundred. It was haphazard. It mightn't happen. But when it did, you knew you weren't having that feeling a lot, going to gigs. Joy Division, maybe. See, there's a chasm between envy and desire, OK? Envy is like wanting something that's not yours. But desire is different. Desire comes out of wanting what is yours, and still wanting it even if it's not yet there, but it's not envy. When desire becomes envy, there's a difference. And there's even a difference from the point of view of the fan. One looks up at this person who they can't be, one looks up at some person that they can be. I and U2 were always what you could be.

That's true if you consider the early eighties. But I'm not sure that's the way you're perceived today by a fifteen- or twenty-year-old. To them U2 is that huge band that has sold more than a hundred million records, that puts on these huge shows.

Yes, but when they listen at night when the lights are turned off, on head-phones, I don't think they're listening to lofty ideas, they're listening to some-thing that sounds familiar.

Still, I'm not sure that listening to your music now, they'd feel that they can make it on the same level as you.

It's less true, all right. We've gotten better at being rock stars; that's something I'm not sure we should be proud of. We got good at insincerity, but only to pro-tect ourselves, to be able to continue to be sincere in our work. OK, now it's MTV, oh my God, there's cameras in your face everywhere! We'd better get good at this stuff. But we're not fully believable as rock stars.

The weird thing was that you seemed to work very hard at being rock stars. Some people started off being glamorous, like Prince. You were not and weren't aiming to be. You aimed to be anti-glamorous. After a few years, changes came.

After ten years . . .

At some point, that zealot attitude of "us" against "the system" became obsolete.

Anachronistic.

And then it seems that you went back to school, not to find deeper roots to your music, the way you did with *Rattle and Hum,* but you went back to school in order to learn how to be rock stars.

That's very good. That's exactly how Zoo TV was. The rock star I put together for myself was an identi-kit. I had Elvis Presley's leather jacket, Jim Morrison's leather pants, Lou Reed's fly shades, Jerry Lee Lewis's boots, Gene Vincent's limp. You want rock 'n' roll stuff? I'll give you some.

The flea market.

[laughs] The fly market! As I just said to you, I still think we're not really believable as rock 'n' roll stars, though we've gotten much better at it. And I'll tell you how I know that: because I still travel and I walk through the world without security. I don't take security with me, I never felt the need to, I can get by. If it comes to it, I can look after myself. But not just that: I like the rub of people, and people find me very accessible. People talk to me, people walk up to me—they don't treat me the way I've seen them treat my contemporaries or my influences. They walk straight up to me because they know from the records that even if my face isn't as open as it was ten years ago, I am. And they can tell. Even in New York, I'm walking down the street, and people say: "How are you doin'?" They beep their horns, or they walk up, they're not afraid of me. Maybe I failed as a rock 'n' roll star. *[laughs]* Occasionally, I get some celebrity geek who treats me like one. I just walk on by. People who know our music, they know who you are. They've been in the dark room, they know you better than your best friend, because you don't sing like that to your best friend, you don't sing in their ear.

So I guess that a few people crossing your path these days must think you are an impersonator. Is that true?

I am one more times than I could admit, but let me tell you an amusing war story. I can't give you the name, but let's say I'm recording with a famous singer from a different genre, OK? They come to Dublin, and they can't get into any of the big studios. So they end up in this fairly modest city-center studio. Now, they already think Ireland is the Third World. So they're a little freaked, being here. The only thing that's gonna make this all right is: the big star turns up. I turn up in my car, and it's not such a fancy car. I've made them keep a parking space outside—I'm not very good at parking. There's some of the star's security waiting outside the studio watching this idiot trying to park in the big star's space. "I'm sorry, my man. We're keeping this parking space." I'm going, "No, it's OK, it's me." *[laughs]* The security guy says: "I'm sorry. We can't let you park here, sir." It's like the land of the giants! I'm saying, "No, no,

I'm the Irish singer, please." Because, in their mind, there is no way I could not have a lot of security, and the setup, and the guys coming with the walkie-talkies. That happens all the time. You turn up at a big party in Beverly Hills, and you're not in the car with the entourage, and you're used to walking up the hill. It's just people are very confused. The thing I'm the most proud of, I think, is the life I have, that never have I lost it. We're under the radar of celebrity, really.

You've got some nerve to say that. I don't think that's really true.

Most of the time, our lives are not vivid enough for that kind of coverage. And I think, generally, even the paparazzi have learnt to respect our position on privacy, because, of course, the way to encourage the paparazzi is to hide from them, or try to punch them out. There've been a couple of moments, but in general, I've just said to them: "Look, here I am. You want my photograph? Take it." On the odd occasion, I've gone out for a drink with them. No one buys them a drink. They're working for a living, you know. And I've learnt to like a lot of them. So I do feel people are very respectful of my privacy in general.

But what are those peers you are alluding to most afraid of, then?

Well, my friend Michael Hutchence used to say: "This is a business of star-fucking, and stars are the worst starfuckers." So, there is the syndrome of "Somebody's not taking my photograph. I don't exist if somebody is not trying to get my autograph. My last album must be crap." At an unconscious level, we're attention-seekers. And I'm sure I must be one of them. But I think I get enough of it in the work, to really not want it in my private life. But maybe not . . . because I'm finding myself, oops, by accident, talking to you for publication, shaking the hand of the odd president in front of the world's media. I mean, what would your pocket book of psychology make of that? "Haven't you got enough attention?" So if you find yourself in those situations a lot, you must want to be there. I probably want it both ways, but the emphasis must always be towards privacy. I just love the retreat of Dublin and Ireland. It has given me the best of both worlds, to go out and play at being a star, even though I don't think I particularly look like one or act like one off the stage. But then, when I want my other life back, I get it in Dublin, Nice, and New York. I spend a lot of time in New York. People are really cool to me, even if they recognize me. Even the cops. New York's finest, so many of them are Irish. And after what happened with 9/11 and U2's support for the city, there's a lot of affection. I really get looked after. Sometimes I'm hailing a cab, and a cop car will pull up: "Hey, Bono, we'll take you anywhere you wanna go." That's the greatest.

Are you implying that you saw a few of your peers getting out of touch?

I'm just saying you don't need all the accoutrements that a lot of my friends have.

But why do they have to have them in the first place?

I don't know. I think it's the status. It's a very hierarchical business. What table you get in the restaurant tells how your career is doing. It's happened to me many times, where you turn up at a restaurant or a club and they haven't got the booking right and you have to queue or get turned away. The paparazzi are taking your photograph as they see you looking a little embarrassed and taking your guest by the hand and retreating. That could have been sorted out by security or an advance party calling ahead, but it's not my style. So maybe there are good reasons, sometimes, for having an entourage. But I don't want to stray too far from the street. I'm not saying I'm not good at the penthouse life—but I'm also good at the pavement. That's a source of pride for me, that I'm good at both. I'm good at the high life, I'm good at the low life. It's the middle where I lose it.

So you don't see yourself as a celebrity, then.

No, I'm not a celebrity.

Who the hell are you, then?

I'm a scribbling, cigar-smoking, wine-drinking, Bible-reading band man. A show-off *[laughs]* . . . who loves to paint pictures of what I can't see. A husband, father, friend of the poor and sometimes the rich. An activist traveling salesman of ideas. Chess player, part-time rock star, opera singer, in the loudest folk group in the world. How's that?

Mmmh . . . I'll let you off just this once.

3. EVERYBODY GETS OUT OF HERE ALIVE

It took me some time to ask Bono about his closest friends: his fellow musicians in U2 and their manager, Paul McGuinness. I thought Bono and I had to get closer in order for him to talk about them, which he eventually did in a very revealing way. It was a Saturday afternoon in his study, and the mood was very relaxed.

Have you heard the story about how Mick Jagger and Keith Richards met up for the first time? I guess they were about sixteen, waiting for a train to London. Richards actually approached Jagger because he had seen him walking with these ultra-rare records from the Chess catalog. Can you remember a similar encounter between you and Edge, something you'd refer to as the founding scene of your friendship, both personal and artistic?

Well, Edge was in Ali's class at high school. They were a year behind me. I'd seen him hanging around the corridors of school with albums under his arm.

Which albums?

I remember there was a group called Taste.

Oh yes, of course. They were Rory Gallagher's first band.

And then I remember Edge picking the guitar, sitting down in a corridor, once. He was playing Neil Young's "The Needle and the Damage Done." I was trying to play it as well. I was envious because I could tell that he could play a little better than I could. *[laughs]* What I didn't realize at that time is that he could play a lot better than I could. He always had that thing about him, that he wouldn't nominate himself to run in the race. But if he was put in the race, he would want to win it. It's a strange thing, and I don't know where it comes from. He has a healthy disrespect—and respect—for his own ego.

What do you mean?

He knows what he's capable of, and he would not push himself forward. He would rather hang back in the shadows and be discovered.

So what you're implying . . .

[laughs, interrupting] What I'm implying is I'm his manager. Whereas Larry was different. Larry, who started the band, would tell you that he has no interest in being a rock star. But he's the one who started the rock band. So that's a little disingenuous, because he's the guy that loved T. Rex, Bowie, and the great pop stars. It's a strange thing. So he, in a way, though he didn't hang around in the shadows like Edge, once he was discovered certainly made attempts to run back there. But "Me thinks he doth protest too much," because I think Larry's really great at being in a rock 'n' roll band, but he doesn't think he is. Has all the instincts, but the way it appears is that myself and Adam were the show-men of the group.

Adam was already the "cool guy" in your school, right? He was more of a hip dresser than the three of you, which maybe was not such an outstanding achievement.

Yes, but he, like myself, has got it wrong.

You mean more wrong than you?

No, it was both. In terms of sartorial elegance and expertise, as the two show-men of the group we have proved ourselves inept over the years. Whereas the two supposed shy men of rock 'n' roll are very good at it. They always look good, they never put a foot wrong, and they never want to lose their cool. My only excuse is I never wanted to be cool, I always wanted to be . . . hot. *[laughs]*

You probably were more impressed by Adam than he was by you. Wouldn't you say?

Yeah, I think that might have been true. I was fascinated by him. I'd never met anyone quite like him.

What do you mean? What was he like?

Well, he had been expelled from an upper-class public school in Ireland, and arrived at this free school with a posh accent, wearing a caftan that he had picked up on his holidays at age sixteen, hitching through Afghanistan. He'd had "Afghanistan '76" written on his T-shirt, and his hair was corkscrew blond hair, but in an Afro. He looked like a negative of Michael Jackson.

Maybe he wanted to look like Jimi Hendrix, the way Eric Clapton did when he was in Cream.

That's right, Hendrix was a big hero in Ireland. And he has a lot in common, in a certain sense. Adam has a very unique sense of where the one is, in terms of where the beat is in the bar. His timing is very unique. Most rock 'n' roll is made by people who love 4/4, but his timing is much more 5/8, much more of a jazzman. I heard somebody saying, when Jimi Hendrix was taught guitar, he couldn't keep 4/4 time, the simplest time. Now Adam can, but it's not really where he wants to be. *[laughs]* I think it's probably because he listened to a lot of jazz, to Jimi Hendrix. That's where he was coming from.

Ever since I met you, I've always heard you address Edge as "Edge," but do you remember a time when you called him Dave?

Yeah, I think probably for the first year. By '78, I think he was The Edge.

And did he call you Bono first or Paul?

He would have called me Paul up until, maybe '76. I was known as Bono by my friends in Lypton Village.* Edge and Adam and Larry weren't really a part of Lypton Village until later.

Was it easy for them to start calling you that? Maybe a few people found it irritating and kept calling you by your given name?

The thing about these kinds of nicknames is they're contagious. You don't have to ask people, they just start doing it. I can't remember when Ali started calling me Bono. I was sixteen, I'd say. Edge had another name from Lypton Village.

And what was that?

"Inchicore." It's the name of a small town on the outskirts of Dublin City.

So who had this preposterous idea to call him The Edge?

I do preposterous in this band. It had something to do with the shape of his head, his jaw, and an insane love he had for walking on the edges of very high walls, bridges, or buildings. Before Bono, I was "Steinvic von Huyseman," and then just "Huyseman," and then "Houseman," then "Bon Murray," "Bono Vox of O'Connell Street," and then just "Bono."

* Lypton Village was the name of the surrealistic street gang Bono and his friends were part of, where name-giving was one of the rituals. (See Chapter 6)

"Bono Vox of O'Connell Street"—now that's an aristocrat's name. There's nobility in it.

Well, yes. *[laughs]*

Weren't you a baron or a count?

What my friends had in mind is close to count. *[laughs]*

When he started the band, Larry was not even fifteen, and you were sixteen and a half. Didn't you feel like a grown-up amused by the nerve of this kid?

It was his band. I think, for a minute, he wanted to call it the Larry Mullen Band.

What sort of music did he want to play?

He loved glam rock. That was his thing. The Larry Mullen Band wasn't really a very glam-rock kind of a name.

It sounds like a jazz-blues band from the mid-seventies.

He was the star. When he sat behind the kit, definitely, the room changed temperature. There was something going on. He played the drums like his life depended on it. And I think, in some very real way, that was true.

And by the way, why didn't Larry and Adam get a nickname, like you and Edge did?

I think the "Junior" [Larry Mullen, Jr.] certainly added the jazz-blues band bit. I convinced him to do that. Adam Clayton just sounds black anyway. But they had unofficial names: Larry was "Jamjar," and Adam was "Sparky."

So would you say Larry was the most dedicated musician of the bunch?

Edge was pretty good—I mean, no, Edge was more than good. But Larry was really impressive, I thought. Just the drum playing, the way the sound just fills the room, and the silver and the gold of the cymbals. His kit was a bright crimson. We'd never seen anything like that. I mean, we'd been playing shitty guitars.

And he had a perfect kit.

I mean, his kit was like a cheap copy.

But it looked great.

It looked great. It was bright and shiny. And he looked great behind the kit. Adam knew all the right words. He knew what to say; he had the lingo; he was *[adopting ghetto voice]* "down with his big bad self." He had all the musician talk. But what we didn't know, until a few practices, is that he could not play a note. He arrived with a bass guitar and a bass amp, and he looked incredible. He had all the gear, had all the right terminology. He looked funky, he acted funky. We didn't realize at the time he couldn't play a note. And so big was his bluff that we looked pretty much everywhere else to why we were sounding so shit. Him!

You mean you didn't realize it in the first place.

Well, he was the oldest, and he looked the most professional.

On a more personal level, I have this feeling that the one you had to feel the closest to was Larry, because you shared some difficult experiences in your teenage years. He lost his sister and then his mother in those years. Was it something that helped you get closer to him?

We always kind of hit it off, actually. Then, as now, Larry does not let many people in. But when you're in, he's a very loyal and reliable friend. I'm a kind of a loyal and unreliable friend. But there's nothing he would not do for you. The thing that stuck us together was that I had this experience of bereavement. I had lost my mother when I was fourteen and he had lost his when he was sixteen, and we both had to deal with fairly authoritarian fathers. As Larry would tell you himself, we both ran away with the circus. So, while the tent was being put up on the outskirts of Europe, we were still outside, and would look at the elephants, and talk a lot. We still do, on occasions.

What did you discuss the most with Larry—and wouldn't as readily with Edge or Adam?

The moment, the *now* that we wouldn't miss out on, the moment we were in, because of the place we wanted to get to in the future. Because Larry wasn't sure about where we were going, and I wasn't sure about where we were.

So Larry's the first one you really got close to?

I'd say Larry and I were pretty close friends. We shared a room on tour. We were the odd couple, really, because he's completely meticulous.

And you're not?

I'm just not. My suitcase would just blow up, and there'd be stuff all over the floor. Larry used to bring his own sleeping bag, because he didn't like to sleep in the sheets of these really cheap hotels. He would actually sleep in his sleeping bag up on the bed.

So he wouldn't catch any fleas or lice?

I remember one time I slagged him off so much that he said: "OK." He threw away the sleeping bag, and he left the sleeping bag at the bottom of the bed. He slept in the sheets. When he woke up, he was head to toe in this rose-colored rash. So people used to laugh at the two of us.

Insiders have written accounts about the tacit division from the very beginning between you, Edge and Larry, the Irish Christians, and then, on the

other side, Adam and Paul McGuinness, the English skeptics, with business sense and posh backgrounds, raised by military fathers. Is this real or an invention?

Well, Adam and Edge were friends. They came from the same suburbs. They were kind of middle-class and they both had British passports. But in terms of fun and frolics, going out, drinking wine, looking sharp, and living the life, I think Paul and Adam had a lot in common. They became friends. Myself, Edge, and Larry were kind of zealots. And we were determined that the world, in all its finagling attempt to corrupt you, to take you away from where you should be going, would not get us. But it's like that old story of the guy who's hiding from the world by climbing up the mountain backwards. He gets halfway up the mountain. He finds a cave. He just looks left and he looks right, he looks up and he looks down, to make sure the world hasn't followed him. Then he looks back into the cave, that's dark and that's quiet. Then he hears something. What's that? It's the world! *[laughs]* There's no escape. We just didn't know that, then. But it turns out that that's a much more subtle threat than sex, drugs, and rock 'n' roll. Self-righteousness, self-flagellation, these things are as dangerous as what you might call the worship of the self. At that time, we were determined that we would never change. The music business would never change us, success would never change us. But if you think about it, that's a terrible thing. That would be awful, not to change. And of course you should be changing. Paul and Adam just wanted to have fun, and get out there, and see what the world had to offer. We knew what the world had to offer—we didn't want to buy it. So we went in a completely different direction. But there was a lot of respect from us to them, and from them to us.

But have Paul and Adam tried to talk you out of this zealot attitude over the years? Or did they remain silent and respectful?

No, they were very respectful. I remember Paul saying, when we put out our second album, *October* [1981], which was a kind of religious experience of an album to make, very un–rock 'n' roll: "Look, these are not questions I'm asking, but they're questions I'm interested in. Anyone with a brain should be interested in these questions. And though you won't find many people in rock'n'roll who are prepared to be so open like you are on this album, you look to black music, it's full of songs like this. Look to Marvin Gaye, look to Bob Marley."

That's a case you're often making. You're presenting ideas of what U2 did or what you yourself are doing now by pointing to black artists. It's interesting, because very few black artists have had a big impact on the rock audience, apart from Bob Marley or Prince.

Yeah, it's the Irish, we are the white niggers. Paul had the overview, because he was a few years older than us. Chris Blackwell, who had founded our record company, Island Records, also discovered Bob Marley. So he was very supportive. So you have your manager and your record company who are totally supportive of what looks like completely eccentric behavior in white rock 'n' roll. But if you look to writers and painters and poets, then you'll often find the search for the ecstatic, the trauma of religious experience.

Which writers, painters, and poets are you alluding to here, specifically?

Well, in music, Patti Smith, Bob Dylan, Marvin Gaye, Bob Marley, Stevie Wonder, the list is endless. Poets: Kavanagh,* maybe an even greater poet than Yeats, John Donne, William Blake. Emily Dickinson—she was a great influence on me. All the Renaissance painters, torn between God, patronage, and the desires of the flesh.

Have you discussed Marley with Blackwell? And would you say, based on what you learned, that Marley went through the "trauma of religious experience"? What is it that ultimately keeps black and white artists apart? I mean, Bob Dylan and Johnny Cash went through that as well.

Chris Blackwell was—is—a real support on this level. Again, another critical character in our lives. Like Paul McGuinness, he seemed to understand that

---

* Patrick Kavanagh (1904–1967) taught poetry at the National University in Dublin.

sometimes the best influence you can have is not to try to have any. I mean, Chris was this great producer of music; he could easily have turned up in the studio and asked us the hard musical questions: "Where's the single? What are you on about? Why doesn't that groove?" He had faith we would find our own way. I think in an odd way he had faith in our faith. But as regards Dylan and Cash, they nearly were exceptions. White music is so much more uptight spiritually. Most black artists came from the Church anyway.

In a nutshell, what did you find out about yourself from your manager, Paul McGuinness?

I found out what I was capable of.

Which was?

I mean, more than anyone in my life, he is a person who believed in me and gave me the confidence to realize my potential as an artist. He has an enormous and sharp intellect, and mine was very unschooled and haphazard. On many occasions, he would sit me down and say: "You have what it takes. You must have more confidence in yourself and continue to dig deeper. And don't be upset or surprised when you pull something out from the depth that's uncomfortable." *[laughs]*

So you discovered things that, on first glance, you'd rather have kept hidden? What were those?

The gauche nature of awe, of worship, the wonderment at the world around you. Coolness might help in your negotiation with people through the world, maybe, but it is impossible to meet God with sunglasses on. It is impossible to meet God without abandon, without exposing yourself, being raw. That's the connection with great music and great art, and that is why it's uncomfortable, that is why cool is the enemy of it, because that's the other reason you wanted to join a band: you wanted to do the cool thing. Trying to capture religious experiences on tape wasn't what you had in mind when you signed up for the job.

What about your own sunglasses, then? Do you wear them the same way a taxi driver would turn off his front light, so as to signal to God that this rock star is too full of himself and not for hire at the moment?

Yeah, my insincerity . . . I have learnt the importance of insincerity, the importance of not being earnest at all times. You don't know what's going on behind those glasses, but God, I can assure you, does.

What else did Paul McGuinness encourage in you?

He said to me when I was very young, like twenty-five: "You have something that very few artists have." And I said: "I don't think so, Paul." He said: "No. You see the whole equation." And that is . . . a curse and a blessing. But it's a very interesting thing, and I'm not sure I understood what he meant back then. I've never really discussed it with him since, but I think I know what he means, which is: the gift is at the center of the contradiction, but the circumference is full of other stuff you have to figure out if you want the gift to really grow.

A blessing, I understand. But why should it be a curse?

It's an end to laziness, it's an end to being a passenger on a train somebody else is driving. You are responsible, no one else—not the record company, not the management. You've to develop other muscles in your bodyguarding of your gift.

I don't think you've talked much about your relationship with Edge, Larry, and Adam in terms of their families. How close did you get to the families of your fellow musicians? You told me that in order to escape your father's sternness, you wanted to go to places where you felt warmth. Was, for instance, going to Edge's place as warm a feeling as going to Guggi's or Gavin Friday's?

Edge's family are extra-special people. They're very laid back, they're cool in the extreme. They're not looking for the obvious. They're both academics, they're not very material. Edge's father was very successful in business. I'm sure he could have been even more successful, but he couldn't be arsed. *[laughs]* He'd rather hang out, he'd rather play golf. He and my father used to play golf on occasion. They got on pretty well, though my dad did complain once that Garvin was a little bit of a stickler for the rules. *[bursts out laughing]* He said: "He's learnt that fucking manual off by heart." But they both loved opera. In fact, it was a great moment when we played Madison Square Garden some years back, when they were both drunk and singing a duet from *La Traviata,* walking down Madison Avenue. It was the kind of place where you could always crash out. I remember coming back at four in the morning, and Mrs. The Edge would come down, rubbing sleep out of her eyes, and ask Edge if he was hungry, and . . . *[gives a bewildered look]* I thought this was just a different universe, completely. I was expecting, like: where is she stashing the weapons, OK? *[laughs]* As soon as he says: "Yes I'm hungry," she'll bring out the howitzer! But he'd say: "No, no. I'm OK, yeah. You go back to bed, I'm fine." And then, it was all very easygoing. And his brother, Dick, was a bit of a genius. The government were paying for him to go to college in computer engineering. More than just a scholarship where they pay your studies, they were paying him to study. He was that good. And then he joined the Virgin Prunes. So there were two mad musicians in the house for the Evans family to deal with. But they were very . . . *open* is the word. It felt like an open house. And Mrs. The Edge was always interested in what you were.

Did Edge's mother work?

She was a schoolteacher, and then, I think, she might have just helped Garvin. Her name was Gwenda, and they were both Welsh, so they had this kind of singsong accent, which made it all the more inviting. Then, they had a garden shed that we used to play in, which is about the size of this room, maybe a little smaller, a very small thing, and they let us play in this bunker, which is about 4 foot by 3, maybe 5 by 4, but that'd be pushing it. So you could just fit the drum kit in, you could just kind of stand, but it was great for a while. I just met Garvin recently, and jokingly, he was wondering what it would be worth now on eBay. He said: "Is it the time, Bono, for the garden shed?" I explained to him that we haven't had a whole lot of luck on eBay, trying to unload our giant lemon spaceship [from the PopMart tour].

I'm curious about your first impression when you entered The Edge's room. Was it very tidy, very organized, the way I'd fancy it?

Oh, I don't remember his room. I remember Adam's room. Adam's room was like a nightclub, by age sixteen. He had ultraviolet light—UV, you know—incense burning, albums everywhere, and a soft chair. *[laughs]* Oh yeah, I'd never seen a room like Adam's.

What sort of atmosphere did you feel at the Claytons' place?

The Claytons had a very elegant kind of house. I mean, it was a very large detached bungalow in a nice neighborhood. I had never seen anything like it myself, coming from a just regular lower-middle-class street. They kept it very well.

Was there a garden?

They had a nice garden. I remember they had this white shag pile carpet. I said to Adam: "Wow! If we had a carpet like that in the house, you wouldn't be allowed walking on it." He said: "You're not. Take your shoes off! *[laughs]* No one's allowed walking on it. We're hardly allowed in here." But his mother was very glamorous, and his father was a pilot, which is again a very glamorous occupation. He was very wry, Adam's father, liked to go fishing. His eyes are never far from rolling at all the fuss around him. He was from the East End of London, and never wanted to forget that, despite having made it to the officers' mess in the RAF. His mother was very able in an argument. So we had many discussions long into the night about life, death, God, and the universe . . . and why we couldn't walk on that white shag pile carpet.

So what kind of people were the Claytons? As laid back as Edge's parents?

No one could be as laid back as Edge's parents. I think Jo Clayton was ambitious for her son, very worried, because he'd already been expelled from one school, and now he joined a rock band, and was hanging out with some very strange-looking people: us. So she was very sweet to us on the surface, but I think, beneath it all, very concerned that her son had fallen into the wrong crowd.

Had Adam been thinking long and hard about becoming a professional musician? Did he feel like he'd fallen in with the wrong crowd?

Adam was looking for the wrong crowd. There was nothing else he wanted to be other than a bass player. There's a joke in the band that goes: Edge wants to play the drums, Bono wants to play the guitar, Larry wants to be the singer, Adam . . . only wants to play the bass! Adam and his younger brother Sebastian were great. They were always laughing, I do remember that. They had that kind of English potty humor. They'd put socks over their penises and kind of walk around, trying to embarrass their sister Cindy. I mean, Adam always loved nudity. He's always been that way. He, when we were in school, used to streak down the corridor, naked.

So he was more of an exhibitionist than you. Great!

Yeah, I know. I remember the first time, we were just teenagers. Ali was talking to him, and she felt some humidity on the side of her leg *[laughs]*, and he was peeing, not on her leg, but near her leg. He'd whip that thing out at any opportunity. He wouldn't want taking a pee to interrupt a good conversation. And he might forget to ask. *[laughs]*

And how did it feel at Larry's place? I guess it must have been a little more somber.

Yeah, I think. Larry's home life was much more like mine, you know. You had this bereaved man, and in some shape or other, no matter how hard they tried to hide it, you were dealing with their unhappiness.

So Larry was living with his father.

His father and his sister, yes.

His younger sister had died as well. What had happened, exactly?

I can't remember the exact details.

Larry was living in the same sort of house as you. Or was it a different background?

Very similar.

Was his father as harsh on him as yours was on you?

His father was very worried about his son throwing his life away with a rock 'n' roll band. His father thought, if he was interested in music, it should be jazz, you know. Learn to play properly. And the only difference was his father would have wanted his son to achieve more than he did in terms of university and all of that. And Larry wasn't interested remotely. Whereas my father couldn't really care less whether I went to college—and I would have quite liked it. That's the only difference.

Did you use to hang around at Larry's place as much as in Adam's or Edge's?

Occasionally. Our very first rehearsal was in Larry's place.

Was there enough space for that?

In the kitchen. There wasn't much space.

Would his father put up with it?

His mother probably told his father that it was a jazz group assembling. She was a spectacular woman. She was just gorgeous in every way. There was no vanity to her. And she loved her son, and wanted him to be a drummer, because that's what he wanted, and facilitated him by letting her kitchen be used for our first rehearsal. We were all standing there, there were like six of us at that stage, and I remember even then, there were girls screaming outside for Larry. He was fourteen, I suppose, and I remember him taking the hose to them: "Go away! Leave me in peace! Shhh!" He's been doing the same ever since. But I really didn't hang out a lot. We went to rehearsals. Finally we got a rehearsal room— oddly—next door to the graveyard where my mother was buried. A complete accident. A little yellow house next door to a graveyard . . .

Aside from music, what were the things the four of you enjoyed doing the most together?

Nothing at first, but then, we realized we shared the same surreal sense of humor.

I never imagined you'd say that. You mean you'd make practical jokes together?

Yeah, we'd do some mad shit together.

Like what?

I think Edge was with me once when we got into Guggi's car. He was seventeen years old and had a car. His father just collected these jalopies, broken-down cars, and would fix them up. I remember we snuck out of the school into his car and drove to a girls' school with a painting that we had done, and went into the school, and knocked on class doors to sell them the painting. So before they got a chance to call the police, we had hit several classes at the girls' school: "Excuse me. We were round here, we have a painting and we're advised that we might find a buyer here in Class C English. *[changes tone]* Hi, girls!" *[laughs]* Just teenage stuff, but surreal. Or we'd do mad theatrical stuff.

What do you mean, "mad"?

Well, I remember, in one of our early gigs, we put on Christmas concerts in the middle of summer. They were called "The Jingle Balls." And so we got on at this nightclub and we did it up with a Christmas tree. We just pretended it was winter in the middle of the summer. Childish things . . . In Lypton Village, we gave each other names and we spoke this other language. Edge fit into that very well in the end, and so did Adam, because they were all very surreal. Larry was just a little more suspicious, but he would be, anyway.

Funny. I mean, the sort of reputation U2 had when the band began was that of a very intense and earnest act.

Yeah, that's why some people who saw Zoo TV were confused—I think you were one of them—and just concerned about the way things were turning out. But actually that's where we came from. Staging, like this Christmas concert in June, you know. We have been playing with theatrical constructs from the very beginning. I had a character called "The Fool," which I played with, which was a forerunner of "The Fly."

OK, I'm willing to accept that you revived a sort of very early U2 tradition with Zoo TV in the early nineties. But it looks like humor had been completely out of the question for the first ten years.

I think we lost our humor a bit. I really do. It was the bends, really. It was just changing pressure, moving from Dublin suburbia to traveling around the world and all that comes with it. This thing we were talking about before, just this sort of determination not to be changed—this zeal, I think, came partly in response to that.

But didn't it exist even before you'd encountered that huge success? *Boy* was sort of tragic, *October* had a terrible solemnity and sadness to it, and *War* was full of anger.

By the time we got to *Boy*, we had taken some of the surrealism out. We had an idea, a construct for the album, and we fit into it. The thing you have to get used to with us is that, when we have an idea, we change shape to fit into it. It's not strange if you're a director or a writer. In order to research a subject, you change clothes and shoes and walk funny. But bands are not supposed to. The subject of our songs, if you like, has always dictated the way we presented them, the clothes we wore, the films we made, the kind of shows we put on.

Oh, really, Bono? From where I was standing, you didn't seem like the funniest guy on a stage in those years to me...

It wasn't a large part of our work, no. But our life, some of our life, lost humor. I think I was the more intense. I don't think I am now. But it was an act of will. Defeat was not an option, though it was much more likely, if you're being honest. I think, you know, I really sensed defeat at any minute, and I was so determined to drown out the voice of failure that I just took out all peripheral vision. I just became very single-minded.

Maybe U2 needed that kind of dedication then. Maybe your audience did.

Maybe they did. Everyone was determined, but no one was more determined than I was. And it could get pretty intense and pretty tense, because this would have to be the best show of our life every night, which, you could say is like: "Chill out, Bono... Chill, OK?" *[laughs]* But ... no! Every night, I am not messing or exaggerating, because in our heads this was the only way to be true. If it wasn't, if you weren't inside those songs, if you didn't live it in that moment, you were lying and you were stealing from the people. We were zealots, we became prisoners of our own cult. *[laughs]* And we'd taken hostages. Paul McGuinness and our road crew were incredible. Joe O'Herlihy, our sound mixer, what a legend! Everybody was working hundred-hour weeks just to push the rock up the hill. It was a high hill, and it was difficult, and our talents weren't really the obvious ones that you need for this particular journey. But it turned out we had other ones, which were maybe more important.

What do you mean by those "other talents" that were more important?

The spark. There was something original about our point of view, even if it wasn't very well expressed. And we were relentless. Just those two things can get you places. When I look back at twenty years, I see the slowest, almost invisible evolution: just tiny, tiny gradations, just on the way of degrees. Just slowly the talent has opened up, and there's moments that looked like we're searching ahead, like *The Joshua Tree* or *Achtung, Baby,* or now. But really, it's just so slow to me. I think, it's taken us this long to figure all this out. I think we're the slowest learners in the world. But you read about the Beatles, and it's just all in ten years. *[imitates sound of a jumbo jet]* But, for us, we've just got to *Rubber Soul* now.

Are you serious?

Oh, absolutely. In my mind, absolutely. OK, I might start to feel ill with envy if John sang "In My Life," sitting in the rehearsal room. And, in fact, all of their songs would make me feel some nausea. But I would say to them: "Your songs have extraordinary melodies that are beyond compare, but our songs have a kind of weight that yours don't. Gravity, you could call it . . ."

It used to be the weight of things to come. But maybe it's a different story now.

It's just weight. We had weight. And weight counts for a lot. There's an incredible moment—I don't know if I talked to you about it—which was after 9/11, when there was a concert for the New York police, the fire department, in Madison Square Garden. The Rolling Stones played an amazing song, "Miss You," so in the moment . . . *[sings] Do-do-doo-doo / Doo-do-loo / How I miss you . . .* Jagger looks incredible. And it was just really a beautiful performance, and it had a lightness of touch that only he has. But then on walked . . . The Who. There were three of them. And in comparison with the effete Jagger, these guys looked like they were longshoremen. They looked like they'd just come up from New Jersey with an iron bar in their back pocket, OK? They put on the guitars and they went into "Who Are You?," and then "Baba O'Riley" and "Won't Get Fooled Again." For the first time in the night, these fire department and these police, who'd been drinking off their grief as they should, and were loud and noisy—"Yeah, there's the Stones! Yeah, there's such and such"— suddenly they stopped. Their mouths fell open. It was nothing to do with cool, it was nothing to do with smart, it was nothing to do with sexy. It was to do with authority—weight, some sort of weight. And our music has that. We're learning the other stuff, even now: figuring out the more unpredictable melodies, the lyrics that can trick you into feeling one thing and then surprise you with another—that's all craft and songwriting, and it's coming and it's great. But that other thing we have, we have it and it's being very strong on this current tour, because we're coming into something. Chris Blackwell used to say: "That's the thing about U2. The band always feels like it's coming, never that it's arrived."

What is the thing you argue about the most in U2? Can you remember when you felt for the first time something like: Oh God, this is wrong; I thought it would never come to this for the four of us?

I might think, if I'm honest, there have been periods of time when I have found each member of the band incredibly frustrating.

You wouldn't use another word?

No, but I'm sure that has happened in reverse about me too. Luckily, it hasn't all come at the same time. *[laughs]* I think that's what you call a solo career. But I think you have to give people some space to lose themselves now and then, and I can remember when each of them had lost themselves, or lost their way in the work, and I found that very upsetting. And then, I don't know, there's probably a period when they felt that about me, but I don't know when that would be.

Can you remember a particular time when you felt the band was resentful of you?

Recording *All That You Can't Leave Behind,* I think I did push their patience the most with our Africa work, just by being on the phone a lot.

Let's get back to that zealot period of yours in the early eighties. How did it come to an end? How did Adam catch up with you, and how did you catch up with Adam?

I think we met somewhere in the middle. Adam . . . we found a third way. He was tired of the world, and I was a little more curious.

Are you all believers now?

Yes. Adam had his own path, and it took him further out into the world. But I would say Adam is, right now, the most spiritually centered of the band.

Because his path was very rough?

Yeah, I think he is the person who is now the most watchful of the sheep as they stray out of the herd. *[laughs]* I do love the image of sheep. You've got to hand it to Jesus. *[laughs]* That is a great one, sheep, isn't it? Because there's something like: pigs are intelligent, they're useful farm animals as they wallow in the muck. But sheep! I mean, they're useful for making jumpers, of course, but they really are pretty dumb. The great image of mankind. And they move in packs as well. They all head off the wrong direction together. There's no particular leader, anyone can become a leader, and anyone can be right for a particular stampede. They're so frightened, and not even aware that they're of great use for making woolly jumpers, or when they're dead making sheepskin coats for secondhand car dealers. *[laughs]*

I don't know how much this has been true or to what extent it's been made up, but the story goes that *Achtung, Baby* was mainly based on Edge's personal crisis at that time, the trauma of his divorce. Has this really been a group crisis or, on the contrary, has Edge's problem stayed inside the borders of his private life?

No, you're right. The fracturing and the fissures in Edge's life were a perfect metaphor for what was going on with the band. There was a lot of tension between us during the making of that album, with Edge and myself wanting to chop down *The Joshua Tree,* and Larry and Adam wanting to put a glass house around it and play to our strength. Because Larry and Adam have that humility, but Edge and myself had the arrogance that it wasn't the sound of the guitar, it wasn't a collision of notes that made up a melody, or a particular bass and drums approach that made U2. We believed that what made U2 was the spark, and that you could destroy all the outward manifestation, and it would still be there. You could put my voice through a distortion pedal, you could ban Edge from playing his echo unit and those silver notes that he plays, you could change the subject matter . . . *[laughs]* you could just deface all that was recognizable in the band, and it still would come through. You could take subject matter that you wouldn't normally associate with the band.

Would you say that the chaos that reigned inside Edge's life gave him the musical nerve to do that?

Ermm, no. It was very hard for Edge to go through that. He's a hard person to fall out with. It took an awful lot, I think, for him to let go of his marriage. He loved Aislinn so much, and his kids were everything to him. So it was excruciating to watch someone so averse to this kind of splitting up. In the middle of it, I think he did just focus on his music as a way of keeping. The intensity of the band must have paled in comparison. So he went on holidays to our argument from his own.

But had his personal crisis isolated him from the band?

Well, we worked very closely together. I mean, I was the one really pushing for the change in direction, and Edge was the one most supportive. There were times when Adam and Larry were, actually, antagonistic. But again, for reasons of modesty, they felt our reach couldn't meet our grasp.

How did Edge's way of dealing with that chaos turn into music? Did it happen in the subject matter of some of the songs, like "One"?

Yeah, subject matter, of course. They are very adult themes. There is a desperate struggle for fun *[laughs]*, which, I think, is, you know, a contradiction in terms. There it is. All these albums, when we tried to escape gravity, *Pop* and *Achtung, Baby*, we always ended up sort of flat on our backs under the weight of the air. *[laughs]* It's very funny.

A few months ago, I listened to all those albums in a row. *Achtung, Baby* comes out as the strongest of the lot, but also the darkest and the hardest. It sounds harder now than it did then. At the time, I thought it was fun, because you'd been experimenting with machines, and your voice was distorted. But with hindsight, it's amazingly violent.

Yeah. "Love Is Blindness" is really something else. And I remember Edge played the solo at the end of this. I was pushing him and pushing him and pushing him, and he played until the strings fell off. Actually, you'll hear strings snapping during the solo towards the end. He was, I think, in tears on the inside, and the outside was just raging.

There's so much self-hatred in that record.

It's a black beauty.

Speaking of black beauties ... I mean, people won't understand—and I won't understand *[laughs]*—if we don't broach the thing that happened during Adam's "difficult period." How did it feel when Adam missed the Sydney show on the Zoo TV tour in 1993? I think you never really told the story from your own perspective. How did you learn about it? How did you face it? How did you live through it? And what happened when you next met up with Adam?

[puzzled] Err . . . What's the connection between Adam and black beauty?

Well, I was thinking about Naomi Campbell.

You've jumped over from Naomi to Sydney.

I had the question ready, but you know what I mean.

[a little embarrassed] No . . . I introduced Adam to Naomi. And he'd always had a thing for her. What people have to understand about somebody like that is that there is a sort of prowess and a kind of big brain in that cat suit, and she is a wildcat—I think she's a puma. But you know, they were in so many ways really great for each other. I think it would not be fair to characterize Naomi as being in any way responsible for Adam's demise and final fall at Sydney.

It was just an association of ideas. I wasn't implying there was a logical link.

Oh, I see. Because I think he was on a road to perdition. *[laughs]* And extradition, and re-ignition—any other "ition" you can find—long before he met her. He had gone out into the world, and was taking the biggest slice of the pizza he could find. He was young, he was in a great rock band, and he was the only rock star in the band. *[laughs]* He had four people's portion for himself. So that's a lot of pizza to eat! *[laughs]* He got sick after a while. He couldn't do a gig because of the size of the bellyache. The real betrayal in Sydney was not between Adam and the band. The real betrayal was between Adam and himself, because there is no more pro a person in the band than Adam. He found it very hard to live with that, and indeed he couldn't live with that. He realized that he had gotten himself quite sick, and he wanted to be better. It took him a few years, but that was a real turning point. As I say, he's a real pro.

A pro who didn't turn up for work.

Yes. We were filming, which made it even harder. It was the first night of Zoo TV live from Sydney. Twenty cameras in the house, steadycams and cranes, extra lighting—lights, action. Or in this case, lights, no action. We went ahead with the show out of respect for the people who turned up and the size of the bills we were going to have to pay if we didn't roll cameras. Adam's bass tech, Stuart Morgan, understudied that night, it was a heroic performance from him, and in fairness a performance deserving to be lit, which he wasn't. He was left in the shadows. *[laughs]* In fact, some people who were there thought it was Adam, which probably hurt him the most, though I might say, if I could, something about Adam's bass playing, and why in the end, it is irreplaceable. The bass can be the blandest of instruments in a rock quartet. Most concerts I go to, and not even rock—jazz, pop, blues—I don't notice the bass. Nobody does. Nobody knows what the guy who gets the girl is doing. In U2 that is not the case. I felt an enormous void that night and I felt I was falling down it. I felt we all were.

But had you seen it coming?

Yeah, yeah, we had seen it coming. But what can you do? He's so fun, he was so good at it. *[laughs]* He was very, very good at it. But it takes a long time to recover from that stuff. You can lose the spring in your step for a few years. I think separation from drink and drugs is probably very like separation from your wife. They say it takes about half the length of time that you've put in it to get over it. So if you've been married for ten years, it'll take you five. If you've been married for twenty, it'll take you ten for you to be really over it. I think if Adam was at it for ten hard years, it probably took him five years to get over it.

What sort of impact did it have on the band?

Whenever Adam got into trouble, we were always there for him. And no matter what scandal was happening, no one cared about the band in those moments. Everyone just cared about him.

Were there moments when you thought it was putting the band in danger?

Oh yeah, for sure, I was always concerned. Because, for us, it wasn't a win until everybody had scored. Everybody had to make it through this alive, to misquote Jim Morrison. Our motto was: "*Everybody* gets out of here alive."

So Adam was dating Naomi Campbell and you had come face-to-face with the paparazzi and the celebrity business. It must have been traumatic for that zealot still breathing, from time to time, inside yourself.

No, no, no. Because you remember celebrity was on the list. It was part of the subject matter. Sliding down the surface of things was the energy of that period. I was the one who agreed to do the cover of *Vogue* with Christy [Turlington], and I had had enough of these po-faced U2ers. We were travelling the same routes as these girls, staying in the same hotels, though we weren't walking in the same shoes. *[laughs]*

Who knows? Maybe in private.

I'm sure Adam tried them on, occasionally, as a great connoisseur of the shoe that he is. But he certainly poured champagne into a few. There was a certain fascination with their power with the populace. It goes back to the silent movie stars. Because in the thirties, Hollywood was never as powerful as it was in the silent age, and there's great power in not opening your mouth.

It's a power you haven't relied very much on during your career.

Which is why I so respected it in the likes of Christy Turlington, who, when she chooses to open her mouth, has a lot to say, thoughtful, considered, and intelligent as she is.

People say there were no bigger stars than Rudolph Valentino and Greta Garbo.

None bigger. And these super models [Christy, Naomi, and company] were the silent movie stars of our age. Blank faces and stares that on one level suggest a kind of erotic acquiescence, and on the other a kind of spitting at the cameras, a kind of annoyance seasoned with mischief. *[laughs]* There was something very powerful. When you got to meet those who were at the top of that particular tree, they turned out to be very clever, very smart managers of their own brand and, in the case of Christy, Helena [Christensen], Naomi, and Kate [Moss], people you'd want to hang out with.

Really?

Hmm . . . They were much more interesting than most musicians. We had a lot of fun, a lot of laughs. We spent summers together. It was great, but it was anathema for a lot of our fans.

Some thought you had lost it completely, or betrayed some sort of sacred cause. You were living the rock-star life.

The funny thing is, those girls, all of them, love and know music more than most musicians. Kate and Christy are brilliant DJs, and always know what's coming round the corner musically. Helena the same, and one of the great conversationalists, hungry for ideas—what can we make happen that night, that year. They can see potential, where others might miss it. And Christy just doesn't miss a thing. Our summers in the mid-nineties were a little heady, a little hedonistic, but Edge and myself fell back in love with music in a way that was largely inspired by those girls and some of our other friends, like Michael Hutchence: great house parties, dancing, swimming in the Mediterranean, night-swimming—there was a great REM song—Michael Stipe, a true poet. Frivolity, exactly the time when we needed some.

There's a word you're not using, which is *decadence*.

I'm not using it because it wasn't decadent, it was just the opposite. Decadence is when you have it all in front of you and don't notice. I noticed everything. And I appreciated it.

What about the rest of your family?

It was a great time for them also. We were all at home, Ali was now closer to the "big girls," as they were known, than myself and Edge. There were young kids to look after, so we kept it somehow grounded.

But living the rock star's life was not what we expected from U2. Isn't it a cliché: here you are now, with a villa in the south of France. Didn't the Rolling Stones have a villa up the road where they recorded *Exile On Main Street* in 1971?

They should have stayed there; that's a great album. I'm one of the people who believes there's more in them. The music has to come out of a life. If there's no life, there's no music. But I think, again, as much as we were playing with clichés, we were also trying to crack them open. You've gotta remember the context here, the context of grunge, the sort of Seattle sound that was dominant at the time. I loved Seattle and I loved the sound, in fact the sound in the sense of a river, as it comes into the delta, the mouth of the river. It's industrial, it's gray, there's rainy skies, there's a plaid shirt, there's ripped jeans, there's thrift-shop jumpers with holes in them, and this kind of umbilical roar from Kurt Cobain. And there arrive in the harbor, plastic pants on a giant cruise ship with a satellite dish at the top going the wrong way up the river. *[laughs]* On Zoo TV, I suppose we were against the obvious definitions of authenticity. Authenticity is about an honest discourse between heart and mind, body, soul. It's nothing to do with the clothes you wear. These white rock stars, they think they're authentic, and that Prince is just some sort of show business Christmas tree. But he has more soul in his little finger than a whole harbor full of those rock bands. Kraftwerk . . . There's another example of cosmic soul.

The grunge movement was very much anti-eighties. It was aimed against the pretension to glamour of the eighties.

But the eighties weren't glamorous. The eighties were ugly: big hair, shoulder pads. I see the eighties as very ugly and very unglamorous. I think U2 are one of the few things you can recommend from the eighties.

The eighties were the reign of fun, fashion, style over substance, the love of money, all those things that people thought U2 were standing against.

We were, and still were in the nineties, challenging them, we just took a different route. The nineties were much sexier.

The nineties were sexier for you, because you had been a zealot during the eighties. Others hadn't been. I mean, look at Madonna. I think the funniest thing about the nineties is that pop artists wanted to go dark and introspective, and acts like U2 wanted to go pop and fight for their right to party. They sort of changed sides and crossed each other's paths. Would you agree?

But *Achtung, Baby* and *Zooropa* are hardly pop. They are as intense and dense as it gets. In fact I remember telling this to a German journalist before the album came out. But he misunderstood "dense" for "dance." The remixes put the confusion to work.

That was in Europe. What about America?

I loved Pearl Jam. Eddie Vedder had an authenticity in that voice of his. They had and they still have commitment as a band. There wasn't much of that in the eighties. In fact, at the end of the nineties, when the PopMart show eventually got to Seattle, the city was really good to us. It was the best show of the tour, outside of Chicago. All the Seattle musicians came down to show support for what we were doing. You know, even Kurt Cobain, before he died, was dressing up in a silver shirt.

Who says *no* the most often in the band? I'm guessing it's Larry.

[laughs] Well, I wouldn't have thought that needed much private detective work. Yeah, he's by far the most cautious person in the band, and does not want to set out on the journey until he has a clear idea of where we're going and how we might get there. How old-fashioned! *[laughs]* You know, he's the most sensible man in the band in that sense.

I remember, when *The Joshua Tree* was released, way before it turned out to be your biggest success, Larry was the one, in the interviews, who was sup-

posed to have convinced you that the duty of U2 was to write and perform timeless pop songs.

Yeah. He and Paul McGuinness are the two people around us who are the most intolerant of what we might call the *artiste*, which is to say they're suspicious of art. *[laughs]* But that's all about control. If I were an artist, I'd want to be in advertising, because I would find it very difficult—and Larry would find it impossible—to hand over judgment of the quality of your work to critics. That's the problem with art: what is and what isn't art is decided by very few people. So those people, because there's less of them, become very powerful. Whereas with a song, it goes on the radio: people hear it, they like it, they put it at the top of the charts. It's not mediated the same way. So I think Larry's always had a suspicion of art, because, then, we're depending on the critics. Any band that has ever depended on the critics is usually broken up by the critics.

Because there's too much pressure on them? Is that what you mean?

Well, that's just no way to live. So he was always looking for the clearer idea, the clearer melody line with the least pretension.

But was he happy while you were recording *Achtung, Baby*?

Well, no. That's what I'm saying. So, therefore, the only way Larry was going to like *Achtung, Baby* is if the songs were great. He couldn't care less about the fact that we were working with technology. And the art project, that was just Bono and Edge being self-indulgent. Whereas the songs—are they any good? If not, let's go home, this place is freezing.

What was his opinion of Brian Eno?

Well, there again, there is a perfect example. Larry would have the least amount of time for process as an essential ingredient. Brian's all about process. The first thing Brian does when he arrives at a session is he redecorates the room—I'm not kidding. He tidies up the place, gets rid of instruments, amplifiers and . . .

people *[laughs]* who are not integral. Then he asks about our approach, what approach are we taking. So there's a lot of time spent on the process. So Larry would have his eyes up to heaven. But then, when a great song arrives at the end of the day, Larry would walk up to Brian and go: "That was a great day." But if the song didn't arrive, Larry would try to stop him being paid. *[laughs]* He'd want Brian to be writing the check for the privilege of being in the room with the band. *[laughs]* It's all about results. If the song arrives at the end of it, that must have been worth it; if the song didn't, he'd rather be home playing with his kids.

How was he showing his impatience?

I think on *Achtung, Baby,* there were a couple of occasions he was nearly at the airport. There was one occasion when he was left behind at what we called "the Brown Hotel" in East Berlin, where everything was brown. At a very tense time, when we had been in Berlin for three weeks, and had produced not one note of any real worth, when things were really tense, Larry was left in the hotel lobby by mistake when everyone else was taken to the studio. I mean, I think the comedy in the situation was eventually spotted by him. But Larry wouldn't mind being left behind if he later had to catch up to something great. He couldn't handle being left behind if he would later catch up with something as brown as the hotel. And there was a lot of brown on that record, before it finally became Day-Glo.

So it took Brian Eno, Daniel Lanois, and Flood to turn black and white into Day-Glo?

And Steve Lillywhite to keep it in focus. I have to say I don't know where we'd be as a band without these people. Daniel Lanois is the finest musician. If you're making an album with him, it's got to be a great album, or someone is gonna die—either you or him. He can't be around average. He can't be around anything that doesn't ring true. He's the definition of a line I used in "Vertigo": *A feeling is much stronger than a thought.*

With Brian Eno, wasn't it the other way around?

You would think he would be egghead over heart, but he's not at all. He listens to a lot of gospel, doo-wop, vocal groups that would bring you to tears. That said, he is hard on old concepts, always looking for the new. But context, fashion are not as important to him as soul. He is—has been—the great catalyst for some of U2's best work: "Bad," "With or Without You," "Grace," "In a Little While." These are very emotional songs that would not have existed were he not in the room.

"In a Little While," I love that. I recognize you in that song.

Well, Brian kicked that one off. He was playing around with some gospel chords, and I just started singing.

How does Flood fit into that picture?

The only man in the world who is a fan of my guitar playing! A true innovator. The explosions at the start of "Zoo Station," where you think the speakers are blowing up, that's him. A dark lord.

I'm remembering a word I meant to ask you more about. It's the first one that you used when I started you on Edge, Adam, and Larry, and that's the word *frustrating* . . . Let's take the example of the recording of your new album. Were there moments when this feeling of frustration returned?

[pause] Ermm . . . On *How to Dismantle an Atomic Bomb*, we got on pretty well, though. [pause] It's very hard sometimes to work on something for a long period of time, prepare for it, present it to the band, and then receive deafening silence, or the sound of a jaw opening and a yawn coming out. But Adam and Larry have very high standards, and usually, if it's really great, they will be very interested. But even then, they won't be hugely excited.

Don't you ever have this feeling of: "God, I know these people by heart. I know the joke he's going to make. Please, spare me . . ." How do you guard yourself against those feelings?

The thing that the three of them have—in excessive amounts—is integrity. They are capable of, on a regular basis, walking away from huge sums of money for doing the simplest things. *[laughs]* And I'm always amused at that. They're unbendable in that sense—flexible, but not bendable. The three of them have very sly senses of humor. So that keeps me interested.

You mean they keep you on your toes?

Yes. They keep me on my toes.

So, this is silly, but . . . Imagine I'm some sort of headhunter, and I'm making a phone call to you. Let's say that Edge has become a doctor, like he'd intended to way back then. So I'm asking you: You're one of his best friends, and I really want you to tell me frankly about the guy. I'm about to give him a job as a director in a clinic. So what's your opinion? What are his best qualities, his shortcomings, and what would you warn me against the most?

Well, first off, please don't make him a director of your clinic. *[laughs]*

Should we appoint him as a surgeon?

This is a surgeon. He will make the smallest incision possible, but you'll need extra ether, anesthesia. But he's gonna probably spend an hour walking around the patient before he finally cuts him open. The area he'll be interested in will be brain surgery.

I heard rumors about weird experiments he enjoys conducting. Should I be afraid of that?

If it's somebody else's head, I think you're safe. *[laughs]* He'll be very responsible with it, and, as I say, he will do the least damage on the way to the problem and on the way out of the problem.

So you're warning me about his tendency toward self-mutilation?

Yeah, I wouldn't let him operate on his own head. *[laughs]* And I'd have a backup emergency power supply, because it could take a long time.

OK, now on to Adam. I'm about to hire him as a landscape gardener. I know he loves nature. I've just bought a huge property, a wonderful place in the south of France. We have vineyards, we're going to set up a golf course, I'm thinking of waterfalls as well. We have heard about this man, Adam Clayton. We know you've worked with him a lot. So do you think he might fit the job?

Well, the first thing I'd say to you is: you want a very, very big budget. And be prepared to spend as much on the garden as you have on the property and on the house. Because, for him, the four walls are not half as interesting as what's outside of them. He sees the garden as God's furniture, and tends to it in a very meticulous way. He will never be seen running in your garden. He will frustrate the rest of the staff by how long it takes him to trim the hedge. But when you stand back, you will see some great and unexpected shapes in the hedge. He moves very slowly, but he'll build a bridge over the river that runs through it, even if he won't use a regular stonemason and he'll use a sculptor.

Excuse me, sir, but that's pretty worrying. You're telling me he's going to be very expensive and that he won't finish on schedule. I'm afraid I'm not going to hire him.

Very expensive, won't finish on schedule. Every artisan will be an artist. And it's only when you realize you have no money left in the bank and you have to sell the place that it will dawn on you that this property is now worth ten times what you put into it. Nothing that he does dates, except his hair.

Last one, of course, is Larry. And, by the way, I have no idea of the sort of job he'd have done had he not turned out to be a drummer.

Ermm . . . So what would I recommend him for? . . . An actor! Because in a way, he is the one in the band who has the most pretense for a person who is so unpretentious. He has created a character that's, I think, very enduring, unknowable, fascinating by doing very little. And I think that the camera loves people who . . . loathe the camera.

Let's say you're his agent. How would you cast him? What sort of directors would you make him work with? What kind of partners and stories?

Well, I think that all great actors are always themselves as well as the person they're playing. It's one of those great contradictions. Daniel Day-Lewis is one of my favorites. As he disappears into someone else, there's always something that rings true, because it's always him. So I think Larry will always have that quality going for him. The actor that he most reminds me of is David Carradine. There's a sort of loner quality about all his roles, even when he's in a crowd. And then, when he laughs, the whole room laughs, because something must be very funny. *[bursts out laughing]*

What would be the breakout role for him?

The highway patrolman in the middle of America. Somewhere like Aimes, Iowa. He would play the highway patrolman who is so distressed at his inability to sort out his local neighborhood, because the farms are closing down, and finally one day he cracks and starts to plan how he's going to rob the local bank.

And what should I be wary of about him?

I'd say . . . don't ask him to do Shakespeare! *[laughs]*

And why is that?

Because he's not an "ac-TOR." "Ac-TOR" is the man who likes the sound of his own voice. You know, the people in theaters. *[puts on voice]* "Hello-o, da-aa-rling . . ." The air kissing . . . He's not an "ac-TOR," he's an "acteur."

And eventually, you, Bono, you've become a top insurance salesman in our company. We're about to hire you as the head of our new venture in online insurance. Does that sound like a good idea to your fellow musicians and Paul McGuinness? What would they say?

They would say: why should we buy insurance from somebody who had never taken any out?

4. WHO'S THE ELVIS HERE?

The next conversation is the third installment from that November afternoon we spent in Killiney in 2002. You'll notice that the mood got heavier. Luckily, we had the MTV awards, pizza, Christina Aguilera, and a few glasses of Chablis to lighten things up.

Your picture has recently appeared on the cover of *Time* magazine with the tag-line: "Can Bono save the world?" You have taken a part-time job as a world ambassador for the DATA organization (Debt, AIDS, Trade, Africa— but also Democracy, Accountability, and Transparency for Africa), a group you co-founded with Bobby Shriver. Before we discuss the roots of your involvement in humanitarian action, I have to ask: Don't you ever feel like the world is just shit and nothing can be done about it?

I do get depressed on occasion, a bit black about the uphill nature of this particular struggle. What we're talking about, in DATA though, in the end, comes from a great tradition. It's the journey of equality. Equality is an idea that was first really expressed by the Jews when God told them that everyone was equal in His eyes. A preposterous idea then and still hard to hang on to now. You can imagine these farmers standing there with sheep shit on their shoes in front of Pharaoh. And Pharaoh would say: *"You* are equal to *me?"* And they'd look in their book and they'd go: "That's what it says here." After a while, people accepted that, though not easily. Rich and poor were equal in God's eyes. But not blacks! Black people can't be equal. Not women! You're not asking us to accept that?! You see, in the Judeo-Christian tradition, we have to accept this: it says that everyone is equal. Now most people accept that women, blacks, Irish, and Jews are equal, but only within these borders. I'm not sure we accept that Africans are equal.

I'm not sure about what you're saying either.

Right now there is the biggest pandemic in the history of civilization, happening in the world now with AIDS. It's bigger than the Black Death, which took a third of Europe in the Middle Ages. Sixty-five hundred Africans are dying every day of a preventable, treatable disease. And it is not a priority for the West: two 9/11s a day, eighteen jumbo jets of fathers, mothers, families falling out of the sky. No tears, no letters of condolence, no fifty-one-gun salutes. Why? Because we don't put the same value on African life as we put on a European or an American life. God will not let us get away with this, history certainly won't let us get away with our excuses. We say we can't get these antiretroviral drugs to the farthest reaches of Africa, but we can get them our cold fizzy drinks. The tiniest village, you can find a bottle of Coke. Look, if we really thought that an African life was equal in value to an English, a French, or an Irish life, we wouldn't let two and a half million Africans die every year for the stupidest of reasons: money. We just wouldn't. And a very prominent head of state said to me: "It's true. If these people weren't Africans, we just couldn't let it happen." We don't really deep down believe in their equality.

Who said that?

I can't say . . . but it was a head of state who was ashamed. It actually scandalized him. We have written off Africans. So the next step in the journey of equality is to get to a place where we accept that you cannot choose your neighbor. In the Global Village, distance no longer decides who is your neighbor, and "Love thy neighbor" is not advice, it's a command.

You're from the same country as Jonathan Swift. You know he had no hope in the human race . . .

"Eat the rich" was a classic. What a great line!

I read *Gulliver's Travels* when I was fifteen, and I found it said a lot about mankind's evil nature. But then, I'm much more of a pessimist than you are.

But it looked impossible for African Americans to have emancipation from slavery! The idea that women would have a vote and run corporations and be prime minister of England, even fifty years ago, was a very hard thing to accept.

I see your point. We've certainly witnessed changes, and maybe we're more generous than our grandparents.

I don't know about that. But what we can say is that there has been in the areas of equality a lot of progress.

My objection is that different civilizations don't keep the same pace. That is what history shows. We in Western Europe and North America live in a postmodern world, whereas Africa lingers on in the Middle Age, or pre–Middle Age. So however well-intentioned we may be, there is an unbridgeable gap. So how do you think we can come to understand each other?

But why is Africa pre–Middle Age? The answer to that question is historical. And let me illustrate this. *[Bono abruptly gets up and calls out to his daughter]* Jojo! Jordan! *[He leaves the room and climbs up the stairs. He returns more than a minute later, bringing back a school manual. He sits down again and starts to leaf through it.]* This is a fifteen-year-old's geography textbook. I was looking at this today, and it tells about it exactly. *[Eventually finds the passage and pro-*

ceeds to read out] "Income gap. Two hundred years ago, it appears that very little difference existed in living standards between the Northern Hemisphere and the Southern Hemisphere. Today, a very wide income gap exists: the North is many times richer than the South. What brought about this gap? The answer seems to lie in colonialism, trade, and debt." They're explaining to this fifteen-year-old kid how the reason why Africa is still in the Middle Age is largely to do with us, and our exploitation through French and British colonialism, but also in their present exploitation of unfair trade agreements, or old debts. You can't fix every problem. But the ones you can, you must. To the degree we are responsible, we must fix. When you ask me to just accept that civilizations are just at a different level, there is a reason why they are. That is my answer.

OK. But let's try this from a different angle. You know that colonialism in France, in the late nineteenth century, was considered a left-wing idea. It was championed by humanitarians.

[laughs] You wanna ask the Africans! Did they feel it was humanitarian?

I'm just telling you what the thinking was at the time in France.

What colonies did France have? Algeria, Côte-d'Ivoire . . . How many? Vietnam . . . France was very generous to a lot of countries there. *[laughs]*

Some people wanted to bring wealth and development to those populations. It may sound unacceptable to our modern ears, because of the evils concealed or brought about. But if you read the literature from that time, you would see that some of the colonialists were actually idealists . . .

But there were many excuses for it! The missions . . . to bring Christianity to the Dark Continent.

Sure, and to bring them the benefits of Western civilization. I'm not saying we have to endorse that today.

But in return, they were robbed of their natural resources: gold, silver, and finally the right to rule themselves. So, however way it was coached or described, in the end, this movement set back that continent by hundreds and hundreds of years. Civilization did not come with colonialism. That's patently clear.

All noble ideas inevitably carry with them the weight of evil.

Why?

Well, look at communism, for instance. Or, you're often telling people that the United States were a great idea, but look at all the wrongs it caused. I don't think you can look at history in a black-and-white way. Every good thing has a dark side.

Right.

Some would say the United States based itself on the killing and the extermination of native populations.

Yes. I think most Americans would admit that America had a bloody beginning, not the founding fathers, but what came after. And the blood is still crying from the ground. Even today the level of violence and gun crime is extraordinary. You wonder if there isn't some kind of relationship with its violent past. However, outside of that genocide, the peoples who made America their New World came to cling to the idea that everyone could be equal. They might have inherited some bad Karma from the abuse of native culture and peoples, but they were holding on to an idea very tightly as they arrived on the shore and ports of America, and it was equality. I guess politically it's an idea that came from France originally, and it is still one of the hardest ideas to live up to. It's a shame there was a layer before it got there, of abuse, but that does not contaminate the idea. The idea is pure. The place where it was executed may not have been.

Napoleon was the product of noble ideals as well.

[interrupting] I like little guys with big ideas! *[laughs]*

But his campaigns killed hundreds of thousands of people! It's the equivalent of a genocide. But Napoleon still had many supporters among the conquered peoples, because he was spreading the ideals of the French Revolution, like freedom over tyranny. Generous ideas quite often bring about bloody results. So often, the good and the bad are closely intertwined.

Right, it's true. Look: evil encroaches in tiny footsteps on every great idea. And evil can almost outrun most great ideas, but finally, in the end, there is light in the world. I accept God chooses to work with some pretty poor material. But I'm much more amazed by what people are capable of than I am by what they're not capable of, which is to say evil doesn't surprise me.

I think you underestimate evil.

The jungle is never far from the surface of our skin. No, I'm never surprised by evil, but I'm much more excited about what people are capable of. And we're talking about the journey of equality here. Well, it's ongoing. There's been some incredible progress but, I'll accept, just more than there has been terrible regression. You're right. With science comes $E=MC^2$, out of which we have fusion. You know that famous quote from Oppenheimer? In July 1945, at the testing of the first nuclear experiment, in the desert of Alamogordo, in New Mexico, when he realized what his science had uncovered, he made the famous quote from the Bhagavad Gita, the Indian holy book: "I have become Death itself."[*] So . . . Please, please, please! Don't ever see me as a sort of wide-eyed idealist who only sees the good in people. Cockeyed, maybe.

It's a very important point.

I do see the good in people, but I also see the bad—I see it in myself. I know what I'm capable of, good and bad. It's very important that we make that clear. Just because I often find a way around the darkness doesn't mean that I don't know it's there.

---

[*] J. Robert Oppenheimer's quote is: "I am become Death, shatterer of worlds." The Bhagavad Gita says: "I am death, the mighty destroyer of the world."

How do you find your way through darkness? I guess, just like anyone, you stumble from time to time.

I try to make the light brighter.

And what does the trick for you? Give me an example.

Harry Belafonte is one of my great heroes. He's an old-school leftist and holds on to certain principles like others hold on to their life. He told me this story about Bobby Kennedy, which changed my life indeed, pointed me in the direction I am going now politically. Harry remembered a meeting with Martin Luther King when the civil rights movement had hit a wall in the early sixties: *[impersonating croaky voice of Belafonte]* "I tell you it was a depressing moment when Bobby Kennedy was made attorney general. It was a very bad day for the civil rights movement." And I said: "Why was that?" He said: "Oh, you see, you forget. Bobby Kennedy was Irish. Those Irish were real racists; they didn't like the black man. They were just one step above the black man on the social ladder, and they made us feel it. They were all the police, they were the people who broke our balls on a daily basis. Bobby at that time was famously not interested in the civil rights movement. We knew we were in deep trouble. We were crestfallen, in despair, talking to Martin, moaning and groaning about the turn of events, when Dr. King slammed his hand down and ordered us to stop the bitchin': "Enough of this," he said. "Is there nobody here who's got something good to say about Bobby Kennedy?" We said: "Martin, that's what we're telling ya! There is no one. There is nothing good to say about him. The guy's an Irish Catholic conservative badass, he's bad news." To which Martin replied: "Well, then, let's call this meeting to a close. We will re-adjourn when somebody has found one thing redeeming to say about Bobby Kennedy, because that, my friends, is the door through which our movement will pass." So he stopped the meeting and he made them all go home. He wouldn't hear any more negativity about Bobby Kennedy. He knew there must be something positive. And if it was there, somebody could find it.

Did they ever find anything redeeming about Bobby Kennedy?

Well, it turned out that Bobby was very close with his bishop. So they befriended the one man who could get through to Bobby's soul and turned him into their Trojan horse. They sort of ganged up on this bishop, the civil rights religious people, and got the bishop to speak to Bobby. Harry became emotional at the end of this tale: "When Bobby Kennedy lay dead on a Los Angeles pavement, there was no greater friend to the civil rights movement. There was no one we owed more of our progress to than that man," which is what I always thought. I mean, Bobby Kennedy is still an inspiration to me. And whether he was exaggerating or not, that was a great lesson for me, because what Dr. King was saying was: Don't respond to caricature—the Left, the Right, the Progressives, the Reactionary. Don't take people on rumor. Find the light in them, because that will further your cause. And I've held on to that very tightly, that lesson. And so, don't think that I don't understand. I know what I'm up against. I just sometimes do not appear to.

I think that someone in your position has the ability to do things that other people can't. People who run relief agencies don't get to talk to Tony Blair. Still, aren't you in danger of being used by those politicians, who will in the end do what they have been elected to do, which sometimes isn't a lot?

I'm available to be used, that is the deal here. I'll step out with anyone, but I'm not a cheap date. I know that I'm being used, and it's just at what price.

So what's the price?

Well, as an example, so far, from the work DATA has been involved in with others, we got in late 2002 an extra five billion dollars from the United States for the poorest of the poor, and a commitment for another twenty billion over the next few years in a combination of increased aid to countries tackling corruption and a historic AIDS initiative. From a conservative administration, that was unthinkable in the development community. Even a year ago [2004].

Would it have been possible if you hadn't represented that organization?

A lot of people were involved, but I think most would agree that we helped dramatize in a new way as justice rather than charity, as something the Left and Right could work on together, getting radical student activists to work together with conservative church groups. We had rock stars, economists, popes, and politicians all singing off the same hymn sheet.

Did this start with the Drop the Debt campaign?

I was talking about DATA in the U.S., but you're right, the model was formed by Jubilee 2000 in Europe in their campaign to eliminate Third World debt. In 1997, I was asked to help out in a campaign to use the occasion of the millennium to cancel the chronic debt burdens of the poorest countries on the planet to the richest. Politicians were looking for something dramatic to mark that moment. It would be the abolition of an economic slavery. Some of the countries like Tanzania or Zambia were spending twice as much of their national income servicing old Cold War loans than they were on the health and education of their populace. It was obscene.

But what is it exactly that made them borrow so much in the first place?

Well, you can say it was irresponsible borrowing, but it was also irresponsible lending. In the sixties and the seventies, the West was throwing money at any African country who wasn't siding with the Communists. The Cold War was being fought in Africa. People like Mobutu, the dictator in what was then called Zaire, stashed this money in Swiss bank accounts and let his people starve to death. It is completely unacceptable to make the grandchildren of those bad decisions pay the price for that. As I say, this was not about charity, this was about justice.

How much have you succeeded in canceling?

About one-third of all such debts, which adds up to a hundred billion dollars' worth.

And you feel you were an important part of that success.

In truth, I think the place where I had the most impact was the United States. The movement already had a lot of momentum in Europe and especially the U.K., but in the U.S., Jubilee 2000 had been a lot slower to catch on. We were running out of time to grow the grass roots. I had to go straight to the decision-makers, or at the very least the people who knew those decision-makers.

Who were they?

The best phone call I ever made in my opinion was to the most extraordinary woman in the world: Eunice Shriver Kennedy, sister of John F. Kennedy, the woman who in her forties, after having changed the world once advising to elect JFK to president, changed the world once more by starting the Special Olympics. A legend and a lesson in civic duty. All the Kennedys are, and I'm not just saying that because they're Ireland's Royal Family, but because I've seen how hard they work.

What advice did Eunice Shriver give you?

She told me to ring her son Bobby, which I did. And he immediately put the family Filofax to work for me. Remember Filofax?

In a different lifetime, yeah.

Well, it was contacts. And more than just giving me numbers, he called them and often accompanied me to those appointments.

Would a member of the most famous Democratic family have influence with Republicans?

Actually, some. But there were more than a few meetings where he would hide in the corridor outside. Mind you, his brother-in-law Arnold Schwarzenegger had a lot of Republican friends. Arnie called a congressman from Ohio called John Kasich, who became an important guide through the Republican side of the Congress.

So you feel that without you, the American side of the Drop the Debt campaign would not have been as effective.

Myself and Bobby Shriver. I think that if you asked President Clinton how he got a hundred percent of the bilateral debt canceled for twenty-three countries, he would say that DATA's forerunner Jubilee 2000 more than helped. If you asked him how it made it through Congress, he would say: "A lot of footwork by a few people." And I'm certainly one of them. Bobby Shriver and I, Larry Summers, the then treasury secretary, we were dead in the water without John Kasich. President Clinton believed in it, but we had to fight hard to get his way. It's funny, I thought the president of the United States was the Big Cahuna, the Boss. But he's not. In the United States, the Congress is in charge. When President Clinton announced his commitment to full cancellation, we thought we cracked it, we were jumping up and down. But then I started getting calls: this isn't gonna get past Congress. And that's how I found myself inside the body politic, trying to figure out how it lived and breathed, how it behaved— a rock star wandering around the corridors of power rather than placarding at the gates outside. Strange. Every few weeks I had to travel to Washington, D.C., to go and meet all kinds of unexpected people, in an attempt to get debt cancellation accepted in the United States. It was uphill. Myself and Bobby Shriver were entering a world not just of ideologue politicians, but one of bankers and economists, and a certain elite who guard America's piggy bank. For most of these people, especially the bankers, it's against their religion to cancel debts. Bobby had a background in finance, but I was way out of my depth.

So what was your line in that part?

I had one answer and two questions.

I'm not surprised you'd start off with an answer. What was it?

Go back to school. Bobby fixed me an appointment with Professor Jeffrey Sachs at Harvard, which completely changed my life. He emboldened me. He turned the math into music. I spent a lot of time with him on and off campus. He's a man who sees no obstacles to a great idea.

But did you also meet people who didn't think that way?

Yes. I also asked and got to meet very conservative economists like Robert J. Barrow, for example. I wanted to get to know the people who might oppose the idea.

What was he like?

I liked him. In the end he wrote an article for the *Wall Street Journal,* offering us "Two Cheers."

OK. Now tell me about the two questions.

The first, I have just mentioned. "Who can stop this from happening?" I wanted to meet the people who could roadblock us . . . to roadblock them.

And the second?

The second was: "Who's the Elvis here?" In whatever area I was, I wanted to know who's the boss, who's the *capo di tutti capi* here. "Who's Elvis," I used to ask, at banking? And they'd say: "Well, in development, it's the World Bank, it's Jim Wolfensohn, it's the people running the International Monetary Fund." So I used to go and meet them. It's Robert Rubin, who was the treasury secretary of the United States, his signature was on every dollar; it's Paul Volcker, who was the legendary chairman of the Federal Reserve, the Alan Greenspan of his age. I just went all the places they didn't expect me to turn up. I didn't go because I wanted to, I went because we had to, to get it through the Congress. It wasn't enough just to talk to President Clinton. Oddly enough, Bill Clinton's staff used to call him Elvis anyway. That was his nickname. The Southern twang, I guess. But it turns out Elvis wasn't enough. In the United States, the president is not the most powerful force—the Congress is. We needed a Colonel Tom* to get our bill passed. And Colonel Tom was the Congress.

So it was like a crash course in how power works.

That's what it was.

So how did you put that knowledge into practice? What were you able to achieve?

On debt cancellation we won the day. It was close, but with a lot of help from a few people, particularly John Kasich. He was incredible. He passionately made the case to the Republicans. In a floor fight in the House of Representatives, he shouted down opposition to the bill and we made it. It took him months, and me months traveling back and forth from Dublin. Internationally, it was no small victory. If the U.S. hadn't moved, everyone else would have gotten out. As I say, there was a hundred billion dollars in play, and I'm very proud of our part, however small it was.

So you think your photo with these politicians paid off.

Well, there is three times the amount of children going to school in Uganda now, three times the amount of children as the result of debt cancellation. That's just one country. All over the developing world, you'll find hospitals built with that money, real lives changed, communities transformed. And if it didn't go through Congress, then the Europeans could have fudged there. You see, they move en masse. Would we have gotten there without people taking to the streets, banging the dustbin lids and raising the temperature of the debate? No. You need both. What the protesters are asking is to get in the room. So then, when you get in the room, occupy it, make your argument, and don't leave till you get the check.

It's another kind of power: star power.

*"Colonel" Tom Parker was Elvis Presley's manager.

You know, celebrity is ridiculous. It's silly, but it is a kind of currency, and you have to spend it wisely. And I've learnt that much.

In the U.S., you went from friend of Bill Clinton to flashing a peace sign in a photo op with George W. Bush . . . Please explain, because I'm getting confused here . . .

I was in a photo with President Bush because he'd put 10 billion dollars over three years on the table in a breakthrough increase in foreign assistance called the Millennium Challenge. It is an amusing photograph. I had just got back from accompanying the president as he announced this at the Inter-American Bank. I kept my face straight as we passed the press corps, but the peace sign was pretty funny. He thought so too. Keeping his face straight, he whispered under his breath, "There goes a front page somewhere: Irish rock star with the Toxic Texan." *[laughs]*

What an amusing and self-effacing guy. It's hard to buy that, don't you think?

You know, I think the swagger and the cowboy boots come with some humor. He is a funny guy. Even on the way to the bank he was taking the piss. The bulletproof motorcade is speeding through the streets of the capital with people waving at the leader of the Free World, and him waving back. I say: "You're pretty popular here!" He goes *[Texan accent]*: "It wasn't always so . . ."—Oh really?—"Yeah. When I first came to this town, people used to wave at me with one finger. Now, they found another three fingers and a thumb." Isn't that funny? *[laughs]*

So you liked this man?

Yes. As a man, I believed him when he said he was moved to also do something about the AIDS pandemic. I believed him. Listen, I couldn't come from a more different place, politically, socially, geographically. I had to make a leap of faith to sit there. He didn't have to have me there at all. But, you know, you don't have to be harmonious on everything—just one thing—to get along with someone.

You put other stuff out of your mind: tax cuts for the rich and an up-and-coming war in Iraq?

You become a single-issue protagonist. You represent a constituency that has no power, no vote, in the West, but whose lives are hugely affected by our body politic. Our clients are the people who are not in the president's ear. My mouth, because it is, belongs to them. Our clients are the people whose lives depend on these Western drugs, whose lives will be radically altered by new schools and new investment in their country. That's a position I take very seriously. They didn't ask me to represent them. Jubilee 2000 asked me to represent them, and, yes, Jubilee 2000 is a North-South, pan-African, pan-European, and pan-American operation, but those people didn't actually say: "Hey, Bono, would you do that?" The ball kind of fell to my feet, it's the truth, and I saw a way past the goalkeeper. What am I gonna do? I'm gonna do what I can. It's already preposterous to have that position. I'll let somebody else be war watchdog.

Speaking of watchdogs, was there uproar within the band when they saw you in some of these photos?

Yes, but they also know the strategy is effective. If it's not, they're going to torture me. They're results-oriented. They also push me to sharpen my arguments.

So being in a band prepared you for what you're doing now.

It turns out that a lot of the things that you learn from being in a band are analogous to politics. And not just politics, even the so-called nasty old world of commerce, anywhere you've got to get your message across. I know much more than you'd expect about these things, just from trying to keep on top of U2's business. We like to say our band is a gang of four, but a corporation of five. I understand brands, I can understand corporate America, I can understand economics. This is not at all so difficult. U2 was art school, business school. It's always the same attitude that wins the day: faith over fear. Know your subject, know your opponent. Don't have an argument you can't win. On the Africa stuff we can't lose, because we're putting our shoulder to a door God Almighty has

WHO'S THE ELVIS HERE?

already opened. We carry with us—this is something that's important—the moral weight of an argument. That's much bigger than the personalities having the debate. I might walk into an important office and people are looking at me as though I'm some sort of exotic plant. But after a few minutes, they don't see me. All they're hearing is the argument, and the argument has some sort of moral force that they cannot deny. It's bigger than you, and it's bigger than them. And history as well as God is on its side.

So you became an insider in the political world. I'm sure you had preconceived notions about politicians. Were those proven wrong or right?

Well, as you get older, your idea of good guys and bad guys changes. As we moved from the eighties to the nineties, I stopped throwing rocks at the obvious symbols of power and the abuse of it. I started throwing rocks at my own hypocrisy. That's a part of what that work was about: owning up to one's ego. These characters in the songs like "The Fly" are owning up to one's hypocrisy in your heart, your duplicitous nature. There's a song called "Acrobat" that goes : *Don't believe what you hear, don't believe what you see / If you just close your eyes / You can feel the enemy . . .* I can't remember it, but the point is: you start to see the world in a different way, and you're part of the problem, not just part of the solution! *[laughs]*

It's probably the same when you start a band. You also have these preconceived notions about the corporate labels and corporate management. Once you get to the other side of the fence, maybe you begin to see things differently.

It is exactly analogous. So who's the devil here? Bureaucracy! It's like a Kafka story. The labyrinth of red tape that excuses inaction. But it's not an excuse, and you have to go through it. Even if a lot of them are not bad guys, even if they're just busy guys, they have to be held responsible and accountable, because these people are in power. Like, Congressman Tom Lantos talks about, as a child, being put on a train to a Hungarian concentration camp and how crowds gathered to watch them being put on the trains, and how this haunted him later in life, not the mistreatment at these death camps, but the blank looks of the passersby, how he repeated the question often to himself: "Didn't anyone ask where those children are going?" I said to him: "Aren't we doing that now with AIDS? We have the drugs, *but . . .*" And he said: "Yeah, we are. This is exactly analogous. We are watching them being put on the trains."

And what should be the response?

I want to find people who will lie across the tracks.

So, are the politicians the train conductors?

No, it's our indifference that should be on trial. As for politicians, I've got to meet and know quite a lot of them; I'm surprised by how much respect I have. They work a lot harder than I thought, they're not paid that well, the most talented of them would definitely make tons of cash in the commercial world, but stay in politics out of a sense of civic duty. People say power is their drug of choice, but in these days the CEO of a large corporation is the one with power. It's true that in the U.S. special interest ruins a lot of politics, and runs a lot of shows, that's the closest you can find to outright evil in politics. The National Rifle Association can buy their way in an argument. How many Americans think it's a good thing that you can buy a gun in a shop? Hardly any! But the ones that do have put so much money into the National Rifle Association that they can get their issue through Congress. It's amazing! Why can't we treat the people that live in wretched poverty with the kind of political muscle they have in the tobacco industry, who hire a bunch of lobbyists and go surround Washington, D.C.? They don't just go, "Cigarette smoking is a fundamental human right. We want to smoke!" No. They fight tooth and nail for that piece of that pie and their customers, and I'm sometimes one of them . . .

So how does DATA "fight tooth and nail" for its clients, the poorest of the poor?

What we're trying to do at the moment, those of us who care about the wanton loss of life and the inequalities of the developing world, is to come together under one umbrella. In fact, we're calling it the One campaign—not a reference to the U2 song, but that'll come in handy. We have to stop doffing our caps and shyly begging for crumbs from the table of the rich countries. We've got to get organized. We have to be able to hurt people who harm us, who obstruct the necessary legislation to put things right. We want to be able to take out radio ads in the constituencies of obstructive politicians, and explain that it's not just money they're cutting off. It's lives, mothers, children dying, like I have seen with my own eyes in a hospital in Malawi—three to a bed, two on top and one underneath. The statistics have faces, they're living and breathing. That is until a decision in D.C., London, Paris, Tokyo, Berlin goes against them, then they stop breathing.

And has your strategy been working?

We've already done it in a small way with a congressman who should now remain nameless, who wanted to be famous for cutting foreign aid until he started to hear from every church and high school in his district that his obstruction was killing kids. We had ads all over the radio. In the end, to his credit, he apologized. You see, that's political muscle; that's what people can do if they work together and invest in a movement. Politicians are about "pig roasts": it's what people are talking about when they're barbecuing chicken that counts. It's what church people are saying, "soccer moms" as well as college students.

What will happen if your dialogues don't result in any real change?

When there are so many lives at stake, I think we will have to consider civil disobedience—certainly, taking to the streets in numbers that will surprise the status quo. There are more regular people than you can imagine who care about these issues and are ready to more than put themselves out to make poverty history.

You take a lot of moral positions in our conversations, but you're wise enough to know that it's not necessarily morality that will help your cause triumph.

The moral force, finally, I do believe in the weight of it. But the apparatus is not moral. The route through it is a very cynical one.

You said it was a labyrinth. Did you find your way through it?

There were ways you could gang up or surround difficult people. If a politician had a hard heart, maybe the person who organized his schedule would not. "Staffers" became allies. After all, they were the ones running the show. Proper politicians were older, but the people who ran their offices were my age or younger. So if they weren't U2 fans, they probably knew one. I found in a lot of cases their idealism still intact.

Sometimes we run into people who are the same age as us but who have made different choices. They'd say to you: "I'm standing on the same ground as you, but in my position I can't help because in my job I am stuck." They tend to be schizophrenic. How do you confront that?

I have to say that I applied the same strategy that we did as a band. When we got to the United States, or France, or Germany, in the early eighties, you had all these people in their silk jackets with the radio stations on their back, just that glazed look in their eye. I used to ask them how they got into this, and the most jaded, hardened record executive would start saying: "Oh, I used to work in a college radio station," or "I went to see Jimi Hendrix at the Fillmore," "I saw the Rolling Stones with Brian Jones"—Really, how was it like? I would get them to remind themselves why they came to the party, because often they'd forgotten. It's the same for the politicians: a lot of them came for the right reasons, but just forgot. And of course politicians are a little like priests and cops. They're either there for the best or the worst reasons: to serve or to abuse their power! *[laughs]* But the latter are the few, not the many.

Just like politics, it seems like people enter the music business for either the best or the worst reasons. Have you had to deal with much corruption there?

U2 has had a pretty good time of it in the music business. Our manager, Paul McGuinness, protected us from so much, he really was a cut above the rest, and instilled in us a sense that we had to be awake to the business as we were to the art. Yeah, we have had to deal with some bullies at a corporate level in the music business, but in the end I don't have "Slave" written on my face, like Prince did in the early nineties. U2 is in charge of its own destiny. We own our master tapes, we own our copyrights, we run our own show, the music business does not own us.

You own your own stuff. That's almost unheard of, isn't it?

Well, there was a cost to that, as I told Prince when he asked me. We took a lower royalty rate, and on those big albums, we were paid less. But we own it. I asked him: "Why are you wearing 'Slave'? He said: "I don't own my stuff, they own it. They own me." And then he asked me like you just did: "How did you pull that off?—Eh, lower royalty rates." You know, most people want the money in their hand, not down the road. There's no excuse in the twentieth century for intelligent people signing a deal they don't understand. That said, Prince deserves the best deal in the world because he is the best in the world. He's Duke Ellington to me!

Back to politics for a second. Do you hear a lot of: "I would love to help you but I can't" from politicians?

One congressman wouldn't even look at me. He was in charge of yes-or-no'ing foreign appropriations. He was a big shot and a big problem. He would talk to me like almost through an interpreter. He was just kind of upset that he, a hard-working guy, had to talk to this rock star from Ireland. You know, I kind of agreed with him. He was saying: You're not gonna get this money, because I know where it's going. It's going down a rat hole, these guys have been ripping us off for years. Because Africa's first problem is not natural calamity, it's not their corrupt relationship with Europe and America. They're the second and third problems. The first problem is their own corrupt leadership. Eventually, we convinced him that the money would be well spent, and later, when I came back from Uganda, I took him pictures of a water hole. I said: "There's the money. It didn't go down a rat hole, it went down a water hole, Congressman!" I have a lot of respect for that guy now, but he was tough. He was a tough guy. In the end of course it wasn't me that persuaded him, it was the chorus of voices in the background—the movement. This unusual panoply of powerful voices from Church leaders like the Pope to sports leaders and student bodies, what Bill Clinton later referred to as a big tent. *[laughs and puts on Southern accent]* "When you've got the Pope hanging out with rock stars, that's what I call a big tent." You see, Jubilee 2000 could get a crowd of forty thousand people to surround the G8 summit in Cologne and hold hands. So it's not just, Let's have our little photo with Bono in here, and get him out of the room. You know, there is some firepower in the background.

Have you ever said to yourself: "This is more complicated than I thought. These people may be right, I may be wrong"?

Oh yeah. When it came to understanding the big issues—and outside that fantastic phrase: "I have met my enemy and he was partly right"—I realized that a lot of the aid for instance had been incredibly badly mishandled over the years, creating worse situations. It's not enough just to ask for money. I learnt that the skeptics and the cynics had a real point, and that without strict conditionalities, there was no point in giving. You're actually propping up sometimes the most evil despots by aid.

I think the most useful people are the ones who are out in the field, who work there and know the population. I don't count myself among the skeptics or the cynics, but . . .

. . . But you're pessimistic!

A couple of years ago, I was in Tuvalu, a tiny archipelago somewhere in the middle of the South Pacific. It's all sand, all flat. They can't grow anything there. And these people get help from the European community. I talked to an Italian civil servant who lived in Fiji. He'd regularly visit these small islands to make sure that the money was well spent. He said the islanders don't go fishing anymore—they eat junk food and they watch TV, and they lie

asleep all day. Now that I'm mentioning it, it sounds like I'm describing life in some parts of Paris suburbia ... Now they have been given money to build solar panels. And then they asked: will that make our washing machines work? He said: probably not. So they said: we won't assemble them. And then they said they wanted a nuclear plant! And there are a whole bunch of civil servants there, benefiting from that aid, who obviously don't do much for their fellow men. So, without education, I'm afraid there is no point in giving aid.

That's the story of aid for the last thirty years, but this is no longer the story. That story has come to an end.

Money is not the only problem in those places.

Well, with AIDS, it is. And with some things, it is. But the waste of resources, the lack of good leadership is often the real problem.

When you discuss the problems of Africa, it seems like you think that idealism is the solution.

But I'm not dealing with idealism! None of my work is based on idealism. It's pragmatism. OK, maybe on debt cancellation, I'm arguing it as justice rather than charity. But in terms of dealing with Africa now, I'm looking for a Marshall-type plan for Africa.* That's pragmatic!

I can't help but remember what you said earlier: "At one time, it looked impossible for African Americans to be freed from slavery." But it was not only Westerners who were responsible for slavery. It was also the Arabs and other Africans.

My reply to that is: yes, but we're not talking about Arabs or other Africans. We're talking about us, our inherited wealth from that exploitation.

* See Chapter 15.

But why are Westerners still trying to solve the problems of Africa? How come Africans aren't doing it by themselves?

If we see aid as investment, and the debt burden of these countries as unjust, and offer fairer trade conditions, Africa will be able to take charge of its own destiny. The reason for the T for Trade in DATA is, in the end, aid is not the way forward for the poorest people in the world. Trade is the way forward. We have to let the poorest of the poor trade with us. And, at the moment, we're not letting them trade fairly with us. So when you say, "Why can't Africans look after themselves?," that is the only way forward for Africa: Africans taking charge of their continent. But at the moment, we won't let them! Even after twenty-three countries whose debts we've canceled now, there are still countries paying back to the World Bank and the IMF more money every year than they're spending on health and education. These are dignified people, and they wanna get up off their knees. But it's us that has them chained to the ground!

But why, then, has no African leader just come forward and said: "We don't need the white men to solve our problems. We can do it ourselves!"

But that's what NEPAD was: New Economic Partnership and Africa's Development. This is what Thabo Mbeki was doing when he put together African leaders in a new kind of partnership, away from patronage. That's what we're talking about: a new kind of relationship. But you can't self-determine if you're carrying that kind of level of injustice in trade and in debt. How about this? If Africa got one percent more trade, one percent of global trade, it's the equivalent of three times what Africa receives every year through aid. Africa receives about 21 billion dollars in aid every year. So 70 billion cash would come into the continent, for one percent increase in trade. This is the way towards self-determination. This is what we're working for, away from the nipple of aid. Africans are sick of the cap in hand. They deserve equal and as fair access as anybody else to the pie. So I'm not for some sort of paternalistic attitude to Africa. I'm against it. But in order for that to happen, we have to break a certain chain. And colonialism is still there in a certain sense. Slavery is present. Economic slavery is what we're talking about, where people make cheap goods for us in the West, but aren't paid.

Lasting presence and involvement are the things that really count, don't you think?

Well, for example, the Global Health Fund at the moment is a new and necessary approach that's set in Geneva, to deal with AIDS, TB, and malaria. It's outside of the UN, but Kofi Annan has asked for 10 billion dollars a year. It has a four percent overhead only, and out of the four percent overhead, they are hiring accounting firms like PriceWaterhouse and Stokes Kennedy Crowley in every country that applies for this. And they police and audit where the money is being spent. This is a new approach to foreign assistance or aid. In the past, aid has been tied to commercial contracts: they'd give you five dollars, but four of them you'd have to spend on French or English or German products, or consultants. It was corrupt and rotten. But those days are over. There are people who are working on this a lot harder than I, giving their whole lives to champion reform of aid, who are not going to let that happen. There will always be abuses, but the increase in foreign aid will only be for places where there's clear and transparent process, where there's good leadership, and where we can see where the money's going. The bright stars, if you like, they get hothoused. The countries around them that have no poverty-reduction programs in place and no good ideas on how to spend the money will lose out. They won't be able to gain access to these new funds, because the people whose taxes they represent won't let them, and they're right.

5. THE SHORTEST CHAPTER IN THE BOOK

I heard nothing from Bono until February 2003, when someone from Principle Management called and asked for my address. The next day, a gendarme delivered a letter by motorcycle into the hands of my stupefied twelve-year-old son Antoine, declaring: *"De la part de Monsieur Jacques Chirac"* ("On behalf of Mister Jacques Chirac"). I opened the envelope and read the card:

Mister Jacques Chirac, President of the Republic, requests the presence of Mister Michka Assayas at the ceremony where the insignia of Knight of the Legion of Honour will be presented to Mister Paul Hewson, a.k.a. Bono, at the Élysée Palace, on Friday the 28th of February 2003 at 12 hours 15—Lounge suit required.

Established by Napoleon, the Legion of Honor is a distinction that usually rewards those who served the French state. "Chevalier" is the first rank, but you may become an "Officier" or even a "Grand-Croix" in the long run. Each ministry provides a list every year, and Bono was proposed by the Ministry of Culture, which traditionally honors artists from all over the world, making them in this way honorary Frenchmen, which is without a doubt the greatest honor a non-Frenchman can receive.

For some time, I was lost in reverie. But then, and this probably is my way of responding when something goes to my head a little too much, I concentrated on a detail. What the hell was a "lounge suit"? When I found out, I just had to face the awful truth: I had no matching trousers and jacket. I went ahead anyway. So for the first and probably last time in my life, I was invited into that main courtyard of the Élysée Palace, which I had seen so many times on TV. It was a small gathering: Mr. and Mrs. Paul McGuinness with their son Max, the ambassador of Ireland and his wife, the Irish painter Louis Le Brocquy's son and his Vietnamese girlfriend, whom Chirac flabbergasted with his knowledge of Asian civilization, a French lady lawyer and friend of Bono's, and an astounded official from Universal Records in Paris, who was standing in for the missing chairman. Plus, of course, Mrs. Hewson herself, Ali. There also was an old school friend of Bono's, a girl with the radiant glare of a fifteen-year-old; Catriona, Bono's assistant; Lucy Matthew, who works for DATA (she had accompanied Bono in Africa with the ex-secretary of treasury of the United States, Paul O'Neill), and a wonderful woman who works in Geneva for the United Nations and clears the ground for many of Bono's meetings with politicians.

Chirac produced a speech, which was not so bad. Obviously, his ghostwriter had been fond of U2 at some point in his life. Notwithstanding, I had to make an effort not to burst out laughing when the president pronounced the words: "Zuh . . . Edge." "That's cool!" pronounced Bono when the speech was over. The bastard, he was not wearing a tie, and he had managed to get me wearing one. Of course, he gave me a mischievous wink when he presented me to my own president who—as all big shots I have come across in my life—looks like some kind of mechanical creature when you look at him in the eye from a close distance. Nothing personal, I had the same impression about his rival Jospin.

Bono talked to the press, and was very impressed by Chirac's knowledge of the terrain. The president had spent more time in Africa than any head of state and was genuinely trying to understand the issues, he said. After one private meeting at the Élysée, Bono was asked: Did he really believe the president was as passionate about Africa as he said?—Yes, said Bono. "My job is to turn that passion into cash."

We were all—not including Chirac—invited to a celebratory lunch at the Hôtel de Crillon, where, a few years before, U2 and crew had been ordered to clear off for the benefit of African heads of state coming over for a summit. Bono made a speech. So did Paul McGuinness, who had just had the time to hastily buy a coffee-table book presenting views of Paris. I remember the smile on Bono's face when he read my words of wisdom on it:

"Congratulations! You managed to get me moved by Chirac, and that sure is no small deed." Then the solemn mood flagged. The girls insisted on staying overnight and celebrating in Paris. They wanted to do some shopping as well. Bono went along with them, with his Legion of Honor hanging on the lapel of his jacket, the decoration looking like a fake, oversized thing on his chest. He proclaimed that he was extremely proud to have been made a "Maurice Chevalier" of the French state. I asked Bono whether he knew that Maurice Chevalier was the singer of the old classic "Thank Heaven for Little Girls." "And so we should, Michka," was his answer.

The company reassembled for dinner at a very traditional bistro, L'Ami Louis, favored in its time by President Mitterrand. I presented Bono and friends with a personal award: a toothbrush (with toothpaste), for nobody had planned to stay beforehand. Bono kept it all evening as a trophy in his breast pocket, the nylon white hairs of it proudly protruding. I did not go so far as to offer underwear, though. We finished the night in a couple of trendy clubs that the record company guy knew about (it always takes a foreigner to discover those places in your hometown). What happened here? We drank, Ali danced, Bono talked enthusiastically with strangers. And we kept drinking. I remember my behavior became extremely enthusiastic. At some point, I asked Bono something like: "And our book? What about the book?—It's going to be the shortest chapter in the book," said Bono.

A few days later, I wrote a letter to Bono to thank him again for that evening. I also mentioned the fact that I could not get through to him on his mobile. Then I received an e-mail:

Michka,

I'm e-mailing because I can't speak with a toothbrush in my mouth after that night. Sacrebleu . . . it was great to see you . . . to meet Claire* and to attempt to drink Paris dry. My number (+ 353 +++++++++) hasn't changed so you are obviously still drunk.

Your friend,

Bono

*My wife's name is actually Clara, but that was a good try.

6. THE TATTOOIST

During the winter of 2003, Bono did a lot of what he called "footwork" on behalf of DATA in the United States. That occurred during the very period when the U.S. and their allies cast no doubt on their intention to invade Iraq. From what I grasped from Principle Management's camp, Bono was reminded, somewhat firmly, by his colleagues that he still held a job as singer and writer in U2, and that an album was due for production that year. I got the information that Bono was due to give a performance on May 25, 2003, at the Pavarotti and Friends concert, a TV charity event that the maestro stages every year in his hometown of Modena (in Emilia-Romagna) for the benefit of his foundation for ill children. Other guests included the three remaining members of Queen, as well as Deep Purple, Eric Clapton, Lionel Richie, and local soul singer Zucchero. Bono had a duet programmed with the tenor. This was no Lollapalooza. I proposed to come over. Bono thought that was a good idea, and that maybe we could spend some time together. So I flew there. Bono rehearsed with what seemed to me a full orchestra. You could see Pavarotti sitting on a chair at a close distance, covered in a sort of flashy red smock of a light fabric round his neck, the kind I remember the barber would make me wear as a child in the mid-sixties. It was hanging loose on his massive features, so it made the impression of a big red balloon with a bearded smiling head on the top of it. Bono was wearing his usual Fidel Castro khaki cap. He rehearsed two songs: the first was a version of "One," accompanied by his acoustic guitar and the orchestra. But the important number was the duet of Schubert's "Ave Maria," for which he had written new lyrics. He sang: *Ave Maria / Where is the justice in this world? / The wicked make so much noise, Ma / The righteous stay oddly still / With no wisdom, all of the riches in the world leave us poor tonight / And strength is not without humility / It's weakness, an untreatable disease / And war is always the choice / Of the chosen who will not have to fight.* The day after the performance, the lyrics to Bono's revised "Ave Maria" were reproduced in every national paper in Italy.

As soon as Bono and team set foot outside the dressing room, it looked as if every possible media person in Italy was in the place. Bono stopped every two yards, speaking in front of a camera. Then there was a press conference held in a tent. Here, Bono seemed more like royalty than a celebrity, as everyone politely guffawed each time he made a joke. It was an impression that was confirmed later that evening. A dinner was set up at the restaurant owned by Pavarotti in the countryside. There, it turned to Beatlemania, except that it wasn't girls but women cooing over Bono. I swear I saw a few of them twisting their high heels on the gravel driveway, in order to catch a fleeting glimpse of him.

At the second floor of the restaurant, which had been reserved for our crowd, media people kept queuing, thirsting for the great man's words of wisdom. All of a sudden I was sitting next to Gandhi: not a bad promotion, I thought, for a guy who used to climb on piles of speakers at his own concerts. After an amazing round of desserts and grappa, we went down the stairs again. We passed in front of the resident band. They were performing "Unchain My Heart." Grappa-inspired, Bono picked up the mike. I'm not sure he knew the song. The diners cheered. When we left, grown-ups still seemed to chase after us. And it was not over. When the motorcade stopped in front of Bono's hotel in Bologna, he was greeted by a crowd of a hundred youths who cheered ecstatically. One of them brandished an acoustic guitar; another one waved the cover of *War*. Bono seemed more to be sucked into the hotel lobby than to actually enter it. Then I was left to walk to my own hotel. The sudden quietness and solitude felt weird, on the brink of being eerie. I felt I had been thrown out of an interstellar spaceship, let loose in an arbitrary spot.

The next day was a different story. I was meeting Bono in the lobby of the Grand Hotel Baglioni at midday, whence we were scheduled to leave by car and have lunch together. A crowd was still hanging around, kept away by crowd barriers and the usual guy in a black suit. In five minutes Bono was down in the lobby with Sheila Roche and his tour manager Dennis Sheehan, who said we had to use the other exit, as there was no way we could break through that crowd. On the double again. Then, as we went down the stairs, Bono muttered something to himself and said it was not OK, that this behavior was too much of "a pop star thing." So up we went again. We tried for the main door. Bad idea. The cheering crowd massed ever more tightly, traffic was blocked, and we could not take the smallest step forward. So Bono had to settle for the pop star thing and use the back entrance.

We quickly arrived in a quiet and narrow street in Bologna's Centro Storico. The empty restaurant that had been booked was so dark I first thought they were out of business for the day. Bono decided to settle for the café next door instead, a nondescript place, equally empty, where he chose to sit at a table outside. We ordered some pasta and a plate of local ham and salami. It was a brave choice of venue on Bono's part, and one that eventually got on my nerves (though I didn't show it), since we were interrupted every two minutes. A girl on a bike approached us and took Bono's arm, glowing, crying *"Che fortuna!"* ("What luck!"). Then two policewomen asked for autographs. At one point a local resident thought it was a good idea to put on "Pride (In the Name of Love)" at the highest possible volume. I must admit I was the nervous one. Throughout, Bono was as quiet as if he were sitting in his own garden. I think that reflects on the conversation, where the mood got more and more—dare I say it—"spiritual."

Remember what you told me back in Killiney? "You should ask me to draw a tree at some point." *[Bono laughs out loud]* Maybe you should have thought twice before saying that, because I want you to draw a map of the route you took to get from home to school.

It's a long one, though, because I went into the center of the city, and back out. *[proceeds to draw a map on the back of a scribbled sheet]* This is all the North Side, OK? I was at a place called Ballymun, a mile from the Tower Blocks. Actually, the Seven Towers. I'll put them in. *[draws with unconcealed pleasure]* It was an incredibly long journey: five miles into Dublin city center. And then I'd take another bus all the way, because you couldn't get to Mount Temple [his school]. That's very important, because most kids are not in the city. They're out there in the suburbs. At twelve or thirteen, I WAS A TOWNIE *[writes the phrase in capital letters]*. So I used to hang out in record shops.

Do you remember the names of the stores?

Yeah, Golden Discs. And that's a great one: Pat Egan's, in a basement. UV light. Punk rock lived there later. *[scribbles them on the sheet]*

Lots of things seemed to happen there.

Lots of things. Gambling. *[keeps on drawing]* Very important thing in here. One of the biggest institutions in my life: "Lost and Found." CIE, bus company. They knew me by name in there, because I lost something every week. I lost all my books. I lost everything I had, all the time. And I still do. Like, I lose my phone every week now. I don't seem to have a very good short-term memory. For instance, especially now, from traveling around the globe and having people driving you in taxis, chauffeurs, and so forth, I know not to store this information, because it's not my hometown. So I have no idea of directions. Even now, in my own city that I grew up in, I'm starting to forget where I'm going. *[resumes drawing]* Now, along the road—Glasnevin—was the Ink Bottle primary school. First kiss. And botanic gardens, beautiful botanic gardens. River Tolka. I used to lie along the banks of the river Tolka, among the flowers—poppies, they were—and just dream. It was a Protestant school. There weren't many Protestants in the area, so I had to go out of the area to visit the place. It was a tiny little thing with a tiny little yard. The headmaster was very good to me, to all of us. We used to kick the soccer ball over the railings into the river, and then we'd have to call school off and we'd all climb over the railings and chase the ball all the way along the river to get it back, so we'd spend miles going. On a sunny day, he kind of turned his back and waited for us to kick the ball over the railings and into the river, because I think he liked it too. It was very good memories for me, that school. Though, my first day at school, somebody bit my friend. So I banged his head off the railings. So I remember very quickly getting to a place where people wouldn't want to bite me. *[laughs]*

The first thing you drew on this map was these Tower Blocks.

I had very strong feelings about it at the time, because I remember when they pulled down the trees and fields, and started to develop the housing estate. This was to be the first high-rise experiment in Ireland. We used to play in the foundations. Then we heard they had lifts in them. We thought: Oh, this is gonna be great, this is like being modern, and Dublin's going like everyone else. Just as everywhere else in Europe was discovering that high-rise doesn't work, in Ireland we were just starting. They moved inner city communities away from their own self-managing, and policing, and real community spirit, put them in high-rise buildings. It started very quickly to descend into a dangerous place. Lifts would break down. People'd get very upset that you'd have to walk up the stairs. I remember walking up the stairs to see my friends, it was piss coming down the stairs, and stink. These were really nice families, good families, living next to people who were sociophobes, who were feeling freaked out about their new address. So when we used to go for a walk in the fields, we could come across the gangs from the Seven Towers, and that was the jungle. Violence, as I told you, is the thing I remember the most from my teenage years and earlier. This was like a working-class area that we lived in, fairly—maybe working-class, lower middle-class—but, you know, the difference between the incomes of people who lived here and people who lived there might be very little. It might be like a car. My old man had a car, so we were rich. And that was a reason to be tortured.

So the other kids who lived there resented you?

Oh yeah. Dublin was very violent. Then, the drugs came in, round 1978. There was very cheap heroin. The people who were smoking dope ended up smoking heroin, as they gave it to them for nothing. And then when people were really strung out, that became an unbelievably violent place.

Teenagers at that time seemed to feel like the old world was being destroyed. Don't you feel as well that punk rock was a way of responding to that?

I think what punk rock gave to us was that you could knock everything down and start again, either decide who you wanted to be: a new name, a new pair of shoes, a new way to see the world. Everything was possible, and the only limit was your imagination. That became further true with DJ culture. You didn't even have to play an instrument—you just had to have the imagination.

Maybe punk rock happened in reaction to the ugly new architectural landscape that was springing up, which was close to a nihilistic statement in and of itself.

Oh yeah. The violence of suburbia starts with its ugliness. The inner city communities, those redbrick houses, they actually had something attractive in texture and tone, those tiny houses my grandparents grew up in. There was more to them than this new suburbia. You know, in Ireland, in the seventies, a lot of these places were built by corrupt builders. They didn't put in plans for shops and amenities. It was just cookie-cutter housing schemes. In a way they defaced Dublin, these property developers. And the violence that returned to them, a generation later, we all had to live with it. Because in housing schemes like Tallaght, I think it's 27,000 young people between the ages of twelve and eighteen walking the streets every night. It's like an army. There was nowhere for people to go, nothing. Women used to push their prams for miles. This is a violence done to them. It's a great place now in comparison.

I once read an interview with Mick Jagger, where he said: "When I was twelve, I loved to play the fool in front of my friends." I figured you weren't like that, I presume your mood would have been more somber. Is that so?

Well, no. I was full of mischief and fun. Probably until I was fourteen. And I think everything changed when my mother died, and our home became an empty house, with all the aggression between my father, my brother, and myself. But up to that, I was full of fun and mischief.

Yeah, you mentioned that.

I mean, I had all of that. Then, later, I found that fun and mischief again with my friends and the Village, as we used to call ourselves. We invented a Village, which was an alternative community, called Lypton Village, and we used to put on arts installations, when we were sixteen, seventeen, with manic drills and stepladders. See, the alcohol level in our neighborhood was so high, people going to the pubs a lot, and we were young, arrogant, and probably very annoying kids, but we didn't wanna go that route. The pub looked like a trapdoor to somewhere very predictable, so we wouldn't drink. We used to watch *Monty Python*. We invented our own language, gave each other names, and we'd dress differently. We would put on these performance-art things, and in the end we formed two bands, the Virgin Prunes and U2. But I did have what you French would call *joie de vivre*, I was fun. You know what Ali said to me ten years ago? She said: "You know, I fell in love with you because there was mischief in your eyes. You were bold as brass, and you were fearless, but you made me laugh. You've gotten very serious." That was true towards the end of the eighties. I started at this point to dismantle my earnestness, and set fire to my ... *[pause]* self!

Were there people you admired in Dublin back then? Colorful characters who influenced you?

No, I didn't have the sense. The people that were really big influences on me were my friend Guggi. He was a kind of a genius. He was not put into the same school as I. He went to technical school, because he could draw, right? And he had a very unique point of view, from very early on. And Gavin Friday— Fionan Hanvey—he was very aesthetic. He made decisions on your character based on your record collection. He was into Brian Eno and Roxy Music. These were the people that I felt normal around. And I had no other people I looked up to. On a level of pure friendship, Reggie Manuel, who was the nattiest dresser, and Maeve O'Regan, who brought me a love of books.

Who's Maeve O'Regan?

I've always had girls who are friends, as opposed to girlfriends. Even when I started going out with Ali. Maeve O'Regan and I were very close. She too had a boyfriend, a smart lanky long-haired American basketball-playing Neil Young fan who made me feel very inadequate. I felt so square next to my bra-burning brown rice hippie pal. She was ahead of me. Girls of the same age are always much more advanced.

Your friends Gavin and Guggi went on to become serious artists: one is a painter, the other an avant-garde conceptual artist. Whereas you chose to do something much more popular. It seems like you took two different paths.

It seemed to them at the same time that it was two different paths. But I don't agree. I just think it's all about communication. And it's just a freak that the thing that I do, a lot of people are in. It is the currency. To sing and write and be in a rock band is the route to pop culture, whereas to paint and to do performance art has a very limited audience.

Come on, you must have known even then . . . These things don't happen by chance.

Yes. Nothing happens by chance. You don't end up in front of twenty thousand people on a stage by accident.

So how did you end up making a fool out of yourself in front of twenty thousand people?

I had a bigger hole to fill.

What do you mean?

A rock star is someone with a hole in his heart almost the size of his ego.

Yesterday, for an hour and a half after rehearsal, clusters of people surrounded you. When we had dinner at Pavarotti's restaurant, people kept approaching you. And it felt almost like harassment. And I thought: when is this guy ever left alone? Your life is certainly different from the life of a solitary artist like your friend Guggi.

He spends so much time on his own. I'm envious.

That ego must sometimes be a very heavy load to carry. Weren't you ever tempted to get rid of it?

Oh, I think I can just about bear it. Just about . . . *[laughs]*

You have always been in a band, you have always relied on others. Maybe you're missing out on the kind of truth you can only find in solitude.

But maybe I know it. Maybe I'm looking for the other half of the story. Maybe I have the first half instinctively, so therefore I don't need to spend hours. And maybe I had a glimpse of that when I was younger. I think, when I spend time on my own, a few things happen. After some hours, I start to laugh out loud. I do. After a few days, I'm having a great time. I go for a walk, and I read, because it's so fresh for me. Then, I'm brought back not to any new insight on the world, but to what I already knew. The noise separates me from my instincts. See, I always believed in instinct over intellect. The instinct is what you always knew; intellect is what you figure out. So for me it's not really a question of sitting and figuring it out. You know what I mean? That's not really gonna help me. What I need is silence in order to find my own voice again. I kind of know what I want to say, I just need the time. Not that I know what I want to say in terms of "I know what I've got to say, now I'm gonna write it," but I know that when I start writing, it's going to come out anyway, so my intellectual life is simply as editor, sorting through the debris. It's not that I'm trying to figure anything out. That's the difference. A novelist is just trying to figure things out.

I don't think so . . . I think a novelist has no clue about what he's grasping. There is that fantastic phrase that I always quote, by the Franco-American writer Julian Green: "I write my books because I need to know what's inside of them." It's not that you draw out a map, make a big plan, and then fill in the gaps. That's what I would say bad writers would do.

Yeah. But you're talking about the discovery there, you're talking of trying to discover what is the truth. Whereas I'm not really looking for that. If I'm considering anything, all I'm on is the obstacles to truth.

I think that's the reason why you are a "community artist." Why did you choose this path, the one where you are never alone? I mean, you never even considered becoming a solo singer.

Here's what happens to me: pretty much everything. You know, the way people who are searching for water, they have one of these forked sticks, wooden branches from a tree, that are called diviners? They hold the two branches and they walk to find water. When they're near the water, the branch starts to tremble. Have you heard about this? Divining. Well, for me, I just go where the thing's going off. I choose that pretty much in anything I'm doing. So wherever I feel more myself, wherever I feel the inspiration is, I want to be. So, in my case, being in a band, I feel completely freed. That's where I dig the well. But it's the same on anything. It's like that game that kids play, hide-and-seek. When they find it "warm," "very warm," "cold," there you go, and then you put your finger in your brother's eye! [laughs] But it's blind man's bluff. That's what it's like for me. I just kind of go "there." It's the same when I'm writing, it's like a very strong instinct. That's the answer to why I end up there. I didn't figure it out, I just did better work there. Why didn't I go on my own? I spent a lot of time on my own as a kid. Maybe that's another reason for wanting to be in a band. I didn't like being on my own as a kid, because I would have liked a bigger family. I was always envious of the families on the street. Like, Guggi had a big family. And Gavin, all my friends had a big family. I'd be kind of sitting there, and I'm sure it's the same for you. Did you have a very busy life as a kid?

Well, not really. I was raised by an old Hungarian nanny in the countryside near Paris. I had glasses, I was clumsy, I was quiet. My older brother was better-looking. He was very popular, artistic, had lots of friends, and I worshipped him. So I thought I really had to find a trick of my own.

[laughing] I like that phrase, "trick of my own."

What I always admired in people like you, who are in bands and do community work, constantly relying on other people, is their patience. Whereas I would rather spend moments looking through the window, or rather the modern equivalent: spending time on the Internet, doing nothing, really ... Getting bored is what fires me with the spark, eventually. I always wonder: what does it take to deal with bureaucracy as much as you do?

Well, you certainly need a lot of humility to depend on others. You need to put yourself second a lot of the time, or third, or fourth. The way we function as a band is a real phenomenon, in some ways more than the music. It's not an organization; it is, as they say, an organism. But that's family. Family makes people very strong. I didn't feel like I had one. I mean I've always envied people with a strong sense of family and community. They're always very strong.

There is one thing about your life that I find quite unusual and extraordinary for a rock star. You have been monogamous for twenty-five years.

I wasn't set up for marriage. I was not the kind of person that any of my friends would say, "He's the marrying kind." But I met the most extraordinary woman, and I couldn't let her go. I have somebody in my life, after a long time, I still feel I don't know. And we have a real sort of almost creative distance between us, that Ali manages. Relationships need management. She has an incredible respect for my life, and she's a very independent spirit. So I don't know how others would have made it through a married life with that length of time, but that's how I have. I don't know how you have, or how anyone else does it, but I think that's what it is. And of course, respect and love. I'm still in love.

But falling in love with another person happens to everybody. I'm sure it happened to you. What is the inner force that has kept you from breaking your marriage?

Breaking my marriage? Maybe a strong sense of survival. I can't remember his quote exactly, but there is a writing by Jean Cocteau where he says friendship is higher than love. Sometimes, it's less glamorous, or less passionate, but it's deeper and kind of wiser, I think. At the heart of my relationship is a great friendship. That's in fact, in many ways, the key to all the important doors in my life: whether it's the band, or whether it's my marriage, or whether it's the community that I still live in. It's almost like the two sorts of sacraments are music and friendship.

But you're the singer and front man in a band, and it's not just any band. I'm sure you've been tempted. Don't you ever feel that no matter what you have decided, love needs to be incarnated?

That's not what the Chinese say.

I had never heard you mention your Asian origins.

Yes, for the missing years, I was in China, standing on my head and studying under the Great Noodle Maker.

OK, let me put it another way. To my ears music has always been sexual. It is certainly what happened during the last U2 show I saw, during the Elevation Tour of 2001. Especially the opening song, "Elevation," that you performed in naked light. A rock show is not only a release from sexual tension. It can also arouse your sex drive. Think of *groupies*.

We never fostered that environment. If you mean *groupie* in the sense I know it, which is sexual favors traded for proximity with the band, it sounds like a turnoff to me. When there is no equality in the relationship, it's less interesting. Taking advantage of a fan, sexual bullying is to be avoided, but the music is sexual, and particularly our music does have this thing. It's like the lovers' row, like one ongoing conversation and argument. And the songs being in the first person, it's quite weird. Sometimes, you can end up fighting with yourself, or the erotic love can turn into something much higher, and bigger notions of love, and God, and family. It seems to segue very easily from me between all those.

But when you're onstage, do you think of, at some point, one imaginary face, or do you fancy one imaginary body, or one imaginary girl?

Usually, I'm just struggling to hit the note, or concentrating on the song. It's not like a technique an actor would tell you, a method that you actually go through. But what I will say is when it's really going off, you have the sense that you're really in the song, and the song is really in the room: all of you, crowd and performers, disappear into it. It's an extraordinary thing. I mean it really is. I think people who come to a rock show, especially at one of our shows, just turn into the perfect audience. I don't know who that audience is. What I'm saying is they're not an amorphous mass of faces to me. I think a lot of times performers do not play for the crowd. Despite what people think, great performers appear to need a crowd, more than not so great ones. It's not the twenty thousand people who may be in the arena, or the one hundred and fifty thousand people. I think they all turn into one person, it's probably the truth. One of the persons turns out to be, in my case, your dad, or your love. But it looks like, and factually is, that you're being so revelatory and revealing to people you haven't met before.

People who listen to your music have this impression that they know you, better than your best friend. That's what you told me once.

One of the great ironies of these concerts is that our songs are very intimate: incredible intimacies shared with people whom you've never met. And I wouldn't trust that. Who would trust that? That's a very bizarre way to live your life.

What do you mean?

On the surface, people who are so open and raw on a first date, you mightn't trust that, would you? *[laughs]* I mean, you're going to a bar, you meet some-body and they tell you their life story in ten minutes. I generally dodge that. On one level, you can look at these concerts and go: God, this is like Hitler's night rallies.

The thought has sometimes crossed my mind.

Well, yeah, I suppose we even played upon that. You know, Zoo TV was play-ing into that whole idea: the night rally. But finally, it turns out that people are much more conscious than you think, and you can't really influence them. If you tried to get them to turn on the person to their right, they wouldn't. In fact, people are much smarter than that.

I guess many people attending a rock show have had that. It's the same for a child when he watches a perilous circus act on TV. When the acrobat is walk-ing on a wire, something inside that child wants him to fall, you see? *[Bono laughs]* **Maybe I shouldn't tell you that, but during that show I had this ap-palling fantasy of someone with a gun in the audience. I felt that Mark David Chapman* thing could happen there. Did it ever cross your mind?**

Yeah, we had that. As you know, I don't travel with security. I grew up around a low but significant level of violence. We always feel like a row or an argument or a grievance in Ireland or France could end up with a bottle smashed in your face. Guns are not pervasive. In America, any crackpot can get their hands on a gun, and we've had a fair share of crackpots over the years. At the end of the eighties, we campaigned for Martin Luther King Day. I remember, in Arizona, we got into trouble, and we had some death threats. Normally, they happen. But occasionally, you get one that the police and the FBI take seriously. There was a specific threat: "Don't go ahead with the concert. And, if you do, don't sing 'Pride (In the Name of Love),' because, if you do, I am gonna blow your

* The man who shot John Lennon.

head off, and you won't be able to stop this from happening." Of course you go onstage and you put it out of your head. But I do remember actually, in the middle of "Pride," thinking, for a second: "Gosh! What if somebody was organized, or in the rafters of the building, or somebody, here and there, just had a handgun?" I just closed my eyes and I sang this middle verse, with my eyes closed, trying to concentrate and forget about this ugliness and just keep close to the beauty that's suggested in the song. I looked up, at the end of that verse, and Adam was standing in front of me. It was one of those moments where you know what it means to be in a band.

Are you hinting that there were times when you were unsure about being in U2?

There was a period in my early twenties when we nearly knocked the group on the head. We nearly called it a day.

When was that?

1982.

Oh, that Shalom Christianity* thing?

I mean, it wasn't a "thing"! It was a very well-thought-out and finally flawed attempt to wrestle the world to the ground and try to deal with some of its ails and its evils. I nearly became a full-time *[laughs]* instead of part-time activist at that point. At that point, we were angry. We were agitated by the inequalities in the world and the lack of a spiritual life. It's not only me, Edge is like that.

Is Edge the same nature of believer as you?

Edge is a wiser man than I am, more meditative. I have total admiration for the way he's able to keep his feelings, ego, et cetera, under control, and yet, that's my biggest worry for him.

* A Christian group Bono, Edge, and Larry Mullen joined by 1981, whose purpose was to study the Scriptures.

We say in French "eaten away from the inside."

No. But I wouldn't underestimate the level of rage beneath those sweet notes that he plays. He can throw a dig. He nearly knocked me out one night.

Really? What happened?

It was back in the early eighties. Everything had gone horribly wrong onstage with the band fighting, rather than the audience. I threw the drum kit into the audience. I think it was in Newhaven, and Edge hit with a right hook.

What caused the argument?

It was the last in a long line of reasons. Too many miles on the same bus, sore throats, sorer hearts from missing home. When I introduced the song, counting it in, one-two-three-four, the band ignored me. Don't ask.

So, even way back then, you thought you had to deal with all the evils of the world. Do you think it stemmed from reading the Bible as a child?

You see, I had to find that at the very bottom of that lies the feeling of justice over charity. I mean, charity is OK, I'm interested in charity. Of course, we should all be, especially those of us who are privileged. But I'm much more interested in justice. The Drop the Debt campaign was a justice issue. Holding the children to ransom for the debts of their grandparents, that's a justice issue. Or not letting the poorest of the poor put their products on our shelves whilst advertising the free market, that's a justice issue to me. These things are rooted in my study of the Scriptures. I guess, like most people, the world just beats them down into not expecting that things can change or be any better. When you've sold a lot of records, *[laughs]* it's very easy to be megalomaniac enough to believe that you *can* change things. If you put your shoulder to the door, it might open. Especially if you're representing a greater authority than yourself. Call it love, call it justice, call it whatever you want. That's why I'm never nervous when I meet politicians. I think *they* should be nervous because I'm representing the poor and wretched in this world. And I promise, history will be hard on this moment. And whatever thoughts you have about God, who He is or if He exists, most will agree that if there is a God, God has a special place for the poor. The poor are where God lives. So these politicians should be nervous, not me.

I'm surprised at how easily religion comes up in your answers, whatever the question is. How come you're always quoting the Bible? Was it because it was taught at school? Or because your father or mother wanted you to read it?

It's strange, I couldn't know. Whenever I hear people talking from the Scriptures, I always manage to be able to see past their sort of personality, to see past the difficulties of the environment I was in listening to them, and the hypocrisy. I always manage to get to the content.

When was the first time something happened when you thought about a line from the Scriptures? When you first said to yourself: yes, I can see beyond that and see how it applies to such and such situation?

Let me try to explain something to you, which I hope will make sense of the whole conversation. But maybe that's a little optimistic. *[laughs]* This was not the first time, but I remember coming back from a very long tour. I hadn't been at home. Got home for Christmas, very excited of being in Dublin. Dublin at Christmas is cold, but it's lit up, it's like Carnival in the cold. On Christmas Eve, I went to St. Patrick's Cathedral. I had done school there for a year. It's where Jonathan Swift was dean. Anyway, some of my Church of Ireland friends were going. It's a kind of a tradition on Christmas Eve to go, but I'd never been. I went to this place, sat. I was given a really bad seat, behind one of the huge pillars. I couldn't see anything. I was sitting there, having come back from Tokyo, or somewhere like that. I went for the singing, because I love choral singing. Community arts, a specialty! But I was falling asleep, being up for a few days, traveling, because it was a bit boring, the service, and I just started nodding off, I couldn't see a thing. Then I started to try and keep myself awake studying what was on the page. It dawned on me for the first time, really. It had dawned on me before, but it really sank in: the Christmas story. The idea that God, if there is a force of Love and Logic in the universe, that it would seek to explain itself is amazing enough. That it would seek to explain itself and describe itself by becoming a child born in straw poverty, in shit and straw . . . a child . . . I just thought: "Wow!" Just the poetry . . . Unknowable love, unknowable power, describes itself as the most vulnerable. There it was. I was sitting there, and it's not that it hadn't struck me before, but tears came down my face, and I saw the genius of this, utter genius of picking a particular point in time and deciding to turn on this. Because that's exactly what we were talking about earlier: love needs to find form, intimacy needs to be whispered. To me, it makes sense. It's actually logical. It's pure logic. Essence has to manifest itself. It's inevitable. Love has to become an action or something concrete. It would have to happen. There must be an incarnation. Love must be made flesh. Wasn't that your point earlier?

Exactly. But you see, I sometimes think that I'm religious without knowing it.

[laughs] But that's very interesting. You're like one of the Three Wise Men, the Magi who were studying the stars, with nothing religious on your mind! And you're looking at your maps, going: *[gets into a comedy routine]* "Here it is . . . OK, it should be over here . . . There's something funny going on over there . . . Is it the aurora borealis? No, it's a single star. My coordinates suggest: we must go this way. OK, something should be happening extraordinary round about . . . *[pauses for dramatic effect]* there. Oh shit, what's this? A little baby! Oh, we stepped into the Christmas story, I thought I was reading astronomy."

I'm going to ask you a very naive question. Why are so many people religious but don't own up to it? Do you think you have an explanation?

I don't know. But religious instinct comes out as gambling, as horoscope reading, as yoga, it's everywhere. It's supposed to be a secular society, but I look around: everybody's religious. They're superstitious, they pray when they think they've got cancer. It's not that far below the surface. We've gone two hundred years since the Enlightenment, but science is starting to bow again.

Yes, but some people won't use the word *God*.

Yeah. Well, because ever since, you had to prove something, or it didn't exist. Such thoughts were outlawed by thinking people, post-Enlightenment: "God is dead." But as I told you once before, I saw a fantastic thing written on a wall, in Dublin. It said: "God is dead. Nietzsche." And then written underneath, sprayed out, it was: "Nietzsche's dead. God." *[laughs out loud]* It's so good! I mean, I do think, now, at the start of the twenty-first century, people are beginning that adventure again. We have the Eve gene, we have science talking about the big bang, we have so much in science that was, if you like, contradictory, that has become less and less so to the idea that there is God. Different disciplines work on different parts of the puzzle. I'm not a scientist, mind you, I'm in a band with one. I'm not a monk, that's obvious, I'm an artist. I'm looking for clues through my music. Am I going off again?

Yes. Actually I was about to wander off myself, but I don't think I'm straying that far. You said, "Intimacy needs to be whispered." What about the whispering in "She's a Mystery to Me," the song you wrote for Roy Orbison? What's the inspiration there? Are you whispering, or was someone whispering to you? To me, that song is some form of incarnation of God—one of the few I would believe in anyway. To me, it's a religious song, a mystical song. The melody is like the one you hear in your head when you're in a cathedral. You can't say that of many other U2 songs.

There's probably some mechanical reasons for this, you know. Like, we're very attracted to suspended chords to the fifth. Edge has that in his guitar playing. You hear it a lot in religious music: Bach. That happy-sad feeling. Agony and ecstasy. It's that duality that makes my favorite pop songs.

One of the reasons I'm sitting here today is because you and Edge wrote that song. It's the song I throw in the face of people who say they don't "get" U2.

And their jaws drop when they listen to it. For me, it's way up there with the Beach Boys' "God Only Knows" in the pantheon of great songs. So I won't leave this place until you tell me how that song happened.

That's a funny one, that. Edge's wife, Aislinn, was the most extraordinary girl, who could surprise you with kindness when you least expected it. She gave me a copy of a soundtrack for David Lynch's film *Blue Velvet*. We were in London playing a concert. I left the record on "repeat" and fell asleep. When I woke up, I had a melody and words in my head. I presumed I was singing something from the soundtrack, but then realized I wasn't. I wrote it down. At sound check that day, I played the song to everybody and started going on and on about Roy Orbison, what a genius he was, et cetera. I told them that this could be a song for Roy Orbison, we should finish it for him. After sound check, I continued working on it. After the show, I was banging on and on about Roy Orbison in this song when a very strange thing happened. There was a knock at the door. John, our security man, was announcing the guests for that evening: Roy Orbison, he told me, is outside. He'd love to say a few words.

What? You mean you had no idea he would be coming over?

I had no idea he was there, I had no idea he was coming over, and neither had the band. They all looked at me like I had two heads. In fact, I was just getting a very large one, *[laughs]* feeling that somehow, God had agreed with me about Roy Orbison! He walked in, this beautiful humble man. He said: "I really, really loved the show. I couldn't tell you now why exactly, but I was very moved by the show. I'm wondering: would you fellows have a song for me?"

That story's even better than the one I would have made up myself.

Later, I got to finish the song with him, got to know his wife, Barbara, his family, and the song became the title of his last album. It was an extraordinary thing to record with him. I was out standing beside him at the microphone, bringing him through the song. I couldn't hear him singing, because he hardly opened his mouth. We went back into the control room, and it was all there. He not only had an angelic voice, but a kind of way about him too.

But the lyrics are extraordinary as well.

[trying to remember, whispering in a low voice, fumbling his way through the words to a forgotten prayer] I couldn't tell you what it was about. It was a disturbed sleep. The subject of the song was kind of haunting me, I suppose. I don't know why, I'm always attracted to subjects like you can't really get a grip on, like sex or God. *[muses for a while]* I think I sometimes confuse them both!

"She's a Mystery to Me" is not just a "very good song." It seems to come from a different place.

That's a good question. What's the difference between a very good song and a great song? Answer: I think, very good songs, you can take the credit for. But great songs, you can't. They feel like you stumble upon them. Of course, then, there's the bad songs. I wish you didn't have to take the blame for them. It's annoying, really, that you can only learn so much in the way of craft. You know, the muse is wayward. But I think you can put yourself in places where they might happen. For some people, that's chaos. And that, for some people, is falling in love. That, for some people, is rage. That, for some people, is railing against the world. Or for some people it's a surrendering to the world.

And what makes it for you?

All of the above. *[laughs]*

Depends on the different stages of your life, I guess.

Yes. I don't know if I said that elsewhere, but one thing that it comes down to, I think, is a certain honesty with yourself. Did we mention that before?

No. I guess it's implicit.

That's what sets you free. You describe the situation that you're in. Even if you've nothing to say, let that be your first line.

I'm sure that when you heard Roy Orbison sing it, you felt some miracle happened.

I couldn't believe it. I couldn't believe that he'd ask us for a song, because his songs are the most evolved in the book of pop. "In Dreams" is probably the greatest pop song ever written, in that it has a structure unlike any other. Most pop songs have a structure A-B-A-B-C-D—verse, chorus, verse, chorus, middle eight, et cetera. If you listen to the structure of that song, the sections don't repeat. It goes: A-B-C-D-E-F-G. It breaks all the rules. Try singing it someday.

God forbid! So what's your favorite lyric in a song?

Kris Kristofferson, "Help Me Make It Through the Night."

How does it go?

[sings] *I don't care who's right or wrong / I don't try to understand / Let the devil take tomorrow / Lord tonight I need a friend.* You know that one? *Yesterday's dead and gone / (Bom/Bo-bo-bom) / And tomorrow's out of sight / (Bom/Bo-bo-bom) / And it's sad to be alone. / Help me make it through the night.* I could say that's my favorite country song.

And what's your favorite religious song?

"Amazing Grace."

And your favorite U2 song?

We haven't written it yet.

Would it be something obvious like "One"?

"Stay (Faraway, So Close)," that's one of my favorites. I also like "Please" from the *Pop* album.

The funny thing is that they're the most operatic songs that you could pick, the ones that . . .

. . . would take you through a journey, to a place you couldn't imagine before then.

This one stopped abruptly. Before Bono left, the waiter asked for a special favor: "Mister-ay Bono, can I ask-ay you something? Can you write your name, your wonderful name, on my shirt?"—"Gosh, are you sure?"—"To Paolo!" *[Bono complies.]* "Thank you. You're great! You're the greatest!" Then Bono added, mischievously, "You know, I do tattoos as well . . ."

7. AT THE BOTTOM OF THE GLASS

Four months passed without my hearing anything from Bono. All that filtered through was that he was "very busy," which was not exactly breaking news to me. During that period, Bono, on behalf of DATA's campaign Keep America's Promise to Africa, had ensured a $289 million contribution from the U.S. Senate; had been made a Doctor in Laws at Trinity College in Dublin; had illustrated the booklet for a modern version of Prokofiev's *Peter and the Wolf*, produced and narrated by his old friend Gavin Friday. He wanted to show his gratitude toward the people at the Irish Hospice Foundation, who had taken great care of his father (whose features inspired him to draw the character of Peter's grandfather), as all royalties derived from the book's sales went to that institution. He also enthused about the new album that U2 was preparing: "It has to be a monster, a dragon, and this is!" he claimed.

Actually, the gestation of that dragon seemed somehow painful. I got the impression that the band, tired of Bono's endless traveling around and his second job with DATA, were holding him hostage in order to speed things up. In late September, a magazine sent me over to Dublin for a quick piece of travel writing. At that time Bono was in his house near Nice. Catriona arranged a meeting for me at the Ocean Bar, right across from U2's Hanover Quay

Studios (it is said that band and crew, using a little motor boat, often come here for a bite). At some point her phone rang.

"It's my boss," she said.

"Our next conversation will be on the phone," warned the Godfather, after having described in a lyrical tone the sun setting on the Mediterranean Sea.

A couple of weeks later, I had a phone appointment. It was a Sunday morning. I was in the countryside near Paris, in the house where I was raised. It felt weird to talk to him in a place where all my child's memories still linger on and where the world, in my view, seemed very small. On the street below, my son was playing with a friend, both of them crouching on an old trolley formerly used to carry wooden cubes. Sometimes their screams would disrupt the recording of the conversation, here and there shot through with their cries of excitement. This time again, I was struck by the serene tone in Bono's voice.

Maybe you remember the handwritten letter I sent to you right after Bologna. I don't know if you got it.

Yeah, I'm sure I did.

I want to hear your thoughts, so let me remind you what I wrote. "After spending a day with you in Italy, I saw a whole new dimension to your character. You are what people make of you: you are there, as you say, to be used. In my view, you try to represent what's best inside of them. So there's one big question here. Since you are such a flexible and pliable person putting yourself out to be used, some people may try to take advantage of that, with a different agenda in mind. A violent or fanatical one, maybe. My hunch is that you are well able to defend yourself against such people. But that, in a way, is an interesting question. I have this impression—I don't know why—but I wouldn't want to see you crossed. I mean, why do I feel that way about this man of peace? I'm sure you've been through situations in your life when you could have turned into a monster." Now what would you say?

Well, I despise violence, but violence is something I know a little bit about. *[long pause]* I'm sorry, that last question's taken me aback for a second, but you're not way off. I think the time that I knew that I was capable of all the things that I disliked the most in other people was, oddly enough, one of the most joyful moments: when our first child was born. And I just felt this love for this beautiful little girl who was so fragile and so vulnerable. Some point around that week, I started to understand why wars were fought. I started to understand why people were capable of cruelty in order to protect themselves and their own. And I was very humbled to realize that.

But what happened exactly?

I can't recall. This is one of the great and bewildering things to me: the more you experience love, the more full of it you should be. But the opposite sometimes happens, because you fear the loss of life. You fear the vulnerability that can take the goodness of it away. This might have happened because when I was just a kid, I had the sense that your whole life can change with a death in the family. It's like they say—at least I say—it's the loss of money that leads to the love of it. You know, the people who care about money are never the people who just made a lot. They're the people who have lost a lot. And I think that might be true in relationships, when if you've lost somebody important to you early on, you live in fear of that the rest of your life. I suppose that's one of the things that I would fear, and that might explain the rage that you referred to earlier, which is real in me, at some point, it really is. An odd thing to own up to, but I do know it's true.

I can see it in your eyes.

I've not entered any period of analysis. I haven't questioned myself enough.

Were you ever tempted to go into analysis or therapy?

Maybe that's why I'm doing this. Seriously, you enter a conversation with somebody whom you trust, whom you can talk to about your motives. *[laughs]* I would have to think that it was part of some creative work, before I'd ever do it. Because if I was sitting there and talking to a psychiatrist or something, I would be thinking: "God, I could do other things with that hour. I could take my kids for a walk." But if I'm sitting down with you, an old friend, in doing something that my kids might someday read, then I can excuse it. So, here we are, Michka. These questions are big buttons to press, and I don't know the answer to all of them. Where that rage comes from? Partly, I would say it's a sense that a life can be taken away from you, quickly, in a dumb second for the dumbest reason. That makes me mad, defensive and protective.

Actually, that leads me to another question. You have often evoked the idea of suicide in your lyrics. One of the first songs that you recorded with U2, "A Day Without Me," was about a friend's suicide. One of your most popular recent songs, "Stuck in a Moment You Can't Get Out Of," deals with your friend Michael Hutchence's suicide. Is taking your own life and turning that violence against yourself, like Ian Curtis from Joy Division or Kurt Cobain did, something that you may have considered at some point in your life?

I think everybody, in their teenage years, plays with that thought, and I certainly did. But I was very distressed in my teenage years. I was kind of all over the shop. I didn't know who or where I was. But as I've gotten older, I've become very intolerant of those thoughts. I am tempted to see it as self-indulgence. That was very hard when Michael took his life, because you understand that people can get to a black hole and they just can't climb out of that. In fact, the more they try—as they say, if you're in a hole, stop digging—the more they examine the process, getting lost in their own life, the bigger the hole. And Michael. I often think: Gosh, if he'd just put it off for half an hour, so that despair left him, he'd still be here. But the thing that finally I've got a low tolerance for, is that having seen so many people struggle for their breath and for sustenance in Africa, where I do a lot of work, and watching people beg for their life, it makes me very angry when I think of people throwing theirs away.

Sure, but if someone feels hopeless and despairing, and you tell him: "Yes, but put this in perspective with the real pain and the real suffering that people have in Africa," it doesn't ...

[interrupting] Well, I do think perspective is a cure. *[laughs]*

But very often, it simply doesn't work at all. People may be aware and have access to plenty of information through the media, but knowing that people suffer from hunger or AIDS in Africa will not help them solve their problems.

It's a very real illness, depression. I understand chemical imbalance and all that. But I do think its prevalence has a lot to do with a lack of perspective on your life and a lack of empathy of what's going on in other lives. This may seem hard, but I read a story of a mental hospital that was next to a school, that burnt down. So the headmaster of the school was visiting in this hospital, and, after the incident, decided to recruit patients who were recovering well to get them involved in a community project, and sought out for volunteers to help clean up their next door. And nobody put up their hand. Was this shyness? He was confused. And one of the doctors said: that's why a lot of these people are here, they're *pickled in themselves.* That was the expression I remember from the story, and it stuck with me.

That's a very good phrase.

It is. And of course you're gonna be careful, especially if you're undergoing that kind of analysis, Michka, my friend. *[laughs]* We must be careful not to stew in our own juices. See, if I look at depression from another angle, I could be more positive. If you look at it as a nerve end. A leper would love to feel pain in their hands, as he catches in a door or as he falls into a fire. So perhaps we should see depression as a nerve end, as a thing that reminds us that everything isn't OK. Because, really, everything isn't. There are reasons to be uncomfortable in the world, and we're not gonna take them on 24/7. Occasionally, it is worth asking some very hard questions about yourself and the world that you live in, the inequalities of it, and I think that that's a way to put depression to use—as a nerve end to remind you of what's not right and get about fixing it. But there's another image I could use about analysis, which I've heard, which is "the rusty nail that sits at the bottom of the glass of water." You take it up through analysis, you take it out of the glass of water and you're staring at it, and go: "Gosh, look what I found in my subconscious—or unconscious—I found a rusty bent nail . . ." You look at it, and you stare at it, and go: "Wow. I didn't know that it was there." Then you put it back in the glass of water. *[laughs]* The only difference is: now you know it's there, and the water's been disturbed and discolored. But you didn't take it out and get rid of it. So I think, if you're gonna listen to yourself in these moments, and you discover stuff about yourself that you don't like, that you have a duty to fix them. Because if you don't, then it's either the thing that I said earlier, the "pickled" thing, where it's just self-indulgence, or you just end up disturbing the waters, and it doesn't lead you anywhere. I'm all for it if it leads you somewhere. So I hope this conversation will lead me *[pause]* to the pub!

[laughs] You mean to a positive place.

Yeah.

I was thinking about that phrase you just used: "We must be careful not to stew in our own juices." I feel it applied to me at some point in my life, so I went through therapy for three years, because I thought I was too self-centered, and it was not interesting at all. Contrary to popular belief, you go through therapy to *stop* stewing in your own juice.

And this therapy brought you out of yourself. Did it, eventually?

Eventually, it did. Also, it helped me understand that being depressed, and feeling that you're a failure at some point in your life, is quite positive, actually. It's very good. *[laughs]*

Yeah, but if it brings you somewhere. And it obviously did with you. Yeah. Now, that's positive. I've a couple of friends that have been down that road, and I'm amazed at them. I've one particular friend who's been through that, and he's really practical about the fact that he fucked up as a kid, and just messed around with people, and had never dealt with it. So he kind of went, and it was like taking a car for a service.

Exactly. I was extremely down to earth about it. It's just like: I have a flat tire, I have to fix it. Because I'm not going anywhere with a flat tire. *[laughs]*

Yeah, well, that's it. I'm not against it if I had the time. I think it'd be a good thing to check your thought process. Unless you have a plumb line, the wall can be built crooked. So I think, for me, that is prayer, and my life worshipping God through music.

It's funny, you know, because when I discovered U2's music, way back in 1980, I could feel the faith that emanated from it. Still, your music seemed based on a very depressing view of life. Your sound had that heavy, gloomy thing to it. I mean, you made it a matter of principle to record your first single with Martin Hannett, who was Joy Division's producer.

You're absolutely right about the color of the period: purple turns black. That industrial stuff was just gray. But I think our music, even though working with Martin Hannett, was always shot through with light. Even if some of the subjects were dark, the music had within it the antidote for the subject matter. It was strange. But, you see. You're in your teens, or you're coming out of your teens. This is what people want to read: the great novel, with the moral subjects that matter, because you want to understand life and the forces that make you. So inevitably, in a teenage way, you grapple with the big questions. And I love that about youth. I don't know if I told you this—this is self-indulgent—but Anton Corbijn had an exhibition in an important museum in his native Holland, and he asked me to open it for him. He warned me there was one room just filled with pictures of me. "Giant Bonos," he laughed. "Isn't that how you see yourself? Ha! Ha!" Well, I'm a huge fan of his, and his hugeness—he's a very tall man. So I went along to introduce one of the great photographers of the age and ended up in this room full of Bonos standing and looking at me over twenty years. And I saw this picture. I must have been twenty-two or something, getting into a helicopter for a video. I think it was "New Year's Day." I just saw this face, and it was my first face. The eyes were so clear, and so fearless, and I looked at it. A journalist walked up beside me and said: "What would you say to that person now? You've got one thing you can say to him. What is it?" I was going to be funny, but then I thought I shouldn't. I told him: "I would tell my younger self: 'You're right. Don't second-guess yourself.' " I felt it so strongly. I wish I knew then how right I was. I wasn't wrong. You're supposed to go: "Oh, I was foolish then. I've grown up, and I laugh." I do laugh at some of the music, some of the statements I've made. Some of the image problems do leave me a little embarrassed, a little red-faced. But there's a strength to that naiveté. I wasn't wrong about the world. The world is more malleable than you think. We can bend it into a better shape. Ask big questions, demand big answers.

Well, actually, that's something people tend to say about their youth: "I wish I had been braver back then." Is that the case with you?

Well, I was. We were brave, but we didn't know how brave at the time. Because here's a band who couldn't really play, who forged their own music, because they couldn't play very well other people's, with the audacity to say: "We can be a big success without having to sell out. And we don't have to be embarrassed by our ambition." It's worth remembering that wanting to make big music in a big band was a hanging offense in the music press at that time. "Selling out" was a popular pejorative. Ideas like "street credibility" dominated discussion. We knew a lot of this stuff was nonsense. What street were they talking about and who did you want to be credible with? "Do you have anything original to say?" was our point. "Are the tunes any good?" So we were right about so many things. That naiveté is very, very powerful.

But after growing out of that naiveté, and maybe getting disillusioned, weren't you tempted to become cynical?

Well, I think cynicism often disguises itself as humor.

Irony.

Yes. But finally, Zoo TV was not cynical. It was fun and it was a strategy. The strategy was judo: to use the force of the attacker to defend yourself. And we were being attacked from all corners, because we were very open. That face that

I talked about earlier was an open face. It was wide open. It was ready for a slap, and to be mocked. So we could feel the media about to close in on us. That was an amazing thing that happened. I realized the force of the media at the end of *The Joshua Tree*. We had a big record, and the natural thing to do would be to just make a live album at that point of the tour, cash in and go on holidays. But we decided: "Oh no, we can't do that." So we wrote songs to put on this. We'd have new songs. We'd make a film about our journey through America. We'd make it much more interesting: we'd make a double album, put it out at half price, and rather than being a band who thought they were the center of the world, we would put these musicians that we were fans of at the center of our world, and in the artwork, with pictures of Johnny Cash. We wrote songs—not all great songs—but we would sort of declare ourselves as the fans that we are. And this *Rattle and Hum* thing came out. But the opposite came back at us. It was like: "Oh, this is egomania, they think they are now one of the Pantheon of these great artists, and they feel they can quote our music." I remember thinking, This is exactly the opposite of what we are trying to do!" But we actually couldn't undo that. It was just a given that these so-called fans had now lost the run of themselves. "Egomaniac," "messianic." These were the kind of words that were being thrown at us. So I just thought: "Right. If people want megalomania, let's give them megalomania! Let's really have some fun with this!" *[laughs]* Let's try to communicate with the people who don't like U2 because we're not real rock stars. I don't think it was cynical, it was more fun. And by the way, there's a part of me that kind of would like to be that rock star.

Do you sometimes think about what would have become of you if you had followed your bad or lazy instincts? I'll give you an example. As I reminded you, Adam once said that if he hadn't been the bass player in U2, he would have become an average landscape gardener [see Chapter 3]. *[Bono bursts out laughing]* So have you ever pictured yourself doing an ordinary job, or even following your more base instincts?

[Pondering] The life of crime? You have to have a better memory for the life of crime. So I'd probably be *[confidently]* a property developer. Beach front, a specialty. "Location, location . . . "

It's funny that you should mention that. It's actually one of the questions I wanted to ask at some point. I don't know much about rock stars, aside from you. What do rock stars usually do? They buy cars, they indulge in drugs. And while we're at it, what are you willing to reveal about drugs? Paul McCartney recently came clean about cocaine and heroin. What about you? Maybe we'll have to wait until you're sixty to find out.

If I ever had so much as a spliff, I would not talk about it, because it's too easy a headline: "Bono Denies Smoking Joint," "Bono Admits Smoking Joint." It's an invitation to a debate that I'm not interested in.

Right. But you don't shy away from revealing drunken episodes, do you?

No, but that doesn't make headlines for an Irish person. Bottom line: I think drugs are dumb. Bottom line: I think abuse of alcohol is dumb. Bottom line: I think that cigarette smoking is dumb. And that's it, really. My point about alcohol is that if you abuse something, it abuses you back. That's really it. Whether it's a spliff, whether it's anything, there's a boomerang to it.

OK. And what about a rock star abusing real estate?

[laughing] There's a couple of people that'd surprise you. I remember RZA from the Wu-Tang Clan telling me that his whole thing was buying land. He didn't want any buildings on the land. Just land. Because money was losing its value. And I love that. Bob Dylan, I know he loves land. People who live their life off the abstract tend to holiday in the concrete. [laughs] I do love buildings. I just like places.

I don't want to sound like a part-time psychoanalyst here, but I once read that as a child, you spent your family vacations in a trailer on a wasteland by the sea. Then the property was developed, and you weren't allowed to stay there anymore. Is there a link somewhere?

That was a railway carriage that belonged to my grandfather, in the sand dunes, on a beach in the north of Dublin. There was an extraordinary moment in my childhood when we arrived. The farmer who had sold the land to my grand-father had died. When his son was looking for the contract that my grandfather didn't have—it was just a cash transaction—he had told him he had to get off. My grandfather wouldn't get off, and he bulldozed this train carriage, just smashed it. It was an extraordinary moment I remember as a child. I remember throwing rocks at his glass houses. I was very angry about it.

What was the first house you bought? I'm assuming it was in Dublin.

I bought a tower, a Martello tower, which I think was a French design. The French used the Martello towers to defend themselves against the English. Then the English took it, used to defend themselves against the French. That was a great military idea. There are seven-foot-thick granite walls, and it was like a lighthouse, this one. It had a glass top, a bedroom for myself and Ali, and then a living room in the middle, and at the bottom it had a dining area, with the kitchen in the wall.* We loved it! I have a few nice houses now; I must admit that one of my deepest fears is that I'd become that awful person who would just buy property and leave it there, not even use it, appreciate it, when there's people sleeping in the street. That would be the sort of person I would hate as a teenager. That would have been my nemesis. I know I'm a little self-indulgent now, but I will say I enjoy them. As I perhaps said to you before, decadence is when you don't notice what you have around you.

So you've been investing in real estate, mainly.

I was never the sort to put money under the mattress, rather make something out of it. I love art, some of my friends are artists, so I buy a little bit here and there. I love places to build an environment, admitting that I've made money buying and selling such places. I have a much harder time selling than buying, though.

* Located in Bray, fifteen miles south of Dublin, the tower that Bono bought belongs to a series of seventy-four towers erected by the British War Office around the coast of Ireland during the Napoleonic wars. They actually derive their names from a place in Corsica called Mortella, where stood a round tower that the English had besieged in vain in 1794. Napoleon is believed to have used the coast of Ireland as a "back door" for invading England. Forty feet high and eight feet thick, these small round towers have flat roofs to which a lookout could climb up and set fire to a bundle of wood to signal the arrival of an invading ship.

You mean you do this as speculation?

Most of the time it's not speculation, but I wouldn't rule that out.

You bought a place in Paris. Are you going to buy a place in every big city in the world?

When I fall in love with a place, a city, I'm curious about how people live and where people live. I'm anxious to get out of the hotel, experience a little bit of the real life of that city or town. I might want an apartment, I might want not to feel such a tourist, the eye of a traveling rat, you could call it.

Just before we hung up, Bono invited me to come to London for the next week, so we could resume our talk there. He told me that U2 had booked Air Studios to do some work on their next album.

8. THE OCCASIONAL MISSING LEG

I arrived at Air Studios in London. When I got there, the mood was very tense. On that day, the band was busy rehearsing a former version of "Crumbs from Your Table," with Bono strumming the guitar as well as singing and giving directions to the band. A couple of cameramen were lurking around. When operations stopped for a while, Bono took me to the cafeteria, where he promptly briefed me. A couple of days before, an array of about forty of the best classical musicians in Britain had to be dismissed from the recording. Why? Well, said Bono, it was a typical U2 situation: "We only found out the songs weren't working when we played them in front of an audience. The orchestra looked bored. The band could feel it: they were bored too. Conclusion: finish the songs before you bring a fucking orchestra to play them." He added that Chris Thomas had concluded the day by saying it had been the worst he'd ever spent in a studio in his whole career (he started out as an assistant to George Martin on the Beatles' *White Album,* and worked with, among many others, Roxy Music, the Sex Pistols, and the Pretenders). Then another sort of trouble set in. A camera crew had been given access to film the band, and they were starting to get on a few people's nerves. It reminded me of what I had read about the Beatles making *Let It Be* while being filmed. Bono saw it as well: "It is the kind of situation," he said in a deadpan voice, "that may force a band to split up. That'll be the only thing that'll make this film interesting. It's like watching paint dry. They must be dying of boredom."

So he called me to his hotel room at noon. He seemed in great spirits. Just before we began to talk, I showed him an article from the satirical newspaper *The Onion* ("America's Finest News Source"), which I had found the day before in a little bookshop. The cover of a recent *Time* magazine that featured Bono with the American flag around his shoulders and the matching headline "Can Bono Save the World?" had been reproduced in this article with a different headline: "Bono to the Rescue." It read:

> *Called "rock's conscience," U2 frontman and political crusader Bono has met with everyone from Kofi Annan to Colin Powell. What has he been doing recently?*
> - *Tirelessly dedicating self to ending Third World debt, no matter how many magazine covers he must appear on in process*
> - *Restoring humanity's faith in the power and the promise and the possibility of rock and roll*
> - *Feeding starving Somalis by dividing loaf into many*
> - *Defeating Bruce Springsteen in epic, five-hour earnest-off*
> - *Vowing to lobby Congress for African aid on progressively larger Jumbotrons until demands are met*
> - *Shouldering the burdens of a post Sept. 11 world/Buying another pair of blue-tinted wrap-around shades*
> - *Revealing that The Edge will betray him three times before cock crows*
> - *Thinking about writing songs about deliverance and redemption; also maybe one about transcendence*

Bono particularly enjoyed the one about Bruce Springsteen.

Then he took me to the terrace of his suite, where he had arranged a photo session for the both of us. There he improvised a kind of drunken speech, celebrating my coming to London, haranguing an elusive crowd at the top of his voice. Then he went back to his room and lay on the couch.

Maybe this is a little abrupt, but I think after reading that strip I showed you from *The Onion,* you will see that it is perfectly coherent. Last time, when we talked, you mentioned that you gave a speech at the preview of that Anton Corbijn exhibition, where in a "room full of Bonos" you were confronted with a huge portrait of yourself from twenty years ago, alighting from a helicopter for the sake of a video. You described it as your "first face." Some journalist there asked you: "What would you say to this person now?" And you said you would have told your younger self: "You're right!" But how about the other way around? Picture yourself today as that young man from 1981 in the long coat, with the intense and innocent glare. He is now looking at the cover of *Time* magazine in 2003, which shows the face of this multimillionaire crusader with blue-tinted glasses. Now what does *he* say to him?

"You're wrong. *[laughs]* For a start, the glasses are wrong. Blue's not your color. Green. Go with the green!" Well. In a way, for me, getting back to taking custard pies in the face for taking a stance on issues was exactly what that younger version of myself was all about. So I think he would approve of that. But if you had said to this twenty-one-year-old one, that one day he's gonna be on the cover of *Time* magazine he *[pauses for dramatic effect]* probably would have believed you. *[laughs]* That's puberty for you. It was late in my case. But the other things in my life. *[pause]* Family, I'd say, he would have approved of. But the complications, the hesitations, the drinking, the well-to-do lifestyle—he would have been a bit hard on me on that one. Because he was a bit of a zealot.

If you were Madonna, I wouldn't have asked you that. Obviously, she'd have answered something like "I've always looked forward to being this person, since the very beginning." But I knew you wouldn't.

I can't answer for Madonna, but in my case that's probably true. At the time that early innocent picture was being taken, I was very strict on myself. I was reading people like Watchman Nee. He was a Chinese Christian philosopher, very concerned about communal responsibility, the death of the self and surface, and no possessions. At that time I lived that way. I lived with no possessions. We were part of a community. Everyone helped each other out sharing what little money we had. I wasn't earning very much. What I had, I'd pass it on. It was like a church that was really committed to changing the world, really. Not in a gigantic way, en masse, but in small ways: individual by individual. I was very influenced by a man called Chris Rowe and his beautiful wife, Lilian. I think he had spent a lot of time in China, the child of a mission there before the Communists threw his family out. He was an older man. He relied on the Lord to provide them with everything they needed. They were living hand-to-mouth, this community. I guess he would have been what you would call the pastor of the church, but he'd be much too radical to wear a collar or anything like that. This was the real deal: a radical group. And I said: "Look, you shouldn't have to worry about money. We're gonna earn plenty of money. I'm in a band, and I know we'll be able to help. We're gonna make it." He just looked at me and laughed. I remember he said to me: "I wouldn't want money earned that way." And I said: "What do you mean by that?" He revealed to me that, even though he had known we were serious about being musicians, and being in a rock group, that he was only really tolerating it. He didn't really believe that our music was an integral part of who we were as religious people unless we used the music to evangelize. I knew then that he didn't really get it, and that indeed he was missing out on our blessing. Such a zealot was he, and such a fundamentalist, he didn't want a part of this rock 'n' roll thing. Maybe it's a compliment to him: we could have been a cash cow.

So he was not the Maharishi.

He was certainly not the Maharishi. He was a great teacher of the Scriptures. For a couple of years, every few days, I would get to listen to him. I learnt a lot. These are ancient great texts, and you can learn a lot from them if you have somebody who can open them up, who has the intellectual capacity, but also the spiritual capacity. Because in the end, they're more than just books. It was hard to leave, but he didn't understand we were kind of shunned. There was a moment where myself and Edge sat around and we thought: "Well, maybe we should knock this group on the head. Maybe it is frivolous, maybe these people are right, maybe this is just bollocks, this being in a band, and maybe it's just ego, and maybe we should put it behind us and just get to the real work of trying to change our own lives, and just get out into the world. There's much to do there." For a couple of weeks, we were at that place. Then we came to a realization: "Hold on a second. Where are these gifts coming from? This is how we worship God, even though we don't write religious songs, because we didn't feel God needs the advertising." *[laughs]* In fact, we ended up at a place where we thought: "The music isn't bollocks. This kind of fundamentalism is what's bollocks."

You just mentioned the Christian zealot background that people associated with U2 in the early eighties. I feel like that's precisely why some people question your activism. I'm playing devil's advocate here, but people who witness your crusade on behalf of the Third World might say: his heart is certainly in the right place, but he is a far cry from the role models he's patterned himself after, from Mahatma Gandhi to Martin Luther King. His heroes were ordinary people living with no material possessions. After all, he is just an outsider, from the showbiz world. What does he know? He does not live with these people. This contradiction that you just pointed out, which you sorted out in your own way, is an important issue in the Christian mentality. It's a contradiction that you faced, and that you still face.

Yeah.

[Interrupting] If a prophet turns up in our time, it seems likely that he will emerge out of a faceless crowd and remain in touch with basic humanity. And that is not you. So, people say about you: just who does this rock star think he is? He's not Mother Teresa! He doesn't work there; he's only giving lectures.

Well, I'll tell you who this rock star thinks he is not. He is sure that he's not Mother Teresa. *[laughs]*

I would have guessed that myself.

. . . that he is not these kinds of role models you mentioned. I'm the person I've ended up, which is a long way from the kind of people who inspired me. But here I am, and I see the embarrassment, excruciating at times, of "Rich rock star works on behalf of the poorest and most vulnerable." I mean, it's a very embarrassing photograph. Yet, you can't deny who you are. And if I gave all my money away, I'd just be a bigger star. *[laughs]* Right?

Possibly.

You know what I mean? We've already got a problem with genuflection. Then people would be finding a donkey for me to sit on. So I actually have figured out that my best insurance from accusation of messianic behavior is to follow Monty Python to *The Life of Brian*.

Which means?

When Brian walks out on the terrace and the people are calling his name, his mother walks out and goes: *[shrill voice of an old common English woman]* "Brian? 'E's not the Messiah! 'E's just a very naughty boy!" *[laughs and resumes normal voice]* So I actually enjoy the fact that I now live very well, and have an irresponsible side, and silliness is something I hold very dear. Because I've learnt that I don't have to live up to people's expectations of who they think I should be. What makes you qualified to help a person who has been knocked down in a car accident? There's only one qualification necessary: that you happened to be there, and you happened to be able to call the ambulance. That's really how I see my role: as raising the alarm. I have a very loud loud-hailer. My bullhorn is plugged into a Marshall stack, and I can use this ridiculous thing called celebrity to the advantage of these issues. That's the only qualification I need. I'm there, I have the loud-hailer, and I'm gonna use it. That's it. When you're lying down there, choking on the road, you're not gonna ask: "Excuse me, have you got a qualification? Are you a doctor? Do you really care about people, or are you just doing this because there's a newspaper report on its way?" You don't care. Just get the job done!

A few years ago, Q magazine ran a list of the most powerful people in the music business. And higher than Madonna or the chairman of Sony Music,

was Bono. So do you think you are one of the most powerful men in the world today?

I don't have any real power, but the people I represent do. The reason why politicians let me in the door, and the reason why people will take my call is because I represent quite a large constituency of people. Now, I do not control that constituency, but I represent them in a certain sense, even without them asking me to, in the minds of the people whose doors I knock upon. That constituency is a very powerful one, because it is a constituency of people from eighteen to thirty, who are the floating vote. They have not yet made their mind up which way they're going to vote. They're the most open-minded, and that's why politicians pay attention to what's going on in contemporary culture and what a rock star might have to do with all of this: because of the people I represent. Now, outside of that, I represent a lot of people who have no voice at all. In the world's order of things, they're the people who count the least. There are 6,500 people who are dying every day of AIDS in Africa for no good reason. It's a preventable, treatable disease. I now represent them. They haven't asked me either. It's cheeky, but I hope they're glad I do, and in God's order of things, they're the most important. So I think that imbues you with a power way beyond anything that you might have an influence on, being in a pop band. It's a certain moral authority that's way beyond your own life and capabilities. The punch you throw is not your own. It has the force of a much bigger issue.

But let me take a down-to-earth example. I have been through moments in my life where I had little money. I recall that at that time it was very difficult for me to live in a world of big ideas. Maybe I was "pickled," as you would say, but I didn't have time for those. The money you have might lead you to develop very unrealistic views about the world. Don't you tend to forget about the problems that an ordinary person has to face in an ordinary life? Most of the time, people are busy paying off a mortgage, raising their kids, et cetera. Aren't you out of touch with reality?

But which reality am I not in touch with? You're working on behalf of a billion people who live on less than a dollar a day. Isn't it more important that

I'm more in touch with their needs than the normal Western life you describe? And by the way, from their point of view, you, Michka Assayas, the writer and the journalist, and me, Bono, filthy-rich rock star, are exactly the same to them. There is no difference in the way you live, in the way I live.

What makes you say that?

Because, if you are at the level of begging for a meal once a day, or medication, there is no difference.

I see your point. When I went to India, I felt like I was being perceived as coming out of a television commercial.

So they would say to both of us: how are you in touch with reality? Both of you live this rarefied existence! You live in Paris, in your apartment, and you go out to the cafés, and you have a nice life. And there's Bono, he lives in his realm. But we are both so far from their experience. So, if you wanna look at the world, two-thirds of the planet are living hand-to-mouth. We live in the other third—the West—and in that third, we're up at the top third of that. And OK, now, of that third, I might be higher up the ladder than you, but compared to most people who live there, there's no difference. We eat well, we can afford medicines, we have time off, and we don't have to worry about our children.

It's true, but maybe my point is less general than that. It's just that, when things come easily, you tend to forget about the way people really feel. You think about them in an idealistic way and start to look at issues on a very large scale. You don't communicate with what's inside those people, with what's at the core of them. Maybe with your music.

See, I don't know. I think that the things that really communicate universally are humor, grace, and strength of character. These are things that people read, no matter whether you're in northern Ethiopia or London. People can read who you are. I must say I quite enjoy being lost in Africa, wandering around, where people have no idea who I am, but even when they do hear that you're some sort of rich rock star, it doesn't really change the way they talk to me. I

'Hungry in a way that couldn't be fed'
U2 in Atlanta, November 1981

'If we weren't able, we had the faith'
An early gig in the Dandelion Market, Dublin, 1979

'Paul McGuinness gave me the confidence to realise my potential as an artist and continue to dig deeper'
After a gig at the Project Arts Centre, Dublin, 1978. Seated left to right: Adam, Edge, Paul McGuinness, Bono, Aislinn Evans, Larry. Standing behind left to right: Guggi, Gavin Friday

'I don't trust a
performer who's
content with
the distance
between him and
the audience'
California,
May 1983

'I have somebody
in my life, after a
long time, I still
feel I don't know'
With Ali,
Long Island, NY,
October 1987

'The subject was so much bigger than anyone on the stage'
Live Aid,
July 1985

'I learnt a lot of my lip from Bob, I had a sense that the impossible was possible from him'
With Bob Geldof, Band Aid, November 2004

'Being in U2, each of us is more than he would be if he were one whole of something else'

U2 celebrate at the 43rd Grammy Awards in Los Angeles, February 2001

'I still think we're not truly believable as rock stars'

ZOO TV, Wembley Stadium, August 1993

SHARON VS. ARAFAT ■ THE DEATH OF DANIEL PEARL

TIME

CAN
BONO
SAVE
THE
WORLD?

Don't laugh—the globe's biggest rock star is on a mission to make a difference

4 March 2002

'A lot of the things you learn in a band are analogous to politics'
The Labour Party Conference, Brighton, September 2004

**'After a few minutes, people don't see me. All they're hearing is the
moral force of the argument'**
Third World Debt Relief, US Capitol, September 2000

'You don't have to be harmonious on everything to get along with someone'
Walking to the Oval Office with George W. Bush, March 2002

think, maybe here it might, but not there. As you say, I'm much more involved with what's really important, which is survival. I used to think, to go back to your first question, it was a big deal. Now I realize that money's only a big deal if you don't have it.

Let me go back to that bad experience in the studio that you mentioned yesterday. You keep telling me that your strength is your reliance on an organization, on a group. And I'm sure the sort of conflict you experienced yesterday has occurred more than once with U2. I've thought to myself: there must be some secret in there. How come these people who have known one another since their teens, who have been through so much together—getting ultra-famous, marriages, in some cases divorces, overindulgence, et cetera— have survived together? Why has the band never split up? Or even been in serious danger?

[pondering] Well, I think the band is in serious danger sometimes. It's not something you can take for granted. I think it is much more likely that people part company than it is that they stay together. Because everyone is financially independent, and they don't need to work. That's always a danger. I think we've been pretty good at getting out of each other's way. There's times when people can really just try your patience, and I'm sure there's times when I have really tried the band's patience, like when I'm not around, for instance, and they're trying to finish the album. There's moments when people are so lost in their own selves, the demands of their own life, that it's very hard to be in a band. But people come out of those phases, and I have, others have. But look: it's every day I'm amazed at that fact, because it gets difficult as people get older, because people want to be lords of their own domain. I mean, everybody, as they get older—I think we've discussed this—rids the room of argument. You see it in your family, you see it with your friends, and they get a smaller and smaller circle of people around them, who agree with them. And life ends up with a dull sweetness. Actually, now that I mention it, it sounds good.

Remember what you said to me: that you wanted to have a family in the band because the family you were born into was not working. But most peo-

ple want to get rid of their family after a while. Sometimes family and friends can be very narrowing.

I think it's claustrophobic, but it's never narrowing, because the friction of different points of view makes you better. And the thing that'll make you less and less able to realize your potential is a room that's empty of argument. And I would be terrified to be on my own as a solo singer, not to have a band to argue with. I mean, I surround myself with argument, and a band, a family of very spunky kids, and a wife who's smarter than anyone. I've got a lot of very smart friends, a whole extended family of them.

You love to be challenged, I have noticed.

To live in Dublin is one long argument. The city loves debate, the din of argument, from chattering classes to the shattering glasses, the big voices of small minds, the itchy bitchy print of some journalists who don't like their job, the irreverence for success. I'd miss this stuff, I'm serious. I like being challenged. You're as good as the arguments you get. So maybe the reason why the band hasn't split up is that people might get this: that even though they're one quarter of U2, they are more than they would be if they were one whole of something else. I certainly feel that way.

There are lots of examples that imply the contrary. I mean, take the Beatles. After a while, they felt being in a band was narrowing.

Did they ever do better work on their own, these luminous, extraordinary talents? Did they, when they lost the tension? John Lennon actually nearly did. But finally his greatness will be remembered as the work he did with his nemesis, Paul McCartney. And Paul McCartney is somebody I'm in awe of. He's such a prodigious talent.

He's magic. You know, for the very first time in my life I really listened to Wings, which was a band that I used to despise as a teenager. I'm not even

talking about my new-wave years. *[laughs]* I have listened all summer long to the *Wingspan* compilation. It sounds so fresh. You forget about the "in-fluences" he may have had.

But time often is forgiving and dismissive of the influences, because they re-cede. We look at *Sgt. Pepper* and we go "Wow! How did they ever think that up?" But of course, if you got into Paul McCartney's bedroom, found his record collection at the time, you would find out. But the clues are gone. *[laughs]* It's like in evolution: there are certain pure situations that hang around longer, but the ones that got them there don't have time to leave fossils. We have a giraffe, we have a horse. But where's the horse with the long neck? The link species disappear.

But to go back to what the Beatles did after they split up . . .

They did good work. Sometimes great work, in his case. But it's not the Beatles.

What do you make of George Harrison? He came into his own as a song-writer by extricating himself from the Beatles . . .

OK. Maybe. But did he have as much fun?

And then what do you make of people who set out to be solo artists from the very beginning? I mean some of your heroes, like . . .

Bob Marley.

Sure! And what about Bob Dylan or Bruce Springsteen?

Yeah, yeah. I've incredible admiration. I think, in some ways, it's easier to re-alize a vision that's singular and in your own head, but it's harder to keep the vision going without argument. Look at Prince. He's one of my fa-vorite composers of the twentieth century. I really believe in him. But he needs an editor. He needs a row. He needs somebody in the studio to tell him to fuck off. "And guess what? There's six great tracks and four of them are pretty average. I'm sorry, sir. Your genius was having a bad day." Does he have that? No chance.

Have you ever discussed this with somebody like Dylan?

Yes. We did. Bob Dylan, in a way, has always been there for me. His music, and occasionally the man himself. No artist alive or dead has meant so much to me. I remember him saying to me once how lucky I was to have a band. I asked him why did he say that. It was at the height of *Joshua Tree* madness. We were on the cover of *Time* magazine, and we had number-one singles, albums. It was very, very exciting, but a head trip too. There was a lot coming at us, just disorienting stuff. And he said: "Imagine going through all that you're going through, now, on your own." I can't imagine what it would be not to have— when extraordinary, ridiculous, over-the-top things just happened to me— Edge or Larry to speak through the side of my mouth about something ridiculous, and laugh to ourselves.

But did Dylan tell you how he managed to get through it?

I think the implication was: by the skin of his teeth. Right? By the skin of his teeth. And not without cuts and bruises.

Well, even in a band, you get them, don't you?

Yes, bruises, and the occasional flesh wound. *[laughs]* The occasional missing leg. I mean, sometimes I do remind myself of the other scene in the Monty Python movie. It's the very first, *The Holy Grail*. It's the knights who say *[ultra-shrill voice]* "Ni!" The knight says *[adopts a thundering voice]* "Stand, all! My valor, my courage is unmatched!" He's taking on anybody. And his opponent cuts off his arm and blood is squirting everywhere. *[laughs]* He goes: "Not a problem . . . Not a problem . . ." And then *[sword and sorcery sound of the other arm being cut]* the other arm goes. He goes: "Nothing! That's nothing!" *[Sound again]* His legs go. Eventually, his head is cut off, and is lying on the ground, in the helmet, just shouting: "Come on, you coward!" As his enemy stands over him, examining the dismantled limbs, he continues taunting: "No, that was nothing . . . a mere flesh wound . . ." he says. There is a danger in describing your survival in battle a little too glowingly.

I'm sure you have experienced bouts of madness.

I might have had one this week.

Aren't there times where you just want to leave everything behind and disappear?

I disappeared for five weeks this year, which was amazing. I haven't had five weeks off for ten years. I wasn't on my own, I was with my family and loved ones, but I wasn't working. You mean, going off for a week? Occasionally . . .

If you had become a solo artist, would you have survived the madness?

No, I don't think I'm as strong as Bob Dylan is. I think he is a very tenacious character. I think underneath all the so-called eccentricity, which I think is just a mask, there's a very true person. He's a good father—I've seen him with his children—with a moral compass, and who can get lost at sea, like everybody. But I think he's very strong. I think I needed company, because I'm more emotional, I'm a more operatic character. I need to be surrounded, even just for the laughter, because if I run out of laughs, then I'm really in trouble.

So you're confessing to some kind of weakness.

I guess so. I think that's probably fair.

Have you ever discussed that with people like Mick Jagger?

I have of course always been interested in the Mick and Keith relationship, more as sort of "I don't want this to happen to me." *[laughs]* They're two extraordinary people who are still working with each other, but can't really surrender to each other in the way that they could when they were kids, arguing and fighting. The real problem in a relationship is when the arguing stops.

That's what I was thinking about.

And you just have that awkward silence. So maybe they're OK, because they're still calling each other names. They've written some beautiful songs together. Even recently, there's one on *Voodoo Lounge* called "Out of Tears" *[sings] I won't cry when you say good-bye / I'm out of tears, out of tears.* That could be, like, from the fifties. Actually, there are two. Keith has a song, "The Worst," which would break the hardest heart. I mean, it's just great. "Mixed Emotions" is another song from a recent album, "Anybody Seen My Baby?"—great tunes . . . I spent some time with the two of them, once. They weren't speaking at the time. There was a really awkward period for the band. Legend has it that Keith had pulled a gun *[laughs]* on Steve Lillywhite, who was producing, and sort of pointed the gun through the studio glass out at him, trying just to spook him. And I called down to the studio. What's interesting about both of them is they're both extremely old-fashioned.

What do you mean?

Mick is like a very conservative man. His children have impeccable manners. Even his clothes, offstage, have a certain kind of yacht-club vibe. I don't think he's an ephemeral person at all. He has a sort of insatiable curiosity about the world around him, and believes that it's worth your while to know what you're talking about. I remember one of his little girls came up to me at one point, and she said *[whispers, adopting posh English accent]:* "People think my daddy's the devil, and he lets them!" *[laughs]* What a great line. The daughter of a man who has written many. For him, I think he climbs into a character. Literally, you can see him, as he starts to sing, get into the skin of this other thing called Mick Jagger, which is this R & B singer. But I think he's very British, very English, very old school, and . . . loves cricket! Now Keith is exactly the same. Keith would light a cigarette for you, talks very respectfully in front of women, would

never make a coarse comment about women, has a nobility in his human relationships, and was tougher than anyone. But no one is tougher than drink
or drugs. He has probably taken a few swipes from both, has taken them on
the chin. But he's still standing and still funny and still throwing a few swipes
back! He's like a Hemingway-type character, *The Old Man and the Sea,* or
something. He's a pirate, actually. But, to quote Dylan, he is the man who has
to be honest to live outside the law.

**I would like to finish this with three quick questions and three quick an-
swers. What is the best piece of advice you've ever heard in show business?**

We put on shows, we do the business. But we're not in show business.

And what advice would you give to an aspiring rock star?

Try to write *that* song: it will manage you, it will dress you, it will feed your kids,
it will direct you in the video. Stop whinging, you could be writing that song
right now!

**That sounds like a sales pitch for a "self-improvement" program. And what
would you warn that aspiring rock star against the most?**

[ponders] Other rock stars.

9. THOU SHALT NOT GO TO AMERICA

Christmas and New Year's Day passed. Progress on the new U2 album was a bit rough. Its release had been moved from spring to autumn 2004. The band had also changed producers: Steve Lillywhite, who had produced U2's first three albums, and remained close to the band ever since, was summoned back. Given that context, I honestly did not expect Bono to have much time. So I was frankly surprised when I received a spontaneous call from him in late January. He was just back from America and planned to stay put for a few weeks, ready to engage in a series of regular phone calls.

So the following conversation took place only a week after that surprising call. Bono was supposed to call at noon on a Saturday. I just sat on my couch, waiting for the phone to ring, slowly sinking into lethargy. By 12:30 P.M., still no sign of life. Then it rang, and a kind of underwater voice came out, apologizing . . .

I was up earlier, and I was reading. There was silence in the house, and I was just reading and reading, then I just fell asleep at that very time. I'm awake again.

You sound tired.

No, no, no. Not at all. That was amazing, that was a deep sleep. Strange, 'cause I don't know when the middle of the night is anymore. I guess it's the middle of the night. *[laughs]*

You must be working late nights with the recording under way. Each time I read a story about a U2 song, it seemed to happen in the middle of the night, or in the wee hours of dawn.

I generally don't like working late at night. *[yawns]* I like the early morning, and when I wake up, I feel excited about the day and the possibilities of it. And it's downhill from there. *[laughs]* I mean, I'm full of energy. I wake up, and so I do my reading and my writing in the morning. Then, in the afternoon, I do the kind of solid work in the studio. Then we break at eight o'clock for something to eat. When we come back, it's either the fun time, there can be some spontaneity in the late sessions. But Edge is much more the spirit in the room the later it gets. There's a phrase after midnight that puts the fear of God into producers and engineers. It's when he says: "I have a little idea I'd like to try." *[laughs]* Because that might mean that they're up through six A.M.

I don't know how it is for you, but my best ideas come when I'm about to go to sleep, or when I feel like I have spent my entire day wasting time, or working without thinking, which may amount to the same thing. I go down to buy a paper, and all of a sudden the idea that I was looking for just happens.

Yeah, the unconscious. Whether it's a collective unconscious or not, whatever pool you draw out from. That's why songwriting by accident is so important, and the getting to the place where that can happen or, as we say, getting to the place where God can walk through the room. Because, if you know what great is, you know you're a long way from it. *[laughs]*

That is definitely my experience.

If you know what great is, you know you're not it. So you have to set up the opportunity to bump into it. And it's a strange thing, because it really might come down to osmosis. It's not the most romantic explanation, but it might be the truest one. The way I could back up this argument is by pointing to artists who have blown both our minds, Michka, as we grew up, people who suddenly just completely lost their gift and started making rubbish music. We don't have to name names here, but you know the kind I'm talking about. You think: How did that happen? How did this person who set fire to my imagination end up with no new ideas, and actually, even incapable of their old ones? Here's my theory: When people are absorbed in the culture, and they're going out, they're listening to music, they're in the clubs, music is just part of their every waking moment, and as a result part of their sleeping times, in their dreams. The life is empty of other lovers. Unless you're in love with the music, or you stop struggling with it in your unconscious when you're asleep, you've other dreams. You're dreaming about moving houses, about whatever other ventures you're involved in. But that's where you did all your great work: you did it when you were . . . *[suspends sentence, searching for the right word]*

. . . missing . . .

Yes. Unconscious.

Is that something you worry about? I mean, you have so much on your plate now. Don't you have the feeling that your dreams are eroding dreams somehow?

A strange thing about all the other work I'm doing is that it's turned music back to pleasure. It's my escape from work. It's where I have the luxury to dream.

Actually, you're getting quite close to a place where I want to start this conversation. Last time we talked, you mentioned your "journey through America." And I think that phrase conjures up much more than it seems to in your case. I'm sure that you know the expression your friend Wim Wenders coined.

"Colonization of the unconscious."

That's right. "The Americans have colonized our unconscious." Let's see how I can get around to this. I am borrowing an idea from the American writer Paul Theroux. This is how he analyzed the Beatles' success in the U.S. In early 1964, he wrote something about how the Americans were deeply questioning their country and the way its ideals had been lost somehow. JFK had just been shot, the civil rights movement, championed by Martin Luther King, divided the country, and it also was the beginning of the military involvement in Vietnam. It was a period of self-doubt, of confusion. So Theroux says that is why young people in America embraced the Beatles and the other British Invasion bands with such enthusiasm. They loved the image of America these groups from the Old World reflected. The Beatles were saying: your music is the greatest, your movie stars are the best, American girls are the greatest-looking, your cars are the ones we want. And in the process, they helped Americans restore their faith in their own country and what it could achieve. About twenty years later, with *The Joshua Tree,* U2 became the number-one band in the U.S. It was a record that reflected your fascination with America. Don't you think that young Americans, at that time, saw you as saviors because you restored their faith in their own country, a faith that was not available anymore elsewhere in the late eighties, when materialism seemed the only option? Don't you think that U2 somehow sold back the dream of America to the Americans at that particular moment in their history?

In the early eighties, America was very uncool in Europe. American fashion seemed at a low point. It was shoulder pads and big hair. There was punk rock, which had given us hope in the seventies that was faded, and it was a very dull moment indeed for American music, with the exception of Bruce Springsteen. Dylan had seemed like he was asleep. Rap was just about to kick off. It had started, but they weren't letting it on MTV. Madonna was singing "Material Girl." Greed was good, from that movie *Wall Street.* The stock market was flying, but it seemed, outside of making money, there didn't seem to be many other ideas around on the music map. Now Jean-Michel Basquiat and Keith

Haring were happening in art. There was the suggestion that something might be under way.

But that was New York ...

That was New York, exactly. There was an incredible mood in the U.K., of almost like the cultural revolution. Just awful. The U.K. music press had broken up the Clash, and there were these bogus ideas left over from punk rock, stuff we were talking about before, like "street credibility." One of these sort of handed-down, Little Red Bookish thoughts was: "Thou Shalt Not Go to America." And kneel at that. But we were Irish. Ireland had a completely different relationship with America, because America was a Promised Land for Irish people. It was the alternative to getting the mail boat to Liverpool or Holyhead, and taking that journey to London on and around the country. But it was much more of a Romantic journey, and in America, Ireland meant something completely different too. Memories of poverty and famine and desperate struggles had been replaced in the sixties and seventies by the Kennedys.

Irish and Catholic.

Irish and Catholic, yes. So Irish people had a completely different attitude. Plus the ballad tradition which was still alive in Ireland was one of the streams that had led into the reservoir of folk music that begat Bob Dylan and so much of American music, country music. These were second cousins of Irish traditional music. So there was a sense that we Irish had more ownership of America. In a way, though Ireland had lost to the British crown its self-esteem and a lot of its land, in America, Irish people were actually in some odd way reversing that. You see, America had been an English colony and, even after Independence, a bastion of Protestantism. The founding fathers of America were as suspicious of Roman Catholicism as the English monarchy. Protestants seemed more able at controlling desires, fleshly, worldly concerns than the Catholics, who were uncouth Irish who had just got off their famine ships and were causing trouble. America was intended to be an outpost of the strictest moralism.

That seems quite at odds with the image that we, as young Europeans, had of America. To me, it looked like the country where everything was possible, where a sixteen-year-old could drive a convertible car.

[laughing] Yeah! But you're talking about the fifties, sixties on. I'm talking about the 1850s, 1860s.

I don't know about that. Actually I was talking about my years as a teenager: the 1970s. Life in America seemed easy and glamorous in that period. So the contrast is very hard to accept.

Yeah. But even in the nineteenth century, some people were not having such strict rules. Some people wanted to drink ale and chase women down dirty streets. That's the Irish for you! After surviving starvation in the hands of the Brits, they weren't going to have a load of Prods tell them what they could or could not do.

What was your idea of America when you were growing up? Did you hear tales about people who went off to America in your family?

Of course, through television, we came across America: the sort of gritty glamour of cop shows, the noise of it, and the fact that it looked like a sexier place. There were so many different people. Everyone in Ireland looked the same. What I'm trying to say is there was no way that we as a band were going to buy this thing of not going to go to America. We loved the U.K. music scene, but we knew we didn't quite fit in with the strict rules of the U.K. music press. As I mentioned, we didn't want to be cool, we wanted to be hot, you see. The music scene in the eighties in London had a lot to do with fashion.

When I first met you, you were banging on about this.

Fashion, really, is what had driven punk rock, not philosophy. People weren't talking about real revolution. It was Situationism that you can wear on your T-shirt. We just wanted to take our music wherever people wanted to listen. In

America, we found people to be much less cynical. Paul McGuinness had an instinct that this would be a good place for us, that we would have to play to what he called "the real America," not just coastal America. That began my love affair with the Midwest. But all the other groups in competition, they would never do that. They would play one date in Chicago, one date in Texas, and that was that.

Do you remember the very first time you set foot on American soil? You took a plane, went through customs, and left the airport. What did you see? Whom did you talk to? Do you remember the smell of it?

Yeah, I do. In fact, we wrote a song about it. It's called "Angel of Harlem." It was December, and we arrived at JFK. I remember from the very first just being in customs, and that Americans spoke louder than anyone else. They were all kind of shouting at each other. But these were just people who loaded the suitcases on the carousel. It was street talk, and it was exciting. Then I noticed that the colors of the paint at the airport, they were not colors you would ever see painted in Europe. They were strange mauves and sort of odd greens and yellows, and there was just a hint of what I now realize was a sort of black influence, and Chinese influence. It was very different. Paul McGuinness had, for a treat, organized a *limousine*. So here we were, with no money, and he got the record company to do a *limousine!* Now, we'd never been in a limousine, we'd never been in New York, we'd never been in America. It was mind-blowing. So we all climb into this ridiculous-looking car with Christmas lights around the windows, and we're sitting there, laughing and giggling. And we're on a *freeway*, tuning in to the radio, listening to different stations, and we came across this station called BLS. That's the very famous soul station in New York, and Billie Holiday was singing. And then we came over the 59th Street Bridge, and see *that* view of Manhattan. I mean, for us, for kids just turning nineteen, twenty, it was Oz! *[laughs]* And Paul McGuinness who had organized the limo, he was the Wizard. *[laughs]* And the tour went so well. I remember we stayed at the Gramercy Park Hotel. The Clash were staying there, the Slits. It was like an American bohemia. I remember the Slits hadn't got guitar straps. They were so punk. Their guitars, they were around their necks by strings. I think Edge put out his hand to shake one of their hands, and the singer, Ari Up, slapped it. She said: "We don't do that."

It's funny you'd mention the Slits, because they were practically the first band I ever interviewed, even before you. The photographer who was there with me was preparing for a shot as Viv, the guitar player, blew her nose into a handkerchief. So when he snapped, she just showed the snot dripping from the handkerchief to the camera. That was the picture.

We saw the Clash in the lobby. They were just so cool, and we knew we weren't. I had a fur coat, which was funny. I remember I walked out to the street. It was snowing in America. I just wanted to take it all in, standing at the corner in my fur coat and my crap haircut. And this unusual-looking man just stops on a bicycle beside me and says: "Hey, honey, where are you going? How are you, sweetheart?" And I was like: Urrgggh! *[laughs]* Not so bohemian after all. I want my mother! Hold on, I don't have a mother. So Irish boy scuttles back into the lobby. It was funny.

Funny, I was thinking about the Virgin Prunes, the group that your friends Gavin and Guggi were in. They were very much into theatrics, bringing out the feminine side, cross-dressing.

. . . which was probably why I was wearing a fur coat . . .

You worked with Brian Eno, who was part of the early seventies glam-rock scene. I don't know if you remember that gatefold sleeve from the second Roxy Music album.

Yes, I remember he wore the ostrich feathers.

That's the one. And you didn't look like him or Guggi, but you didn't look like Bruce Springsteen either . . .

Artiness, arty-fartiness is around the corner from sissy, isn't it? But in a way we were an art group, even if we didn't look like one. Our joke was: we didn't go to art school, we went to Brian Eno. Because every other rock band in the British invasion, they were all "art school." Brian Jones, Keith Richards, John Lennon, Pete Townshend, the Clash were art school. Sex Pistols weren't art school, but their manager was. You see, before we went to Brian, we had our own sort of avant-garde teenage years, our own surrealist performance art and humor: the giving of names, the arguments about Andy Warhol's art and films—one major spat about his film *Bad*. The Virgin Prunes had actually taken over an exhibition space in Trinity College, where Guggi had sculpted vaginas out of fresh meat, flies and all. Gavin had one corner called "Sheep," where a mate of ours crawled around on all fours in a traditional Aran sweater to take the piss out of the folkies. They were running amok. But if you look at those early pictures, the way the Virgin Prunes carried on was extraordinary. I mean this is twenty years before Marilyn Manson. There was a very strong glam cross-dressing aspect. I mean, it is a strange thing. Myself and Guggi, when we were kids, one of the albums we both obsessed on was Lou Reed's *Transformer*.

What a title! Now I'm coming to think of it.

[laughs] Little did we know what the title was about when we were thirteen: transexuals! We were very heterosexual, but that's a different point, isn't it? So were most of the glam-rock bands. It's funny Guggi later found himself in a frock as part of the Prunes. I see I'm macho enough to know that creativity is from the feminine side, and . . . there you go.

Let's go back to your coming to America for the first time. So you arrived when the Reagan era was just beginning.

That's right. But to go back to what we were talking about earlier, U2 would appeal to the ports in that Catholic sense, but we'd also appeal to the Midwest in that Protestant sense.

You were Protestant *and* Catholic. A country obsessed with religion must have got you going.

Yes, it's true. The Bible-bashing televangelists that you would turn on in a hotel—these knock-off salesmen for God—whereas most reasonable sensible people would just change the channel, I was fascinated.

Who was the first televangelist you saw on TV?

It was a preacher who was asking his audience in TV land to put their hand against the screen to be healed. So there were people, old ladies with bronchitis, old ladies with broken hips, and probably people with cancer, all over America, getting out of their armchairs and putting their hands on the TV. It broke my heart. But remember I was a believer. Though I understood the power of the Scriptures they were quoting from, and I did believe in the healing powers of faith, I was seeing it debased and demeaned. But unlike a lot of people, I understood the language. What's always bothered me about the fundamentalists is that they seem preoccupied with the most obvious sins. If those sins, sexual immorality and drug addiction, come out of unhappiness, then I'm sure God wants to set people free of that unhappiness. But I couldn't figure out why the same people were never questioning the deeper, slyer problems of the human spirit like self-righteousness, judgmentalism, institutional greed, corporate greed. You only have to look to unfair trade agreements that keep the developing world in the Dark Ages to see the hypocrisy I'm talking about. These people talk about the debasing of culture. What about the debasing of hundreds of thousands of real lives?

Right. These people go to church on Sunday. I guess they're very generous when the plate comes around. So were you angry with those fundamentalists?

We thought they were trampling all over the most precious thing of all: the concept that God is love. These televangelists, they were the traders inside the temple, that story where Jesus turned over their tables. They were putting people off God, especially young people who didn't want to admit to being

Christians anymore. Because in clubs, on campuses, everywhere, people would say: "You're part of that. They're nuts!" So it was very interesting to be in America at that time. We were fans and critics, getting ready to tell them the best and the worst on *The Joshua Tree.*

But I presume what they caught on to was the best. I mean, on *The Joshua Tree* and *Rattle and Hum,* you told them it was OK to listen to roots music, to the blues, the gospel and country music. At that time, did you ask yourself: "Why us? Why did they pick us to remind them of how great their country is?" I mean, they already had Bruce Springsteen.

Well, I think, Bruce Springsteen influenced us a lot in the eighties. It was also significant. His music had a similar mythology at its heart. Again, that was one of the things that was "against the law": playing music in those bigger halls that they call arenas, basketball arenas. We went to see him in an arena, and he changed our life. He really communicated. For the first time, U2 realized that a bigger venue doesn't have to dilute the power of our music. We realized it could add to the experience: a bigger crowd, a bigger electrical charge. But we'd never seen an audience as engaged on that scale. There were twenty thousand people and you could hear a pin drop if he wanted you to. Now, I went to see the Rolling Stones in Madison Square Garden at the same time, and I had fallen asleep. The sound was so bad . . .

A little while ago, I took care of a huge music encyclopedia. Going through the stories of all these bands and performers, I came to a tentative conclusion. I think that the mystique that was born out of rock music comes in a main part from the performers who utterly reinvented themselves. See, Robert Zimmerman, the son of an electrical appliances retailer in the mountains of Minnesota, reinvents himself as Bob Dylan, tells people that a blues musician gave him his guitar, or that Sioux blood runs through his veins. He invents a mythology of his own. I think that in the minds of our generation, you invented yourself as Bono and fascinated us in the same way. Do you know who Bono is?

I'm trying. It's the hardest thing . . . to be yourself. Maybe I haven't been able to pull it off *[laughs]* . . . yet.

Lots of people wouldn't let you begin to.

Why?

I think they're enjoying your personality crisis. It's a spectator sport, watching you figure this stuff out, reinventing yourself constantly.

That's the great thing about America. It is the land of reinvention. It was never about where you come from, it's always about where you're going. And people accept that beginning again is at the heart of the American Dream. The Irish came over from a death culture, of famine, and of colonization, which of course was emasculation. They found a new virility in America. They began a new life in America. And this of course is at the heart of the idea of redemption: to begin again. This is at the heart of religious fundamentalism too: to be born again. I wish to begin again on a daily basis. To be born again every day is something that I try to do. And I'm deadly serious about that.

One of the most important things you did in America—and I'm talking about the continent, as opposed to the United States—was making a stand about the Sandinista movement in Nicaragua. That was your first public involvement in U.S. politics, right?

Let me think. Well, the first thing of a political nature in America was dealing with Provisional IRA sympathizers in America: the sponsors of the mayhem back home. We only discovered we were Irish when we went to America, in the sense of what being Irish meant. Bobby Sands* was dying on hunger strike in the Maze prison in Northern Ireland. It was heartbreaking, but it was also rabble-rousing. It was all over the news every night in America. The tin-cuppers were going to raise a fortune out of his sacrifice. Remember, there are 45 mil-

*Bobby Sands (1954–1981) was an Irish Republican from Belfast.

lion Americans who consider themselves Irish. The younger generation would come and see us play. Second-generation and third-generation Irish were throwing money up onstage for the revolutionaries who were giving up their lives. But when we'd meet these people afterwards, they didn't really know anything about what was going on.

Did they have much support at home?

Few realized that these revolutionaries were not representing the will of any significant majority. Whatever way you drew Ireland, with or without the border, they were a minority. Even if they were amongst the Catholics in Northern Ireland, they were a minority. Yet these people felt they had the right to form an army and destroy lives. So they were the enemy, as far as we were concerned. Fascists, brown shirts—in this case, green shirts. There had to be a better way.

Did you have any big ideas?

Well, maybe understandably, this began our interest in nonviolence. And here, the U.S. played a role. America had had its own troubles with race relations in the sixties. We started to see similarities with the civil rights movement. We became students of nonviolence, of Martin Luther King's thinking. That all started happening around that time. Then we wrote "Sunday Bloody Sunday" as a way of refuting the armed struggle. So America had brought us to that place. America had made us question about being Irish. The irony was that a lot of people thought "Sunday Bloody Sunday" was a call to arms, a rebel song for a united Ireland. It was about unity, but not in the geographical sense.

Don't you believe in a united Ireland?

Only by consensus. The border was drawn by threat of war, but we have to accept it won't be removed by force. Real division, as the great John Hume says, is in the people's hearts and minds.

Did the Provisional Army in Ireland threaten you at some point?

We were deliberately trying to dry up funds for the IRA in America. I know we annoyed them, but they didn't respond in any organized ugly way, no. We must have pissed them off. We were huge with the Irish-American community. Some small amount of well-organized people were the culprits, passing the hat around raising money for the Irish cause—which really meant putting bombs in English pubs and killing innocents. So we were not very popular, no, with the Provos. And we were let know that back in Ireland in subtle ways.

How subtle were they?

Actually, not at all. After having denounced the IRA from a stage in Ireland in the early eighties, I remember a few incidents. Once, our car was surrounded by a bunch of Provo supporters. One had wrapped the tricolor around his fist trying to smash the windows of the car with his bare hands, screaming "Brits! Traitors!" However real or not, there was one threat of kidnapping, which the head of the Special Branch was taking very seriously. I remember we all had to have our toeprints taken as well as our fingerprints. That set the imagination off . . . *[laughs]* Were they gonna break our legs or post them? I don't want to exaggerate the effect this stuff had on our life. But still, for the rest of the eighties, within some quarters where we used to be welcome, we became personae non grata. In certain pubs and certain places, people would look at you, and think you'd let them down. But, after a while, people realized that it wasn't that we weren't nationalists, or that we weren't supporters of their grievances.

There were very real grievances, weren't there?

Yes. There had been great abuses taken of the Catholic minority, but we, like most Northern Catholics, believed in a peaceful solution. We hated the Irish ambivalence to violence. You know, there'd be a bombing somewhere, some atrocity in a supermarket in the middle of England. Women and children would be slaughtered. Everyone would be shocked by the news, everyone. In Ireland, people would stare at their shoes for a few days. People would be saying: "Oh, they've gone too far, now this is all too much." But then, you know, a couple of months later, somebody would be singing in a pub some folk song, some battle hymn, "A Nation Once Again," or something like that, and the hats would be passed around, and everyone would put in for the Provos. I hated that about us Irish, our duplicity. I just felt that we had to take a position, which was clear—that this violent route was not making the lives of anyone any better. It would not lead to anywhere other than despair, and would make the job of integration for both communities more difficult.

So no direct threats?

No direct threats. Just a sense that you pissed them off. I heard Gerry Adams took down a U2 poster from the Sinn Fein office. He certainly referred to me as "a little shit" in a major press interview. It's not helpful when the leader of an armed struggle who has support in every working-class neighborhood, and a lot of maniacs on his side, calls you a "little shit." It doesn't make your life easier.

Do either of you hold a grudge now that peace is in the air?

Not at all. Since then, Gerry Adams has put out his hand to me. He went to the offices of Jubilee 2000 to learn about the Drop the Debt campaign. He is a very brilliant man. He already knew his way around a lot of our issues. If he and his party deliver disarmament of the paramilitaries, they will be a force in politics. I hope he feels remorseful for the damage the armed struggle caused to Ireland. He would believe that it got us to the place where there is an Irish peace agreement. I don't believe that. But he put his hand out to me, and I respected that. I shook it. In Ireland, there is an expression: "Keep your hands in your pockets when you're talking to these people." Well, I took mine out, and he took his hand over.

So you're optimistic about an end to "the Troubles"?

Yes. Years later, I would have the greatest honor of my life in Ireland when U2 played in support of the Good Friday Peace Agreement in the Waterfront Hall in Belfast in 1998. We got John Hume and David Trimble, the two opposing leaders in the conflict, to shake hands onstage in front of a U2 and Ash audience. People tell me that rock concert and that staged photograph pushed the people into ratifying the peace agreement. I'd like to think that's true. I'd like to think that the extreme Unionists and the extreme Republicans now have the courage to put down their guns. Because it takes courage to trust in the peace process and to return to civilian life. Both sides have suffered too much. It's easy for me to proffer my opinions. I'm not living next door or across the road or across the town from a painful memory. I live in Dublin in a house beside the sea.

10. MY LIFE AS A DISASTER GROUPIE

This conversation happened on the phone, only ten days after the previous one, in mid-February. The man was still in his home in the south of France with family, most of them gathered in the bedroom.

[jocular] Michka!

Oui, c'est moi!

[conscientiously articulating in French] Comment allez-vous?

Fort bien et vous-même ? First lesson. *[laughs]*

Very good . . .

Got a better voice than last time.

Really?

Did you get a good night's sleep? Now I'm really playing it like a doctor . . .

[laughing] I wrote this thing this morning about Elvis Presley for *Rolling Stone* magazine. They're doing a special issue on pop stars, I guess. So, mine's called "Elvis Ate America Before America Ate Him." So I've been up and out, and I'm trying to get rid of those two punk rockers and their mother, lying on the bed here beside me. But they're slowly getting up. Jojo [his elder daughter, Jordan] is fighting off revising for her mock junior's first exams, and Eve is lying down pretending she's ill.

That sounds like a dysfunctional family.

Yes. Hollywood and Holly-weird.

You mean like the Osbournes.

It's very Osbourne in our house. The girls, if I'm very tired, if I had a very late night, they see me shuffling. They say: "You're shuffling like Ozzy." And I say *[Ozzy's voice]:* "Fuck off! Fuck off!" No, I don't swear at my children in my own voice, only in Ozzy's. That's what's great about Ozzy. I get to swear at my children in his voice.

That's a good excuse.

I love the Osbournes. They're a very rare thing: they're a family that loves each other. Also I like his voice when he sings "Iron Man," because he has a voice, in a way, like a machine. It doesn't sound human at all.

Have you ever met him?

I met him once in a lift. It wasn't much of a conversation. "Going up?" was, I think, the remark. *[laughs]* He was getting out at the fifth, and I was getting out at the seventh floor. I didn't have time to explain that I had bought *Paranoid.* And I think it's one of the greatest rock records. He invented heavy metal. God-like genius . . . *Paranoid* is heavy in the nuclear sense.

It's so funny that Black Sabbath came back into style with Nirvana. I thought that heavy metal had been wiped off the map once and for all in the eighties. And then it came back with a vengeance with those grunge bands.

It's visceral. It's boys' music, but it's for a time when being male is a lot more elusive than you think. In your teenage years, music has a lot to do with who you want to be and how your hormones are describing that. And I think that's why hip-hop—*[getting interrupted]* Oh God, that's Elijah now who's coming. Out, you little dwarf! No, that's me.

Now, that's your real personality showing. Not the nice guy I know.

Isn't that true that hip-hop and hard rock, it's very male music? What are you listening to these days, Michka?

Presently? You ... And on that subject, you know, these phone calls are great, because for me it's like expecting the next installment of a serial. *[Bono keeps on laughing his devilish laugh]* So let me go back to what you said last time. I'm quoting you here: "We only discovered we were Irish when we went to America." You took your first political stand against the Provisional IRA and the armed struggle. Isn't it strange that you somehow got involved in the civil war in El Salvador and Nicaragua after that? How did you find out about what was going on those countries, which to a lot of people didn't mean more than a T-shirt or the name of a Clash album?*

Well, the difference between the Sandinistas and the Provisional IRA was that the Sandinistas represented a majority of their country. And so, as ugly an armed struggle as it was, it at least had that behind it. It's true, I heard about the Sandinistas from the Clash. But the more I read about the Sandinistas, the more I became fascinated by their modus operandi, because here was liberation theology in action. When I visited Nicaragua, I was shocked to see how much the people's religion had inspired their revolt. Here was revolution rooted

*Sandinista!, 1980.

in something other than materialism. There was a spiritual coefficient. The reason the Nicaraguan revolution had to be put down was because it had caught fire. That was terrifying for the Americas. It could have spread all through Mexico, and up north. There was one church I remember going to, where they had these murals all around the walls of the church, of scenes from the Holy Scriptures, like "The Children of Israel escaping from Pharaoh." But Pharaoh would have Ronald Reagan's head on him! *[laughs]*

Really? Where did you see that?

In Managua. I remember just being amazed at how the populace were being taught revolution through Bible stories. All over they were being taught that Jesus preached the Gospels for the poor, which he did. But Jesus did not take up arms.

Exactly, that was my point. I mean, you had just made very clear that you did not want to support the armed struggle in Ireland.

I wasn't writing a love song for the armed struggle. I saw it as a disappointing outcome of the reading of the Scriptures. But I was inspired by the application of the Scriptures into people's real life. I remember I had a meeting with the minister of culture, Ernesto Cardenal. I remember him saying that the poetry of their revolution—and indeed a lot of the Sandinista ideologies—were inspired by the Irish uprising in 1916 and Irish poets like Patrick Pearse. He himself had been taught by Irish Jesuit priests, expert in sowing the seeds of revolt. It's true. I'm telling you: wherever you go in the developing world, you'll find the Irish nuns and priests jumping out from behind bushes! It's amazing: we exported revolution through the clergy. We were very good at it, and it traveled very well. I remember saying to the minister: "But there's nothing glorious about people losing their lives, and bloodletting." You may be able to argue for it, facing no other escape route, but it's never glorious. In Irish folklore, even Yeats talked about "the rose that is made red by the blood of the martyrs, that's dripped to the ground." I hate all that stuff.

I think it's nineteenth-century Europe, actually. As a teenager in France in the seventies, I was marked by that mythology. We had the insurrection of May 1968 and what they called the "Leftist movement" thereafter: a fanatical bunch of young people, often the bravest and most ambitious of their generation, who devoted themselves to the idea of revolution. It certainly was glamorous. It went back to the glorious army of the French Revolution, the nineteenth-century insurrections, and then, of course, the Bolsheviks, the Trotskyist uprising, the Maoist Guerrilla, up to the guerrillas in Cuba and Vietnam. It occurred at a sort of junction of Romanticism and Revolution. I realized that the so-called heroic People's Guerrillas were mostly glorified on an aesthetic and idealistic basis, that their supporters had deliberately turned a blind eye to planned starvation and concentration camps in Russia and China, not to mention the massacres in Kampuchea by Pol Pot. The whole point was anti-Americanism, which made perfect sense in Europe. But those causes were excuses and fantasies. Dismal fantasies, actually.

It's not that I couldn't understand where the Provisional Army were coming from, and it's not that I don't understand violence myself, personally. I was just trying to figure out: was there ever any reason to take up arms? On the one hand, you had Martin Luther King saying "Never," Gandhi saying "Never," Jesus Christ, both their inspirations in this, saying "Never." On the other hand, here were the Sandinistas saying "We have to look after the poor, we have to defend the poor." That position had to be studied from my point of view, even if I didn't buy it. I wanted to know more about liberation theology and the Sandinistas. I was very moved by them when I was there. They suffered a lot. Their revolution was very costly, and it didn't turn out their way in the end. Same with the French Revolution. Ironically, it was the French Revolution that inspired America.

We have all heard that dreadful phrase: "You can't make an omelette without breaking eggs."

I know. In the end, ideas are not worth as much as people. Whenever you meet a philosophy where that is not true, and where ideas are worth more than people, you have to be on your guard. A dangerous idea that almost makes sense is a very compelling thing. In a way, when the devil gets it right, it's usually not a wrong fighting with a right, it's usually two half-truths fighting it out. It'll do the most damage. Marxism-Leninism was an extraordinary idea to lead mankind out of its squalor. It was a dangerous idea that almost made sense. There are many.

Just after we ended our last conversation, I remember you told me you had recently met Senator Jesse Helms to discuss the AIDS in Africa issue. You came out of the meeting with a lot of respect for him. You mentioned that it was a disturbing experience for you, since as chairman of the Senate Foreign Relations Committee in the early eighties, he had done whatever he could to suppress the Sandinistas.

Well, you know. Wandering around Nicaragua, seeing their supermarkets empty—nothing on the shelves—seeing their people starving because of the blockade the United States had put on it, seeing the lives lost, as these people tried to escape from the tyranny of the landowners. One percent of landowners owned more than forty percent of the land before the revolution. I remember one very moving Mass they gave out to the people. At the end of the Mass, the priest then picked up a list of the dead. And he called each one of them by name: "Rodrigo Omares!" and all the congregation went: "*Presente!*" *[making it sound like a sort of smothered roar]* "Maria Gonzalez!—*Presente!*" And they were calling out a roll of the dead and the congregation replied: "*Presente!*"—they're present with us. You could see in the eyes of all around me. I could see the cost. This was the other side of America as far as I was concerned at that time: America, the neighborhood bully. And one of the architects on the Right at that time was Senator Jesse Helms, who later did me and everyone working on the Global AIDS Emergency a great favor when he came out in our support. It was a great irony for me, to find myself twenty years later feeling such affection for this old Cold Warrior.

Did you mention what you thought about the past when you spoke to him?

I never brought it up. I took my time with him to press ahead with our work in the AIDS emergency. He did an incredible thing: he publicly repented for the way he had thought about HIV / AIDS. Politicians rarely do that. He really changed the way people on the Right thought about this disease. People said to me: this is the devil himself you're going to meet, and his politics are just right of Attila the Hun. He had personally dismantled the National Endowment for the Arts in America. Todd Rundgren had written a song about him: "Fuck You, Jesse Helms." But I found him to be a beautiful man with convictions that I wouldn't all agree with, but had to accept that he believed in them passionately. This is happening to me a lot. I am discovering how much respect I have for people who stay true to their convictions, no matter how unpopular.

OK, now imagine we're trying to write a script about your adventures in Central America. Now, the credits have rolled and the camera pans over a bird's-eye view of a landscape with forests and hills. What scene would come next?

So ... Walking in the hills, about a hundred miles from the main city of Salvador.

First, what are you doing there?

I'm walking with a friend who has a group called "Sanctuary" that smuggles people whose lives are in danger, out from enemy territory, and brings them to America as kind of refugees. And he has a few programs to help with the poor in El Salvador, and I—myself and Ali—are both involved in one of those programs, working with the campesinos, the peasant farmers. So, we're going to see the project, but it is in rebel-controlled areas.

Who are you walking with? And what do they look like?

Well, there's an American fellow. His name is Dave Bedstone, he's a sort of a Harrison Ford in *Raiders of the Lost Ark* character: adventurer, intellectually and spiritually, and indeed in rough physical terrain. And there's his girlfriend, Wendy, who is from San Francisco: curly hair, keeping everyone's spirits up. And then there's Howard Jules Hoyle, who has driven from San Francisco to El Salvador with a surfboard on his roof. It is "Surf's up, Captain"—if you've seen *Apocalypse Now,* the character of Robert Duvall. He likes to surf. He's very funny, there's comedy in every piece of his body language. Ali, who keeps looking at me with those eyes that say, "Why exactly are we here again?" *[laughs]*

So what project brought you there?

It's a small farm, a co-operative, and I'm just helping out with that financially. Then there's a local guide. It's extraordinary, because as I was walking through this sort of thick green rainforesty terrain, some of the rebels pass us on the road. They're like fifteen-year-old girls, beautiful girls, carrying rifles, and you dare not look at them with anything other than respect. *[laughs]* Then we pass a wall on which is written: FUCK JESUS. So I'm a little taken aback and I go: "Wow! I thought this was the home of liberation theology. What's going on here?" To which our guide replied: "No, no, that's not Jesus Christ. It's *Hay-zoos*, he lives around here. No one likes him. He's working for the other side." *[laughs]* So we continue on along this path, and as we're crossing a road, we see some government troops. They look a little worried, and just as we cross the road, there's a dead sort of *pop-pop-pop*, a sort of dull—couldn't be further from the sound of gunfire in the movies—type sound, because it's so flat, and it whips over our heads. And we just freeze on the road. We don't know what's gonna happen, whether we should take for cover or we should stand still. There's silence, big silence . . . We can hear each other's hearts beating, then laughing from the government troops who were just letting us know that they don't like us and they could take our life if they really wanted to.

So what kind of drama have we got here?

It would have been a comedy at times. If you saw us stop and freeze, there was a freeze-frame in a black comedy: "Rock star craps in his pants." *[laughs]*

What's the soundtrack? Any music?

No, cold silence. Maybe the sound of five hearts put through an amplifier.

Were your lives really in danger?

To tell you how real a possibility that was, the day before, we were driving along the motorway from the airport and we saw a body thrown out of a van on the road. People go missing round here all the time, and some nuns have lost their lives recently. I mean it was a very dangerous time, and in truth, we didn't need to be there. If I'm honest, I was at that time thinking seriously that maybe we should have stayed in the Sunset Marquis at Los Angeles and gone to the beach. *[laughs]* There was no heroism present at this point, just: "Oh shit . . . Why have I brought Ali here?" But, you know, they passed on. And my friend, who now lectures in a university in Oakland, California, is just blank-faced and fearless: "They're just trying to scare us. Keep walking. Not a problem." Not a problem? I thought. What's a problem? Grenades? Anyway, we walked on to the project, feeling like Colonel Kurtz in *Apocalypse Now*, the fire-bombing of the villages shaking the ground underneath our feet. This sounds like gross irresponsibility, but my friend had to get money to these belea-guered farmers. There was a kind of ethnic cleansing with a government health warning. They would tell people: "Get out of your villages, we're about to bomb the shit out of you." Military sponsored by the Land of the Free, terrorizing peasant farmers. It was unbelievable. Because people wouldn't have left their villages; they were their homes. It was carnage, it was awful. It was the other side of America. It's a long time ago now, but in order to remember it, I tried to turn it into music, in the song "Bullet the Blue Sky."

Does that song fully represent the complexity of the experience?

No, but I tried.

So you are the gringo there. Politically engaged rock singer visiting a dangerous place, and meddling, I would suggest.

A tourist, you could unkindly suggest.

[laughs] I was about to say that! Well, you were a political tourist. Have you heard of this outstanding book by Jared Diamond, Guns, Germs and Steel? Its subtitle is "A Short History of Everybody for the Last 30,000 Years."

It's an anthropological book, yeah. I have the book, and I've started to read it. Story of my life!

In his foreword, he is trying to describe why he wanted to write the book. He says he had a revelation walking on a beach in New Guinea with some local politician. Diamond is a white man, his companion was a black man. They discuss their two countries' history and fate, and the man says to him: "Why is it that you white people developed so much cargo and brought it to New Guinea, but we black people had little cargo of our own?" Diamond says he actually wrote the book in order to answer that question, actually taking up his point of view. That, I found fascinating. So did you try to consider the point of view these people in Central America had of you? Were you interested in what they had to say to you? Like: What is your purpose here? Why do you want to help us?

I was just looking for some value for money, you know. *[laughs]* This is something I had gotten interested in. It's intellectual curiosity. I'm a writer.

Right, but you did not go over there as a journalist.

Any writer, if he's any good, is a journalist. And I wanna see things for myself, not through mediation of newspapers and TV. You can sit in the air-conditioning, behind a plate glass of your prosperity, or you can try to smash it and get out. I wanna see things for myself, I don't like to see things secondhand.

So you're claiming to be a reporter.

I'm just curious. You go around lifting stones until you find some really interesting creepy crawlies.

Sure, but from my experience as a traditional reporter, there is a point when you're talking to people, and they start asking you about your life. It's always: "Are you married? Do you have any children? How is life there? What's the price of things?" They ask you about football, about movie stars, often about

the most superficial things in your culture. Did you have that experience with people from El Salvador, or was it completely different?

Of course, exactly that. You know, I've had extraordinary experiences that are two-way. I can't recall the details—too many details—of the lives that I met on that trip: looks, faces, the resolve and the humor. I remember things like that. But I wasn't going there to discover what was going on particularly in Salvador, if I'm honest. My subject wasn't El Salvador, my subject was America.

How do you mean?

I wanted to know what was the on-the-ground effect of American foreign policy, because I was a fan of America. And I believed in this country, more than most people I knew, and I was lost to its music and its literature. But I wanted to know: what did it mean? I went there with an open mind. It's funny, I talked to Sean Penn about this, 'cause he did the same when he went to Baghdad. He's been a couple of times. People say: that is not a place for a movie star, Baghdad. And he said, "I want to know what this is." And on his second trip, he was conciliatory, because he saw there had been progress made. As to the occupation, he didn't agree with it, but he could see that a lot of lives had been changed for the better, if not enough lives. He said that. So, writers are reporters, and we wanna see things for ourselves. Dissent is a very valuable part of the American psychology. I really respect him for that. Anyway, I'm just explaining. If I wanted to really understand the people of Salvador and some of the people whom I was trying to help, I would have stayed there for a lot longer than a week. I was taking snapshots.

So let's keep on going with the screenplay. We had an establishing shot, which was this little group of yours walking on that path in the hills. What would be an important line of a dialogue between you and someone from there, one of the campesinos? Was there a character that struck you? A discussion you had there that was particularly meaningful to you?

If there was any line of dialogue, I'd have to put it in a more Monty Python kind, and adopt a John Cleese accent, and say *[mock Eton accent]*: "Hello-o! So you are a revolutionary, are you? Jolly good. I'm a rock sta-ar." *[laughs]* "Lovely to meet you. What is it exactly that you do? You shoot at people. I see. Now, just explain what exactly has the level of oppression been over the last years. Hmmm, considerable, I can see that. So, how many families run the country again? I get it. Anyone here ever heard of Gandhi? Oh, sorry about that, sorry. No, no, not a moment to bring up nonviolence. Well, there we go." I mean: a sort of twenty-four-, twenty-five-year-old late developer trying to figure out a worldview: are there any circumstances where an armed struggle is correct, to challenge my convictions about nonviolence, and try to figure out: why are the good guys on the side of the bad guys?

So why were the good guys on the side of the bad guys? What did you learn about that?

Communism did not produce freedom or prosperity for anybody. It has pro-duced a hundred years of some of the most heinous crimes ever committed by human beings on one another. So I can understand now why America had such a fear of it in Central America. But the kind of socialism that I was interested in was not of that old Marxist-Leninist order. It was a new shoot of it, which, as I say, did not attempt to put down people's faith, and used the religion of the people to inform them about their rights. And I think that was one of the most important moments of the twentieth century: the birth of that new expression of equality. I know it went sour, but I thought it was a shame that the religious establishment didn't embrace it and try to foster some of the ideas. You know, there was Archbishop Romero, who was shot, and the Pope at the time wouldn't acknowledge him. There were a lot of people who put an awful lot on the line for these ideas: "the Gospel of the poor," they called it. And these people, as far as I was concerned, lived their religion. They were priests who would rather be with the people than with their peers or their superiors. You know, there is an amazing moment, and it's one of those passages of Scriptures, which I have to tell you about, because it's pertinent here. It's when the Children of Israel are wandering through the desert. They've just been delivered from captivity by Moses, but they're straight back to worshipping the Golden Calf. It's business as usual, they have forgotten the God who delivered them. They keep getting warnings, and finally God just has enough and says to Moses: "Get out of the way, I'm gonna destroy my people. Then I'm gonna start again. This experiment has just run out of gas, and this freedom thing is really not working out. *[laughs]* So get away from the midst of these people, because I'm gonna vaporize them. I can, I made them, after all." Of course, Michka, you'll realize I'm paraphrasing here. And then the Scriptures record that "Moses, knowing the heart of God"—this is an amazing line—"instead of running away, runs into the center of the people and says: 'If you take them, take me.'" And God presumably smiles. It was the Gospels in action, people laying down their life for their brother. You know, it's a great line from the Holy Book—sorry to get all religious on your ass this morning: "No greater love has a man than he lays his life down for his brother." This is what I was seeing in Central America.

But before that expedition in El Salvador, you visited Nicaragua. The revolutionaries were in power over there. What impression did that make on you?

I was at the time very inspired by the revolution. Maybe I was suckered by the really nice treatment of the people I met in government, the poets and musicians that I met there. At the same time, though, I do remember on Revolution Day listening to *[sighs]* Daniel Ortega speak for about four hours. With the translator beside me, I'm going: Whoa! What is it about these revolutionaries? They talk longer than I do and I can talk. I don't do paragraphs—but these guys don't do chapters.

Fidel Castro's speeches are marathons, actually.

I know. These guys are the Grateful Dead of political speech-making. They go on and on, and they don't take acid.

It's more like hypnosis, actually.

I could see some of the bullshit that was coming out of it. I talked with Salman Rushdie about that, actually, at some point. Because it turns out that he was at the same Revolution Day speech as I. We were wandering around each other. We didn't know each other at that point. He wrote *The Jaguar Smile* out of that—that was his comment.

And what was *your* comment on the Sandinistas and Central America?

I wrote a couple of tunes that I'm very proud of to this day. And one of them, "Mothers of the Disappeared," has been played all over Central and South America, as an act of defiance in Chile. These women who had their children abducted and murdered by the secret police didn't even know where they had been buried. They had no place, no graveyard to mourn. These women, these mothers, their stories, I will remember, always. You know, I've learnt so much on these sorties, these outings. As I say, I was born in the suburbs. What did I know about the world? I was always bored with my own. *[sighs]* Even where I grew up, I was always sleeping on somebody else's floor. I just have that wanderlust. That's who I am. So I don't know. It's not even about learning—at a certain point, that's my excuse for going there—or end results like writing some songs, writing some articles. It's probably something much more selfish. I like to describe it as intellectual curiosity, but maybe it's just tourism or voyeurism, I don't know. It is who I am. I've greedy eyes.

My French publisher once told me he felt strangely about people like you, who travel around the world to do charity work. Because, he elaborated, the reason why they do that is that they're too bored to stay in one place for more than a week. Obviously, what they do is useful work, there is no denying it. But he thought that the main reason that motivates them is the fact that they can't bear returning home every evening to their wife and children. Or to any other boring daily reality.

I've huge admiration for the media in war zones. They risk their life in the pursuit of truth. I don't care about the reasons they took the job. They do us a great service. Look, the job of life is to turn your negatives into positives. I mean, that's like saying: "All those performers, they're really insecure. They need twenty thousand people a night screaming 'I love you' to feel normal . . . " *[stands up to imaginary critic, dismissing in his tone any intention to be apologetic]* "YEAH. YEAH." *[laughs]* I mean, no one does anything interesting for just the right reason. It's the flaw that makes the frame. Ask any great photographer. You wouldn't write a song if you didn't have a hole in your heart. This is not one of the great insights, is it? You only have to meet war correspondents.

I meet them all the time. And I look at them and I see the same mad eyes that I see in the mirror. *[laughs]* "They're my mad eyes, what are you doing with them?" Oh gosh, they love their wives, they love their children, but they are compelled by what's at stake in these far-off places. They are witnesses, they see how the way the decks are shuffled thousands of miles away can turn other communities into pink dust. That is hard to walk away from. Because our lives do have meaning, our votes do affect lives of people we will never meet. Politics matters. We grew up in a generation where we were told it didn't, and we were bored: "No matter who you vote for, the government always gets in." That's wrong. We have to puncture that. We might find out that the reason the war correspondent is there, is because . . .

. . . he wants the adrenaline rush.

It could be the adrenaline rush. It could be that he killed a kid in a car, and he's trying to save kids' lives. You know, people might have a whole array of real reasons and excuses for being there, but that doesn't matter. They do an amazing job. You can title this chapter: "My life as a disaster groupie." Yes, I am attracted to the front line and the people that I meet on it.

Met someone special on the front line?

I met Don McCullen, the famous photographer. He took some photographs of U2 in peacetime. *[laughs]* And you know, people who've seen the sort of things that he's seen normally don't talk about them, because it's too much. I don't talk about what I see when I come back from Africa. I do not sit down at the kitchen table and talk about lives lost in front of me, or talk about those feelings.

Maybe you should. Because this is how people respond. They don't respond to abstract ideas, but they respond to a certain photograph, to a certain testimony.

Yeah, they do. You know, I'm trying to do it. I pushed on McCullen to do it. And he told me something that I will never repeat, even to myself, because it so disturbed me. I wish I hadn't asked him. Because some images just over-power the eye. They just storm your brain and take prisoner of it. I have so many of those experiences. Sometimes I just don't want to share them.

Of course, I do understand that. But then again, let me put forward an ex-ample. Ten years after World War II, the French director Alain Resnais made a documentary called *Nuit et brouillard*—"Night and Fog." He used archives from the French and German military in order to help people see what the concentration camps were actually like. People did know about them, but they hadn't realized what they actually looked like. That is the purpose of documentaries if they're any good, or of a specific testimony. It can be yours, it can be anyone's. Only after they saw Resnais's film did a lot of people come to fully realize what the extermination was, and some said: "We didn't know, we had no idea." After that, they couldn't say that anymore. That is the pur-pose of true stories. I don't know if I got you right, but I think the thing about not being too precise or too concrete may be a mistake.

No. They come out when they come out. I'm just saying it's not something that I talk about. And it's not something I want to talk about. It overpowers you in moments when you are really not expecting to. You find yourself walking down a street with tears rolling down your face, and pictures that you can never be separate from, but you wish you could.

It seems like the experiences that you had while traveling in Africa are the ones that you refrain from talking about, more so than El Salvador and Nicaragua.

It was different. What is going on in Africa defies all concepts that we hold to be true: our concept of neighbor, our concept of civilization, our concept of equality, of love. I mean, you can just forget about it. What Africa says about Europe and America is withering. It says we've built our Houses of Parliament and government on sand, because if we really believed the things we say we be-lieve, we would not let 23 million Africans die of AIDS. You can't have the benefits of globalization without some of the responsibilities. We are now next-door neighbors through television images, through radio, through the Internet, and *in fact. [laughs]* The thing we forget: in Europe, while we're pointing a finger at America—*we* are their actual neighbors, not America.

You cannot deny there are a lot of European NGOs in Africa.

Yes, Irish, French. In fact, Médecins Sans Frontières are one of my favorites. I met this guy in Soweto—Lawrence Ndou. MSF had kept him alive. He is an advertisement for these drugs that are denied all Africans: drugs that cost nothing to produce. After research and development, they cost nothing. It's a pittance. We've heard all kinds of excuses why we haven't given those drugs out: too complicated. The drug regimen. Africans don't have wristwatches, they wouldn't know when to take the drugs. All this kind of propaganda and rubbish. And I meet this fellow—he looks like a pop star. He's a beautiful-looking man, twenty-seven years old. Six months ago, he was on death's door. The only reminder that he was HIV-positive and had full-blown AIDS was scratches he had all over him from the itching, and scars. I said to him: "That's so great." He says: "Well, I lost my wife. She didn't get on the drugs on time, she was dead before I got to the drugs. So I have two kids, and I look after them." And I say: "Well, it's great that you have survived." He says: "Well, it's not great, because I have a new love in my life, and she is now looking after my children like they were her own." I say: "Well, that's fantastic." And he says: "She is now HIV-positive, and she can't get to these drugs. So what do I do? I give her my drugs, and my children lose their last parent. I share the drugs, and we both die slowly. Or I keep my drugs and let the love of my life die in front of my eyes." There are lots of issues going on in Africa. It's complex. There's corruption, there are problems of their own making, but then there're problems of our making for them, and then there're problems we could easily solve for them.

OK. I hope to hear you talking soon about Africa on a very personal level, with stories and people. Because you sometimes have this tendency to dwell on the abstract. *[laughs]*

Yeah, you're right.

But I will take you back to actual feelings, people, colors, smells, individual stories, because that will anchor everything that you have to say.

OK. Yeah, obviously, the abstract is a lot easier to deal with than the concrete. But I'll try. So, look, we'll make another appointment, doctor, and I will do my very best. So, until then, at the same time: "Tune in five to five, it's *Crackerjack!*"

11. ADD ETERNITY TO THAT

Our next telephone call took place a week after the Madrid train bombings that left 191 commuters dead and more than 1,800 wounded on March 11, 2004. Everyone was in shock; it was the biggest terrorist attack to ever occur in Europe. I wrote about it in my weekly column for the French magazine *VSD*. I wanted to convey how I felt about that act. It was one of those moments I wished I'd been a songwriter.

I wanted to know how Bono reacted to the news—not as a spokesperson or an ambassador for DATA, but as a human being. I mean, how do idealism and goodwill stand in front of that? This is the piece:

Song lyrics may be silly, but they do tell the truth. At the Olympia Theatre in Paris, the Beach Boys' former songwriter Brian Wilson insisted on dedicating "Love and Mercy" to the people of Spain:

I was lyin' in my room and the news came on TV / A lotta people there hurtin' and it really scares me / Love and mercy, that's what you need tonight / Love and mercy to you and your friends tonight . . .

Rather dull words, you might say, nothing original about them. But then again, unfortunately, there's nothing original either nowadays about the Massacre of the Innocents as seen live on TV. Maybe you'll find his words derisory and useless, but that utterance of compassion made me feel good.

As much as anyone, I was caught between subdued anger and a need to cry when the news came on TV. Is there a way to feel intelligent when you see a gymnasium turned into a makeshift mortuary, strewn with stretchers? Some morning, a handful of people board a commuter train, carrying bags filled with charge, all stuffed with bolts and nails. I am refusing to analyze it. Try putting yourself inside the head of a madman, and pretty soon you'll find yourself feeling like a madman too. Moreover, that is exactly the aim of those delirious political and religious sects: carrying the world away into a collective madness at the end of which, of course, truth will prevail, a truth that only its followers detain.

So, love and mercy, then . . . In a magazine called Courier International, *I have just read about the story of Zarema, a twenty-three-year-old from Chechnya. Armed with an explosive belt, she renounced, just at the last minute, to smash herself to pieces in a pub in Moscow, and turned herself in to the police. A Russian journalist got the opportunity to interview her in her cell. There she told him her appalling life story. Her mother abandons her while she is a ten-month-old baby. Then her father gets murdered on a building site in Siberia. It doesn't sound like a great start in life. It isn't. Raised by her grandparents, she is forced into marrying "according to our old customs," as she puts it, some local dealer. Pretty soon, the man gets shot down by a competing gang. At that time, she is expecting his baby. For want of money, she is not able to raise her baby daughter by herself. So out of hand the husband's clan places the baby in another family. Zarema is accordingly parted from her child and sent back to her grandparents' place. They live at the far end of the country. There, she goes out of her mind with grief. So what does she do? She robs the family jewels, which she proceeds to sell to the market, so as to board a plane and to abduct her daughter. But her aunts recapture her just as she is about to do that. They humiliate her and strike her repeatedly, because she has become the disgrace of the family.*

So Zarema sees only one solution. To become at last a "decent person"—I'm quoting her words here—she thinks she has to sacrifice her-

self for Allah and Jihad, so her shame gets washed away and her debt paid off, since the rebels give away a thousand dollars to a martyr's family. At the rebels' hideout, she encounters other suicide applicants. One of them, a nineteen-year-old girl, blows herself up during an open-air rock concert in Moscow: fourteen dead. Zarema sees the bodies on television. Something clicks in her head. Above all, she feels compassion for the young girl who died in the operation, the one whom she saw every day—her companion. "She is the one that I pitied the most," she says. So her eyes open and she gives up the madness. You can say a kind of miracle happened.

Love and mercy: those words do not only make sense for the survivors. In order to fight effectively against the terrorist insanity, perhaps they're more useful weapons than the infiltration of cells, the shelling of villages and the so-called war on terror. Because the nature of that terror is moral and religious as much as it is political, the answer sometimes has to be of the same nature. In one case, love and mercy simply worked.

[in a sort of growl] Bono-jour!

I'm sorry, it's not "Bono-jour." It's "bonjour"!

"Bono-jour!"

Good morning! I'm very happy to hear your voice.

[with a scowl] And what's good about it?

It's been a long time.

I'm a little under the weather today, so I don't know if I'll be of any use to you. But here goes. How are you doing yourself?

I'm fine, but in a bit of a shock about the Madrid bombings. I wanted to read out to you the piece I wrote yesterday. *[so I carry out my threat]* Simple question here: where were you "when the news came on TV"?

[sighing] The news seems to be now on TV every hour of every day. I heard about it on the radio, but it was only when I came in to the studio at lunchtime that I saw the pictures. Heartbreaking.

Do you know that song, "Love and Mercy"?

"Love and Mercy" is one of the great songs ever written. The thing about song lyrics is: with the cadence and the way the melody falls, they can be more articulate than any purely literate response. This is something that any non-English speaker knows. It's a funny thing, but when U2 songs are written, I don't write them in English. I write them in what the band call "Bongelese." *[laughs]* I just sing melodies and the words form in my mouth, later to be deciphered. I remember Brian Eno saying: "Why put them into English, Bono? They're so eloquent as they are." And he had a point. So pop lyrics, in a way, are just a rough direction that you sketch for where the listener must think toward. That's it, the rest is left up to you. Which is why pop music becomes the folk music of the next era. Feelings travel better than thoughts. I can't think of a greater song to be sung than Brian Wilson singing "Love and Mercy." Because, in a way, they're the two feelings that those terrorists sought to destroy.

What song would have you sung had you been onstage on that day?

"When Will I See You Again?"—the Three Degrees.

How does it go?

[sings] When will I see you again? De-de-de-de-de . . . / When will we share precious moments? It's a song about loss. That song can bring you to tears. It's a very strange course of events. We played in Nuremberg on the PopMart Tour in August 1997. There's a venue there, which is where Hitler was to be buried with his generals. They had marked out an area. There's a stadium, the Zeppelinfeld, which is associated with the Third Reich. It is an Albert Speer building. There was some controversy about us playing there. I remember thinking: *No, we should never be afraid of a building. And if people are so scared of it, paint it pink or something like that.* Howie B, my great friend, was deejay-

ing. He has produced U2 and was on tour with us. Jewish. He was very un-nerved by playing there. He said to me: "I'm not sure if I want to do this." I said: "Well, you don't have to if you don't want." But he went on and started his set by playing the Three Degrees' "When Will I See You Again?" It was just the most remarkable thing to see this joyous jazzman with tears down his face, decades later, mourning people of his own ethnic group that he'd never met, but feel-ing it. I really felt this song just chase the devil away. [sighs] Because you should never think about these things on a grand scale: these are families, and sisters and brothers and uncles.

That's how I felt yesterday.

When we played the United States on our last tour, after 9/11, we were among the first bands to go into New York and play a proper show.

I had no idea about that.

Yes. We felt it important to make the same point. These people were not sta-tistics. We used these giant screens to project the names of everyone who'd lost their life. If I turned around and I looked at the screen, I would see "Elvin Romero," "Efrain Romero," "Monica Hoffman," "Stephen Hoffman"—fathers and sons, whatever it was. Everybody in Madison Square Garden could see somebody they knew or somebody who knew somebody, and the whole place wept. And it wasn't just their own grief—they wept for other people's grief. When everyone's dancing and jumping up and down, there's that deep well of pathos because everybody is connected.

It's weird that you should mention simultaneously 9/11 and that U2 concert at Madison Square Garden. It seems to imply that the inhabitants of a big city feel connected to each other through only two kinds of events: when a hor-rible catastrophe happens or when they gather for a rock concert. It's like the most joyful or the most horrible event both produce a strangely similar ef-fect: to make people feel like they're all one. On that night, it was apparently an odd combination of both.

[light chuckle] Yeah, a great rock show can be a transcendent event. A crap one on the other hand can feel like a funeral—your own! But it's an extraordinary thing to get seventy thousand people or seven thousand people to agree on anything. I mean, we've all been to really doglike events. *[laughs]* They just bite your arse and you feel like you've got the worst ticket in the world, and that sound is blowing everywhere but by you, and somebody's pissing up against the fence. Or indoors, it's the same. I mean, in a club, you can feel as far from the singer as in a stadium, depending on the mentality of the singer. It's not about physical proximity. But when it comes right, it is the most remarkable thing.

What's your definition of community?

This is the question that hangs in the sky over our heads at the moment. Through media, we have some strange faces in our backyard whom we weren't calling family until very recently, and we still don't really want to. But if you're going to enjoy having your sneakers and your jeans made by developing communities, you are already involved with those people. You cannot therefore just ignore some of the problems they're negotiating. They're living on your street. There was this old definition of generosity, which is at the very least the rich man looks after the poor man on his street. Guess what? *[laughs]* Now, that street goes round the globe.

So you're saying invisibility doesn't work for either end of the street.

That's why New York never had to deal with race riots in the nineties like L.A. did. The rich and the poor see each other every day, pass each other on the same street, travel the subway. Eye contact is unavoidable. In L.A., you have a mosaic of suburbs very separate from each other, economically, culturally. If they pass each other on the street, it's on an eight-lane freeway. It's an environment for the mistrust and the hatred that can come out of that after an incident like Rodney King.

During one of your first visits to Paris, more than twenty years ago, you told me that you were planning to write a screenplay from the point of view of a terrorist. Do you remember that?

Oh, I do remember it very well, yes. I was trying to figure out how one Irishman could take the life of another Irishman in such cold blood. I was obsessed with the thought that these same people had in every other way ordinary lives. They were milkmen, taxi drivers, schoolteachers. I worked with some people on it. What I was intrigued by was what Hannah Arendt called the banality of evil, her description of the trial of [Adolf] Eichmann, and how he used to walk his dog close to Auschwitz. And he was a lovely man—the sweetest man you could meet while you are walking your dog—and responsible for this kind of evil. It was a subject we were living with here. I don't know if I told you about my own experience of one of the worst bombings in southern Ireland. I just very nearly escaped.

I don't remember you mentioning that.

It just left a little bit of a mark. I told you that I used to have to pass through the City Centre to go home. It was two bus trips to school. I told you I used to go and look around the record stores. There was a coffee shop I used to go to called Graham Southern's, near the bus stop. If I had the money, I'd read a music magazine or have a cup of coffee there. One day, fifteen minutes after I left, the street was blown to pieces. It was a bomb outside. It was a close call— a little street called Marlborough Street.*

Now I understand why that terrorist story was haunting you.

But it haunts everyone who's lived near or close by. That's what the terrorists intend.

I see a distinction between two different kinds of terrorists. On the one hand, you have the bombers from the IRA or the Loyalists, or ETA in the Basque country: they don't look for martyrdom, they fight a war. On the other you have the suicide bombers who want to be martyrs, like that girl Zarema. In modern times, a terrorist's story is that of someone who thinks that he or she

*It might have been one of the three car bombs planted in the City Centre of Dublin on May 17, 1974, by Loyalist paramilitaries. As a result thirty-three civilians and an unborn child were killed.

has to die first, so their people or the whole world will be better off, or saved, because others are going to die as well. It's like *The Pied Piper of Hamlin:* the idea is to have as many people as possible following them off the cliff. It seems like modern terror is as much about self-hatred as hatred. It is intrinsically suicidal.

Yeah. I guess that's a psychological truth, that you can't love anyone else without loving yourself. And I guess you probably can't hate anyone else without hating yourself. But outside of the perversion and the warped mind, we have to tackle the real problems that fester and turn decent people toward indecent acts. I mean, there are some problems that haven't been approached in Ireland, in Israel, in the Middle East. They're not an excuse for this ill harvest we're reaping, but they have to be approached. Love and mercy . . . Mercy is the outworking of love, but love demands that you try to see things from another person's point of view.

Terrorists are focused on big ideas. You're quite aware that there are no greater idealists than terrorists. Most of them revere the notions of God and holy justice. I guess for a person like you, who is deeply religious and idealistic, it must be very disturbing.

I'm a lot of other things as well. But you see, Michka, people who are open spiritually are open to being manipulated more easily, are very vulnerable. The religious instinct is a very pure one in my opinion. But unless it's met with a lot of rigor, it's very hard to control.

Correct. But you've also never seen a skeptic or an atheist smash himself to pieces in order to kill as many people as possible. I mean, atheists would organize concentration camps or would plan collective starvation, but this kind of terror we are dealing with now is of a spiritual nature. You can't hide from that.

It's true. Yeah, smashing other people to pieces doesn't need the same conviction. Most terrorists want to change the material world. Well, add eternity to that, and people can go a lot further to pursue their ends. It's a big prize, isn't it, eternity? It's not a two-term or a three-term presidency. *[laughs]* But of course, this is always a corruption of some holy thesis, whether it's the Koran or the Bible. My understanding of the Scriptures has been made simple by the person of Christ. Christ teaches that God is love. What does that mean? What it means for me: a study of the life of Christ. Love here describes itself as a child born in straw poverty, the most vulnerable situation of all, without honor. I don't let my religious world get too complicated. I just kind of go: Well, I think I know what God is. God is love, and as much as I respond *[sighs]* in allowing myself to be transformed by that love and acting in that love, that's my religion. Where things get complicated for me, is when I try to live this love. Now, that's not so easy.

What about the God of the Old Testament? He wasn't so "peace and love."

There's nothing hippie about my picture of Christ. The Gospels paint a picture of a very demanding, sometimes divisive love, but love it is. I accept the Old Testament as more of an action movie: blood, car chases, evacuations, a lot of special effects, seas dividing, mass murder, adultery. The children of God are running amok, wayward. Maybe that's why they're so relatable. But the way we would see it, those of us who are trying to figure out our Christian conundrum, is that the God of the Old Testament is like the journey from stern father to friend. When you're a child, you need clear directions and some strict rules. But with Christ, we have access in a one-to-one relationship, for, as in the Old Testament, it was more one of worship and awe, a vertical relationship. The New Testament, on the other hand, we look across at a Jesus who looks familiar, horizontal. The combination is what makes the Cross.

Do you know this passage from the Old Testament? God is addressing Moses. He's telling him that He is trying to teach the Jews, but they won't go for it. They keep reverting to their bad habits. And He uses this funny phrase: "Behold, it is a stiff-necked people" (Exodus, 32:9). And I thought, this is the daily experience I have with my children! Sometimes, you're so mad with your child that you want to throw them out the window.

[laughs thoroughly] Yes. There are moments, and I know they have them about me.

Speaking of bloody action movies, we were talking about South and Central America last time. The Jesuit priests arrived there with the gospel in one hand and a rifle in the other.

I know, I know. Religion can be the enemy of God. It's often what happens when God, like Elvis, has left the building. *[laughs]* A list of instructions where there was once was conviction; dogma where once people just did it; a congregation led by a man where once they were led by the Holy Spirit. Discipline replacing discipleship. Why are you chuckling?

I was wondering if you said all of that to the Pope the day you met him.

You know, he loved to play soccer.

Could you please, just for once, spare me the Monty Python digression?

Apparently, he was very good in goal. You'd need to be, in his position.

Do you think you got one of these past him?

Let's not get too hard on the Holy Roman Church here. The Church has its problems, but the older I get, the more comfort I find there. The physical experience of being in a crowd of largely humble people, heads bowed, murmuring prayers, stories told in stained-glass windows, the colors of Catholicism—purple, mauve, yellow, red—the burning incense . . . *[suspends sentence]* My friend Gavin Friday says Catholicism is the glam-rock of religion.

So you won't be critical.

No, I can be critical, especially on the topic of contraception. But when I meet someone like Sister Benedicta and see her work with AIDS orphans in Addis

Ababa, or Sister Ann doing the same in Malawi, or Father Jack Fenukan and his group Concern all over Africa, when I meet priests and nuns tending to the sick and the poor and giving up much easier lives to do so, I surrender a little easier.

But you met the man himself. Was it a great experience?

I was with a few great people: Jeff Sachs, the great economist; Bob Geldof; Quincy Jones, who's been a mentor to me, a deadly serious man, but he kept whispering to me to check out the Holy Father's shoes: ox-blood loafers, as it happens. "These are some funky slippers," he was saying. There were some nervous giggles, but we all knew why we were there. The Pontiff was about to make an important statement about the inhumanity and injustice of poor countries spending so much of their national income paying back old loans to rich countries. Serious business. He was fighting hard against his Parkinson's. It was clearly an act of will for him to be there. I was oddly moved . . . by his humility, and then by the incredible speech he made, even if it was in whispers. During the preamble, he seemed to be staring at me. I wondered. Was it the fact that I was wearing my blue fly-shades? So I took them off in case I was causing some offense. When I was introduced to him, he was still staring at them. He kept looking at them in my hand, so I offered them to him as a gift in return for the rosary he had just given me.

Didn't he put them on?

Not only did he put them on, he smiled the wickedest grin you could ever imagine. He was a comedian. His sense of humor was completely intact. Flashbulbs popped, and I thought: "Wow! The Drop the Debt campaign will have the Pope in my glasses on the front page of every newspaper."

I don't remember seeing that photograph anywhere, though.

Nor did we. It seems his courtiers did not have the same sense of humor. Fair enough. I guess they could see the T-shirts.

Did he really help, eventually?

Without his support and his right hand in these matters, Diurmuid Martin, an Irish archbishop, we would not have gotten such a result. They weren't just platitudinous words out of Castel Gandolfo on that day. Actions followed. They were tactical and strategic, and put the shoulder of the Church to a few doors that had been slammed shut on us.

Just for the last time, I would like to go back to our tour of the dark side of religion. Appalling things seem to happen when people become religious at too early an age or when their experience of life is nonexistent. Don't you think?

Zealots often have no love for the world. They're just getting through it to the next one. It's a favorite topic. It's the old cliché: "Eat shit now, pie in the sky when you die." But I take Christ at his word: "On Earth as it is in Heaven." As to the first part of your question, in my experience, the older you get, the less chance you have to transform your life, the less open you are to love in a challenging way. You tend towards love that's more comforting and safe.

As I told you, I think I am beginning to understand religion because I have started acting and thinking like a father. What do you make of that?

Yes, I think that's normal. It's a mind-blowing concept that the God who created the Universe might be looking for company, a real relationship with people, but the thing that keeps me on my knees is the difference between Grace and Karma.

I haven't heard you talk about that.

I really believe we've moved out of the realm of Karma into one of Grace.

Well, that doesn't make it clearer for me.

You see, at the center of all religions is the idea of Karma. You know, what you put out comes back to you: an eye for an eye, a tooth for a tooth, or in physics—

in physical laws—every action is met by an equal or an opposite one. It's clear to me that Karma is at the very heart of the Universe. I'm absolutely sure of it. And yet, along comes this idea called Grace to upend all that "As you reap, so will you sow" stuff. Grace defies reason and logic. Love interrupts, if you like, the consequences of your actions, which in my case is very good news indeed, because I've done a lot of stupid stuff.

I'd be interested to hear that.

That's between me and God. But I'd be in big trouble if Karma was going to finally be my judge. I'd be in deep shit. It doesn't excuse my mistakes, but I'm holding out for Grace. I'm holding out that Jesus took my sins onto the Cross, because I know who I am, and I hope I don't have to depend on my own religiosity.

The son of God who takes away the sins of the world. I wish I could believe in that.

But I love the idea of the Sacrificial Lamb. I love the idea that God says: *Look, you cretins, there are certain results to the way we are, to selfishness, and there's mortality as part of your very sinful nature, and, let's face it, you're not living a very good life, are you? There are consequences to actions.* The point of the death of Christ is that Christ took on the sins of the world, so that what we put out did not come back to us, and that our sinful nature does not reap the obvious death. That's the point. It should keep us humbled . . . It's not our own good works that get us through the gates of Heaven.

That's a great idea, no denying it. Such great hope is wonderful, even though it's close to lunacy, in my view. Christ has his rank among the world's great thinkers. But Son of God, isn't that farfetched?

No, it's not farfetched to me. Look, the secular response to the Christ story always goes like this: he was a great prophet, obviously a very interesting guy, had a lot to say along the lines of other great prophets, be they Elijah, Muhammad, Buddha, or Confucius. But actually Christ doesn't allow you that. He doesn't let you off that hook. Christ says: *No. I'm not saying I'm a teacher, don't call me teacher. I'm not saying I'm a prophet. I'm saying: "I'm the Messiah." I'm saying: "I am God incarnate."* And people say: *No, no, please, just be a prophet. A prophet, we can take. You're a bit eccentric. We've had John the Baptist eating locusts and wild honey, we can handle that. But don't mention the "M" word! Because, you know, we're gonna have to crucify you.* And he goes: *No, no. I know you're expecting me to come back with an army, and set you free from these creeps, but actually I am the Messiah.* At this point, everyone starts staring at their shoes, and says: *Oh, my God, he's gonna keep saying this.* So what you're left with is: either Christ was who He said He was—the Messiah—or a complete nutcase. I mean, we're talking nutcase on the level of Charles Manson. This man was like some of the people we've been talking about earlier. This man was strapping himself to a bomb, and had "King of the Jews" on his head, and, as they were putting him up on the Cross, was going: *OK, martyrdom, here we go. Bring on the pain! I can take it.* I'm not joking here. The idea that the entire course of civilization for over half of the globe could have its fate changed and turned upside-down by a nutcase, for me, *that's* farfetched . . .

But sometimes I'm not far from thinking the world has been shaped by a bunch of nutcases, or one big nutcase hiding somewhere in some big fancy invisible lighthouse. *[Bono laughs]* **Now, that cartoon stuff of yours has taken possession of my brain. What I mean here is that Christ was not the only one to make those kind of claims. There have been other prophets.**

That's right. But they didn't change anything . . .

Actually, you can look at the history of religion like the history of rock music. Different bands competing for the same market.

Steady on! *[laughs]*

I'm half serious about that. It's just that there was something in the air. I don't think it's so off the wall to say that. You might take that famous quote by John Lennon—the one that almost got the Beatles burned at the stake in

the Sun Belt—in reverse. You might say that in his time, Jesus Christ was as popular as the Beatles.

That's very funny, Michka. I want to avoid remixing here, but I guess we can say that. You know, Jesus . . . He had a real messianic complex. *[laughs]*

He was a bit like you, wasn't He?

No, He only thought He was Bono! *[laughs for quite a while]* No, but seriously, if we only could be a bit more like Him, the world would be transformed. All I do is get up on the Cross of the Ego: the bad hangover, the bad review. When I look at the Cross of Christ, what I see up there is all my shit and everybody else's. So I ask myself a question a lot of people have asked: Who is this man? And was He who He said He was, or was He just a religious nut? And there it is, and that's the question. And no one can talk you into it or out of it.

You said to me: "Nobody goes to church, nobody's religious anymore." But at the same time you're saying to me religion is everywhere . . .

The religious instinct is everywhere.

The experience I have every day is that people look for magic.

They're right to look for magic.

I don't know, really. To us, celebrity is magic, and it's certainly a new cult. I mean, people try to get close to celebrities, because they think they convey some sort of magic, that they bring them luck, actually. Anyway, if we want to sum this up, someone who becomes a terrorist and someone who goes to a U2 concert have something in common. They both want to escape from the materialistic, dull daily life. You see what I mean? Both are looking for transcendence.

But there are two routes out of town. There always were, there always are. There's transcendence and there's the cover version, or the dull copy: junk-food transcendence of drugs, the "easy to digest but finally that's gonna give you heart disease" religion. But I tend to believe that people who just want a cheap way out of their life can find zealotry in lots of places. The true life of a believer is one of a longer, more hazardous or uphill pilgrimage, and where you uncover slowly the sort of illumination for your next step. Religious people, generally, they freak me out. Honestly, I start twitching when I'm around them. But sometimes, maybe weirdos are the only people who really know they need God.

And what about the other ones? What would they need God for?

I look around at the twentieth century: it's not a great advertisement for unbelief. Where did communism bring Russia? Look at what more openness is bringing to China. I will say this for the Judeo-Christian tradition: we have at least written into the DNA the idea that God created every man equal, and that love is at the heart of the Universe. I mean, it's slow. The Greeks may have come up with democracy, but they had no intention of everyone having it. We have to conclude that the most access to equality in the world has come out of these ancient religious ideas. *[pause]* Michka, are you still there?

I'm still here. This is interesting. But I'm realizing, maybe a bit too late, that it's quite hard to steer an Irishman banging on about God and religion.

Do you really think other people are going to be interested in this?

No idea.

Right. That was an unexpected diversion into the catacombs. I enjoyed it, but we don't know if anyone else will. Stop me if I get too self-indulgent. But you know what? I never talk at this length with anybody who's writing or recording. They're usually drinking.

Or falling asleep. But that's OK. I think at some point you tend to forget who you are.

That's good.

And at some point I forget about your personality and bin the set list.

Well, me too. That's good. OK. Let's get lost, as Chet Baker would say. One last thing, though. Can we title this chapter: "For those not interested in God, please pass by"?

12. THE GIRL WITH THE BEARD

We seemed to have found our pace: an hour on the phone every three or four weeks, keeping things sharp and concise. I now think of these conversations as genuine performances on Bono's part. Once you've got him, he is always spot-on.

He was in his villa in Nice and mentioned that he had just gone for a swim and "lain up on a stony beach." He must have thicker skin than I do. In Paris, the temperature had dipped below freezing the night before.

So even though it's the day before Easter, I'm vowing that I won't lecture you like I did last time.

No, I just might need to be.

Well, not always. *[laughs]* When I think back to how you first got involved in humanitarian action in Africa, I picture that famous moment during the Live Aid concert in the summer of 1985. Many remember it, and now you can even download it online: as you finish one of your songs, you spot a girl in the crowd who is waving at you, pressed against the railings. You signal her

to come on the stage, and then, realizing that she can't get past security, you jump off the stage, pick her up, and then you both abandon yourselves in a sort of slow, languorous dance. Probably more than one billion people witnessed that piece of showcase intimacy. Nineteen years later, may I ask: what the hell were you thinking at that moment?

[clears his throat] Well, you should never trust a performer completely.

Yeah, you already told me that.

As I told you, performers are sort of part con men and, if they're any good, part shaman. So, in order to do your job, you have to be completely spontaneous and completely conscious. Though it was a spontaneous act to leave the stage, which was rather high and removed from the crowd, and though the time spent in the crowd resulted in us not performing the hit—"Pride (In the Name of Love)"—the other side of me knew what I was doing. I was trying to find an image that would be remembered for the day.

So you're finally revealing the appalling truth: it was staged.

Partly, in my head, you know. But it's hard to describe this process, because it's like when you're writing: you're looking all the time for the right image. Or when you're performing, you're looking for those moments. As we've discussed before, as a performer, I'm not content with the distance between the crowd and the performer. I'm always trying to cross that distance. I'm trying to do it emotionally, mentally, and, where I can, physically. So it wasn't just about rescuing the girl from the crowd, because I'm not so sure she needed to be rescued, but I was trying to find an image just to communicate how we all felt on that day. That was an overpowering day. It was a day that made tiny everybody that was in it, and the subject was so much bigger than anyone on the stage. I was not happy with just playing our songs and getting out of there. I wanted to find that moment. Of course, afterwards, I got a terrible time from the band. I was almost fired. Because I had climbed on roofs, I had left stages before, I had climbed on PA stacks, I had jumped into the crowds, I had physical confrontations in crowds, but this was the worst one for them, to leave them for what felt like hours, apparently. Larry told me he was going to stop playing. This was a big show for our band, there were a billion people watching, and we didn't do our big song. Everyone was very annoyed with me, I mean, *very* annoyed.

But were you convinced at that very moment that it was the right thing to do, the right image? As it turns out, you were correct.

It turned out, but I didn't know until a week later. It ruined my day. I thought I'd ruined the band's performance. I went home to the hotel and just watched the end of Live Aid, which was Bob Dylan with Keith Richards and Ronnie Wood as guests. I just put it out of my head. A week later, people came back and said that was one of the moments they remembered. I was hiding out in a small country town in Ireland where Ali's family live. We called on a sculptor friend of her family. He was pulling a piece of bronze out of a furnace as we walked in. His eyes nearly popped out of his head. "That's you," he said, "I've just taken out of the fire. It's a piece inspired by what you did last week on Live Aid. It's called 'The Leap.' You see," he said, "you made a leap of faith that day."

Everyone watching discovered that "out of control" aspect of your performance. Did you realize that at the time?

We keep starting these conversations, but the other thing I don't trust is a performer who's content on the stage, content with the distance between him or her and the audience. Whether it's an actor or whether it's a singer, I want to feel like the person on stage can stop playing a role, jump down, sit on my knee, follow me home, hug me, mug me, borrow money from me, make me breakfast in the morning. I've always had that as a performer. I don't want people to feel comfortable in the relationship. I want to feel like it could snap.

Do you remember that girl's name? And did you ever talk with her again? Do you know what she's doing now?

No. Not at all. We both gave ourselves to a moment and a piece of television. And then . . .

. . . no memories.

"I never called, I never wrote." *[laughs]* Actually, I'm not even sure if she was pleased that I singled her out.

What did you feel when she was in your arms?

Oh, I felt she was just a gorgeous girl. I felt her sort of shaking a little bit in my arms. But she might well have just been going: "I wish this rock star would stop sweating on me. I wish he washed."

Maybe *she* hasn't been washing ever since . . .

She might have been there to see the Rolling Stones, or whoever else was on, David Bowie.

When you're in the audience, you want these kinds of moments to be unique, magic, and unrepeatable. You ask yourself: Was that staged? Or is it going to be exactly the same at the next performance, whether in Amsterdam or Houston, Texas?

Sometimes it is. Because what I tend to do as a performer is I remember the happy accident.

And you tend to repeat it.

Not every night, but I will try to find a moment like that again. That's the kind of story of our live shows. Like, for instance, on Zoo TV, I remember one time I picked the camera out of the hands of someone in the crowd, brought them onstage and then filmed them from their eyes right the way down: their top, their belly button, their belt, their T-shirt, their jeans, right down to their toes. There was something very erotic about this girl standing there that I was filming with her own camera. And then I thought: "Wow! Imagine if we could broadcast that on our giant screens . . ." And so on Zoo TV we did that. I used to bring somebody out from the crowd and film them from their head to their toe. It was an amazing moment. It was a private moment, but then made into a sort of mega-moment.

It was a sort of journalistic statement as well, because that's what TV is about these days.

That was reality TV: Zoo Television, where people become the zoo. What was the name of the mental institute that the Victorian English used to visit? Bedlam. People would pay in to poke the mentally retarded people with sticks and watch them being mad. That's what I think the Andy Warhol fifteen minutes has done.

When you think back to those moments, are there any that you regret? Do you ever think: I have no idea why I did that, or who I was back then?

I remember going into a crowd during the *War* tour with the white flag. And I remember the crowd wouldn't let me through, and I started fighting with the crowd. That big jock had started to block my way, and I lost it in the crush, throwing digs to protect myself, making my statement about pacifism and nonviolence. *[laughs]* I don't know what was going on in my head back then. There are pictures, I think from the same tour, maybe, in Los Angeles, jumping off a balcony into a crowd. Robert Hilburn, the great American critic, said it was one of the most exciting moments he'd seen at a rock 'n' roll show and one of the dumbest. *[laughs]*

Well, the two usually belong together. Did you know that James Brown actually started doing this balcony thing in the late fifties?

I didn't know that. I got it more from Iggy Pop. Iggy Pop was my definition of the greatest performer in music. I was sixteen when I discovered him in the record shops we've discussed, in the City Centre of Dublin, seeing the pictures on the Stooges' albums. They set fire to my imagination. He was combatative, physical, manic. I'd never seen anyone like him. Whereas the punk performers looked like they would leave the stage, but they really wouldn't. *He* would.

There's this story I've heard that, for me, sums up the revolution that punk brought to the art of performing. It happened during one of the very few performances that the Sex Pistols gave, way back in 1976 in London. At some point, Johnny Rotten climbed down from the stage, and quietly sat in the theater, watching his own band perform. He became a part of the audience. I would say it was less raw and brutal than Iggy Pop, but just as challenging.

Yeah, not just raw intelligence there, a sophisticated mind at work. Moral outrage is what I got from the Sex Pistols. But as to becoming part of the audience, I remember playing our first tour of the United States. There might be like sixty, seventy, one hundred people in the club. The floor would be empty. I would leave the stage, sit at their tables, drink their drinks and kiss their girlfriends. Fun stuff. I loved that. I loved becoming the audience. U2 came from the audience. I like the idea that you can go back. On the last tour, during "The Fly," I left the stage and climbed over the crowd, and walked out of the back of the arena and got into a taxi and went home.

You mean you didn't finish the show?

That was the last song. Maybe there was one more song to go, but I just did it. I did it because I could. In these concerts, I'm always looking for the image. On the last tour, during "Until the End of the World," I used to reach out and grab a hand, and then bite it. The lovers' row thing, biting the hand that feeds. It was a great image to see in the newspapers the next morning; "U2 still hungry." *[laughs]*

During those early U2 concerts, you could actually sit in the same seats as the crowd. Now you can only pretend to. It's not the real thing anymore.

That's right. It's more difficult now to walk around. We're up at a very different pitch now, I'm glad to report. *[laughs]*

No more slobbering into other people's beer.

I do miss that aspect, but I don't miss it that much. I used to feel sick, worrying about how many people would turn up. I mean I would feel physically ill, because before we go onstage is a very difficult time anyway. It was made much more difficult if we didn't know if there was anyone gonna be there. *[laughs]*

Let me go back to that Live Aid performance in 1985. I think Bob Geldof started the whole thing after he saw a report on the BBC in 1984 about famine in Ethiopia. But how did you get interested?

Well, you know, Ireland has a lot of ties with Africa, because of Catholic missions: nuns, priests. Ireland is very Africa-conscious because, I suppose, as a country, it had its own famine not that long ago. In the mid-nineteenth century, the population of Ireland went from eight million to four million. Two million died and two million went off to become policemen in New York. *[laughs]* Well, no: in Boston, and London, San Francisco, Birmingham, Sydney. But there are very strong ties there. Maybe it's folk memory, maybe it's just a shared colonial past. Those reports from the BBC were extraordinary. I'm sure you had similar in France. It was hard to believe, what was happening. It was really hard. We watched that image of that starving child trying to stand up. You know, it's still stuck on my mind. In a world where there is so much, in a world where there's plenty, in a world of unimaginable prosperity, a child can die of starvation! It's hard to believe. Then later, after Live Aid, when Ali and I went—and the images weren't pictures, they were children standing in front of me, or at least trying to stand in front of me. I remember deciding that I don't want to be, I will not be, in a world where that continues to be true. Now, with DATA informing me, I know that we can be the generation that ends extreme poverty, the kind of poverty where a child can die for lack of simple immunization or having food in its belly. Because we can, we must. Yes, there will always be poverty, yes, there will always be people dying of disease, but no, not that stupid poverty.

True. But most musicians who have done work for Africa have also been passionate about African music. Peter Gabriel, for instance. Paul Simon went

over to South Africa to record *Graceland,* and he worked with the famous Zulu choir Ladysmith Black Mambazo. But you didn't go over there with Edge, Larry, and Adam. You went as a private person, not as a musician.

Well, remember there was a cultural boycott for South Africa. People, many times, offered us to go to Sun City. We turned them down. We were the first band to be invited after the cultural embargo was lifted.* The first band the ANC invited was U2, because we had been part of the anti-apartheid community in Ireland and in Europe. But we hadn't visited the rest of sub-Saharan Africa. Until that moment, there weren't many Holiday Inns for a band to play.

But I am sure that your greatest mentor, Brian Eno, had introduced you to African music by the time of Live Aid.

Oh, he talked about it all the time. He had just made *Remain in Light* with the Talking Heads, and in fact he arrived at the U2 session for *The Unforgettable Fire* in early 1984 with his head full of Africa.

Knowing the extent of your passion for Africa, I am surprised that it has never spilled over into U2's music. I mean your music has always been . . .

. . . fairly white.

Actually, yes.

Let's go further. The Irish aren't white. We're more rosy pink. *[laughs]*

Peter Gabriel was too. But he started collaborating with African musicians early on.

Yes. In Ireland, there were only three black people in the seventies: one of them sang for Thin Lizzy; one of them a best friend, Sharon Blankson, now runs U2's

*Nelson Mandela was released from prison in 1990.

wardrobe; and the other one ate some people. There was a famous incident in the seventies where a medical student at the College of Surgeons ate a couple of people.

Really?

I'm not messing. I think his name was Mohangi. He ate his girlfriend and served her up in a restaurant where he was working. *Mohangi* entered the language at the time.

You're pulling my leg?

It's better than eating it! But you know, there were very few immigrants who wanted to come to Ireland at the time.

I can understand African music wasn't on Irish radio, but why should that have prevented you from trying if you wanted to?

We'd listen to the music, but it wasn't really what we were into at that time. You're trying to find your own voice. I like African music, as it happens, an awful lot. But the concept of world music didn't really do it for me. I felt lifted by Youssou n'Dour and Angélique Kidjo. My favorite African singer is that Egyptian singer Oum Kalthoum. And then Salif Keita, King Sunny Ade: these were all on our record label—Island Records. I loved them. But it turns out that the groove-based music isn't our strength. My voice doesn't sound great singing over a groove. My voice seems to prefer chord changes in the more Western sense. It's finally that. I remember that we were coming up with some pretty good grooves, but the songs weren't very good. With Brian Eno at the helm, we were experimenting with a lot of grooves, but I remember saying to Edge: "I think my voice might need a few chord changes." I am not black. I am white. Might as well accept it. *[laughs]*

But the idea of a rock star who goes over to Africa only when a big catastrophe happens there, and is not passionate about its music, or its people—it's a bit upsetting.

What I'm telling you is, being Irish, I wasn't exposed to Africa as a cultural force, more as a moral dilemma. Yeah, it's a shame. Because Africa's next door to Europe. It's as close to go from where I am now in France to Africa as it is going from Toronto to Jamaica.

You could have swum over there this morning.

I think I was trying ... to get away from you. *[laughs]* I ran out of air, actually. The truth of it is that Africa did not feel like a next-door neighbor to Europe. We grew up thinking of Africa as farther than Australia, which is a pity, because I would have loved to go as a tourist, and Africa needs our tourism. I'm trying to bring my children there now. But, no, I went there as part of a relief agency, an aid worker, and that's not a great way to see Africa.

Still you traveled there, and I'm sure that seeing it for the first time was a shock to you. I would love to hear you talk about your experiences there the same way you discussed your first time in New York. So you are in Africa for the first time in your life. You've just landed and passed through customs. What is your first impression? What do you see? What do you smell? What do you feel? And where are you exactly?

It's Addis Ababa. There's heat, intense heat, and the noise of a busy airport ...

Ali's with you.

It's just Ali and myself. We're trying to meet someone. His name is Steve Reynolds, and he's the guy who's put this together for us. I think I'm enjoying the feeling of mild fear.

What is it that feels threatening?

Well, just because I don't know what's around the corner or where we're going. I don't know. Will there be people at the airport to meet us? Will it work out? It's not unlike New York, actually. It's that same kind of high-pitched chatter, and people shouting across each other. There is a certain molecular excitement in Africa, which you do pick up. It feels like the molecules are vibrating a little faster. So then, we go out onto the streets, and it's the chaos of Addis Ababa.

I've never been there. How big a city is it?

It's a big city. I've been there a few times now. I can't remember where we stayed, that's kind of gone. But before we went off, someone asked us if we wanted to see around Addis Ababa. They said the best way to do was by horse. So I said: "Horses?" And they said: "Yeah."

Can you ride?

No, I didn't tell them I couldn't ride. You should know that about me now.

It's true. *[laughs]*

No, I didn't say anything about not riding. Ali can ride. So, they said: "We can take Haile Selassie's horses." I said: "You're joking!" They said: "Yeah. Now Haile Selassie's gone, the palace has been taken by the Communists."

Mengistu.

That's right. But he's not interested, as it turns out, in Haile Selassie's horses. So somebody has them, and you can take them out for the day. They're giant stallions.

What color? Black?

Black. And I had to get up on this horse. When I was a kid in Northside Dublin, the gypsy horses, they used to let them out in the winters. They'd come into our neighborhood, and we used to ride them bareback. But this is a very different thing. They're about twice as tall.

It's a double-decker.

[laughs] It's a double-decker. You got it. I'm trying my very best not to show our hosts that I can't ride. I've told them I can. So we go through the back streets, and I remember one vivid picture of the people who are with World Vision, which is an American aid agency. One of the women was breast-feeding a child on the horse. *[laughs]* She was so comfortable. She didn't mean to be insensitive. But the Muslim women did not like this and came out and started throwing stones at her because she was showing her breasts. I love it when other people make such a faux pas. It's usually me. But it was incredible to go through the back streets of this ancient capital by horse.

And when the people in the streets saw this white man looking a little funny riding that huge horse, *[Bono laughs]* how did they react? Did they wave at you or did they stone you?

They waved and laughed. Boys with big pearly grins just laughing their head off at the Irish people.

You toured the city, but I remember a couple of years ago you mentioned a story about visiting the countryside, where you saw a treasure in some holy place. Do you remember that?

Yes. The area of Ethiopia where we were working was in the north: a place called Ajibar, near Wollo. The local Communist commander took an interest in myself and Ali, I think just out of boredom. And he befriended us, would ask us questions about where we lived, and even our address. I got the impression he was going to bolt to get the hell out of Dodge, as the Americans say. We were in the hills, where you could see other hills way in the distance. At the top of one of those hills on a large flat mesa, you could just about make out a monastery. We asked "Comrade Gorma" about it and one day he took us there.

On horseback?

No, we went on jeep. Then we got out of the jeep, and then we took, I think, some donkeys. Maybe it was horses. I can't exactly remember how we got up there. But when we got to the monastery, an extraordinary thing happened. All the monks started to panic and got down on their knees in front of this military man, and kind of begged him.

. . . not to harm them.

. . . not to harm them. And it was so shocking to see this. Then they all started bringing him in, and showing him around. He was not that scary a man, but it will show you the memory of the revolution had left these monks terrorized. The monks brought him and those following behind to this silo—I guess that would have been for grain, or something like that. There was a ladder. We climbed up the ladder, and then climbed down another ladder into the middle of the silo where, wrapped in sacks, was a treasure that they'd been hiding. There were crowns, gold crowns, and religious artifacts. I couldn't believe my eyes. I photographed them. I still have the photographs. But the monk offered up the crown to "Comrade Gorma." He put it on Ali's head, and I have pictures of them. I really don't know how priceless they were. I'm not qualified enough to figure out whether they were nineteenth- or eleventh-century. But as we left, we were so sad because we had the feeling these beautiful treasures wouldn't be there the next day. I don't know where this man went. Maybe now he's an antiques dealer. But maybe I'm wrong. Maybe he handed it over and they're in a museum somewhere. But it was Emperor Menelik's retreat. Menelik was in direct line from King David. Ethiopia . . . it's a mystic country. People are so royal looking. You read about Solomon coming to meet and indeed fall in love with the Queen of Sheba. It's like Bob Marley on every corner. They say it's where the Garden of Eden was. They say it's where the Ark of the Covenant is. It's a remarkable, beautiful country. It is bewildering to see the kind of poverty that lives there now.

There is something unexpected in your amazement at the beauty of the place. The experience you have just described is not particularly sad. There is an

element of drama, but you are conveying a real sense of beauty. But each time I have heard you talk about Africa before today, it was only to remind people of how tragic and dreadful a place it is.

I can't agree with that. I always try to talk about the potential of the people and the place. As I say, it's a place of rare beauty. In fact, my book of photographs, *A String of Pearls*, taken when I was working there, was not of the sick and the hungry. They were of the recovering and the well. Because I wanted to convey how beautiful and how noble these people were. Yes, I think it's very important to describe Africa in terms other than tragedy. You have to find a way of describing its myriad of possibilities, its thick jungle and rocky terrains. The Serengeti, the shining temples and calls to prayer . . . Their holy cities, where they play their car horns like musical instruments. Big bloody suns, that's another one. When you see the sun setting, you duck.

Whenever I visit developing countries, the thing that strikes me the most is the happiness in the midst of misery. I mean, you read about war and dismal poverty, but when you're there, you see smiles, you hear laughter, you feel kindness, even joy.

Oh yeah, the absence of self-pity, which is a quality I wish I possessed. It's a quality I admire in people the most: lack of self-pity. It's one of the marks of some of my favorite people. But, oh yeah, the giddiness and the laughter. You know, I used to have earrings, when the two of us were in charge of this orphanage for a short while. I was called "The Girl with the Beard," because I couldn't shave.

I think that just by accident, you've come up with the title of this chapter.

That's what it was, I was called "The Girl with the Beard." Myself and Ali worked on a program where you could teach children through songs or one-act plays. It is still operating, I'm told. We would teach them the things they needed to know in order to not be sick. So I wrote songs and they were translated into Amharic. Somewhere, these songs exist, and one of the plays was about giving birth. We worked with the local nurse. Stuff like how to cut the umbilical cord. There were some bad practices. They would use cow dung, and things like that, which would cause infection. These people are a captive audience. The children would then go around, singing these songs and so teach their parents. It was a three-week program: a song, a play, and a story, and then repeated. That's all we did there.

So your work was about the spirit of the people. It was not just distributing food.

The camp was about feeding, but myself and Ali were in charge of the orphanage. We slept in a tent. In the morning, as the mist would lift, we would see thousands of people walking in lines toward the camp, people who had been walking for great distances through the night—men, women, children, families who'd lost everything, taking few possessions on a voyage to meet mercy. Some, as they got to the camp, would collapse. Some would leave their children at the gates, and some would leave dead children at the fences to be buried. There was barbed wire all around the camp. I always thought this was so upsetting that we should have barbed wire. I thought the place looked like a concentration camp.

But why did they put up the barbed wire?

Unlike the concentration camps, it was to keep people out. It really brought home the problem. There was not enough to go around. Wouldn't you steal food for your family? I would. And again, these people are so royal, they're so elegant, so upright, these women and men. To have their dignity robbed from them, to arrive at a feeding station where it's Auschwitz in reverse . . .

Were people from the outside threatening to loot the camp?

No, I don't remember any feeling of aggression. The barbed wire was precautionary. I do remember a man coming to me with his child—his son. He was so clearly proud of his son. Giving me his son, and saying to me: "Please, take my boy, because if he stays with me, he will surely die. If he goes with you, he will live." Having to say no, and having to turn away, is a very . . . very, very, very, very hard thing to do. One part of me did and, you know, one part of me didn't. That's the part of me that still goes back there. It's a more than uneasy feeling. If you just put it into your own world, and think about your own child, and what it took for that man to say that, it's . . . bewildering.

You did that right after Live Aid, right?

Yes. Having got caught up in Live Aid, I said to Ali: "I just can't get these people I'm seeing on television out of my head. We have to try and do something. In a quiet way. We didn't tell anyone we were going. We just went out, as it were, under the radar.

These experiences have clearly altered the course of your life. Everything you've been talking with me about, all the presidents, all the Popes, all the arguments, I finally realize that it all comes down to this.

I don't think I can talk about this anymore. Let's change the subject.

OK, OK. Coming back to music, has your perception of African music changed after that?

I had a kind of epiphany, but it was a couple of years later, just sitting outside the Sunset Sound Studios in Los Angeles, when we were working on *Rattle and Hum*. The studio was way down east on Sunset Strip. And on a Saturday night, I would watch the parade of Mexican hot wheels, jumping trucks, muscle cars, and people cruising by, listening to rap breaking in America. Nineteen eighty-eight was incredible: incredible sound systems, deep sub-low bass, a cacophony of rhythm, chanting, disconnected voices, hip-hop coming from all directions. Amazingly sophisticated pop music. *[suddenly imitates human beat box and syncopated rhythms]* And I'm thinking: "I know this music. It's African music." The epiphany was realizing that technology had brought African music to the descendants of Africa in America. People who had no memory of their continent of origin, and no direct experience of the call-and-response music that is Africa. Yet through technology, through digital samplers, scratching old vinyl, their music was swimming back up the river through swing, rock 'n' roll, soul, electronica, to its birthplace, which sounds to my ears so like hip-hop. How did that happen? Pure African music arriving through the DNA, through the genes of those people. That blew my mind. It still blows my mind because of what it suggests of a kind of folk memory, of what we all might carry with us from our ancestors. And not just music, gifts, maybe even prejudices.

What about your ancestors?

Oddly enough, Irish music has more than a little in common with African music or Middle Eastern music. It comes from a completely different place than the rest of Europe, well, Northern Europe. Its musical scale is pentatonic, not chromatic, i.e., quarter notes, bent notes. The *sean nós* singers, for example, their melodies they sing unaccompanied can be traced to Northwest Africa. I visited a musicologist in Cairo once who backed up the theory of professor Bob Quinn of University College Galway, who said the sea routes from Africa had brought much more connection even in the pre-Christian era between the west of Ireland, west of France, west of Spain and West Africa. If you look at Ireland's most famous religious manuscript, the Book of Kells, it's like Coptic manuscripts of the same era. Now you'd tell that to my old man, Bob Hewson, and you'd get more than a hairy eyeball. You'd get a clip on the ear. Blackfellows, the Book of Kells. Feck off! You see, a sneaky racism plays a part in everything. The Irish, and I'm guilty of this, think they invented everything.

13. I WOULDN'T MOVE TO A SMALLER HOUSE

"All the presidents, all the Popes . . . I finally realize it all comes down to this," I had just said to Bono when he told me about his experience in a refugee camp in Ethiopia in 1985. Since he started to work for DATA in the late nineties, he'd banged on many doors and met quite a few heads of state. Hence these mental snapshots of a few Elvises of the late twentieth, early twenty-first century—Tony Blair, Bill Clinton, George W. Bush, Vladimir Putin, Gerhard Shröder, John Paul II, Jacques Chirac. Did all of those world leaders have an ear for the melody Bono sang to them? "Annoying question," as he would put it.

It seems to me that you and Tony Blair are jealous of each other's job.

In one of our cases, maybe. *[laughs]* He's a pretty good guitar player—plays every day, his missus told me. I checked his guitar case to see if it was in tune. It was, perfectly. He had a band in college—Ugly Rumours, I believe it was called. Little did he know that might be his nemesis. But seriously, he and Gordon Brown could really change the world if they keep up their work in Africa. They can be the Lennon-McCartney of global development.

You mean continual arguing?

I mean their best work is when they work together.

And what about your arguing with Blair?

Well, there are very few things I would disagree with Tony Blair about. Going to war, when he did, with Iraq would be one of them. But I believe he was sincere—sincerely wrong, in my point of view. But I think the extraordinary thing about Tony Blair was: it was clear, when he went to war, that he was doing the unpopular thing in his own country and with his own party. It wasn't a move to make himself popular. Fairly unusual behavior for a politician. We need more of this. Mind you, less of that.

You didn't answer the second part of my question. When does Bono want his seat in government? Does Bono want to be president?

[laughs] I wouldn't move to a smaller house.

OK, so now, you've visited smaller houses. I mean, you've gone backstage.

Having gone backstage, yes, and seeing the laundry room and how a few live wires are sticking out of the odd wall. It's what politics has in common with sausage-making: if you knew what they threw in there, you wouldn't eat the end product.

What is the most surprising thing that you have discovered about politics?

[pondering] How immense shifts in position begin instinctively rather than intellectually. And how great alliances are made because of a shared sense of humor or a spontaneous comment.

That reminds me of a funny thing I heard once. Someone told me he had spoken to an ex–Cabinet officer who said to him: when you're in school, there

tends to be approximately three groups of people. Some are just obnoxious; some are clever and quite able; but most are just dull and wait till it's over. He said that when he joined the Cabinet, the distribution was exactly the same.

[laughs] That's right. This is the thing: they start in the most unbelievable way to resemble people you know, in every good way and in every bad way.

Power is often very petty stuff. Have you read that book by the Polish writer Ryszard Kapuscinski, *The Emperor?* I know you've read the one about his years as a war correspondent in Africa, *The Shadow of the Sun,* but *The Emperor* is about the last years in power of Ethiopia's last emperor, Haile Selassie. It is an extraordinary account of how power was organized there: an incredibly refined structure totally centered on itself, blind to the devastation happening in the country. Now that's quite an extreme example, but I'm pretty sure that half of President Chirac's day—or any president's—is the same: they deal with who is going to be invited to such and such ceremony, or how to prepare for the next election. Power is often more about itself than about actually doing useful things for the country or the rest of the world.

Yes, I have read *The Emperor,* and it's true. Red tape, whether they're cutting it to open hospitals on the same day as they are cutting the health budget, or the red tape of bureaucracy tying their hands behind their back, the machine of politics makes it hard for change. A good leader needs big scissors to get things moving. Actually, I think a great leader has to have a great ear for melody. By this, I mean clarity of ideas. What I think they might all have in common, the ones that I've met—if they're any good—is an ability to see through the din and clangor of ideas and conversations and points of view, and hear the melody line, and realize: this is the thing we've got to do; this is more important than the others. They're like talent scouts in the music business. They're A & R men for ideas. Bill Clinton was incredible at spotting an idea.

Did you witness that talent of his in action?

Oh yeah! Like, I had to pitch him one.

You mean Clinton caught on to it immediately?

Well, his administration was full of people our own age. I mean, they were people in their thirties. He didn't just have an ear for a melody, he had his ear to the ground to pick up fresh insights, new ideas for the economy, for everything. He had a brain that could remember them all. I had met him a few times, but I remember, as I told you before, having to go to pitch him the Drop the Debt idea for the millennium, Jubilee 2000 stuff.

Describe the scene.

I remember it was a hot day in D.C., and I hadn't expected it to be. I was wearing like a blue cashmere coat, which I thought was pretty smart. I had some big boots on, but I thought the cashmere coat would be a compromise for the salubrious quarters of the White House. But because it was so hot, I had to take it off, leaving me with a T-shirt, combat pants, and boots in the Oval Office. So I looked like a member of our road crew. Our road crew are pretty stylish, but maybe not for the Oval Office.

How were you introduced to him?

He was waiting, sitting in his chair, in this historic office.

Behind his desk?

No. Smoking a cigar. Not behind his big desk, though he talked about his desk. It was President Kennedy's desk. Now every president gets to choose the desk of one of his predecessors.

What sort of vibe did you get when you saw him for the first time? I know you're very instinctive and you have this ability for tuning in to people.

I thought . . . *[laughs]* that he looked more like a pop star than I did. And I thought: he might be thinking that too, because I really did look like I'd come out from under a car. He looked very sharp, as he always does, and he just smiled. His staff and he himself just burst out laughing. I think they thought I was there . . .

. . . to do the plumbing?

I prefer carpentry.

What was the first thing that he said to you?

I can't remember. "Have a cigar," probably. But he was very busy. He was good to see me. We had pleasantries, and a bit of a laugh about probably the first time we'd met, which was very funny. We were going to a Chicago Bears game, and he had offered us to jump a ride with him in his motorcade. But I noticed his concentration was on medium, which is to say he was listening, but not intently, to these pleasantries. It was only when I asked him, did he have any good ideas regarding the millennium? After all, he was going to make the big speech. Being leader of the Free World, it's a historic moment. What did he have planned? Then I noticed his concentration sharpening. "Because," as I explained, "I have a really great idea." I said to him: "The dumb parade and the fanfare, is that all we're going to remember? Or could it really feel like History? Could it really be a new beginning for the people who needed a new beginning most, i.e., the poorest of the poor?" He got on that idea after a lot of questions in and around it, told me that he was already supporting the HIPC [Heavily Indebted Poor Countries] initiative, which was a World Bank initiative. It was a process where they were trying to ease the debt burden, but it wasn't going far enough or quick enough. I was saying that the millennium was the hook to hang this on and to getting the Bretton Woods people, i.e., the IMF, the banks, et cetera, farther down the road. He was very interested and very supportive, but he knew he would have trouble in his treasury, because Robert Rubin, who was the secretary of the treasury at that time, was not a fan of debt cancellation. He, it turns out, was a fan of Alexander

Hamilton, the very first secretary of the treasury for the United States, who, when given a choice about whether the United States after Independence should refute its old debts with Great Britain, decided to pay them, and with that, gain credibility.

But did Clinton click on anything in particular that you said?

It wasn't a new concept to him. What might have been new was how popular a melody it could be, that somebody like myself was interested, and that it might actually be one he could sing on New Year's Eve 1999.

So you'd been trying to achieve a precise goal, there. You wanted him to mention it in his speech.

I wanted him not to just mention it. I wanted him to follow through on it, to raid the bank, the World Bank, as it happens! *[laughs]* Because it was going to cost taxpayers' money to cancel those debts. I didn't realize how much he supported the idea. We wrote many letters, we corresponded, we talked. But until after he left office, I never knew how hard he had to fight. I remember his chief economic adviser, a wonderful man called Gene Sperling, told me just how frustrated the president was at not being able to further my proposal. At one point I had sent him a letter. Gene was called up to the top cabin in Air Force One, and the president was screaming at him at the top of his voice, pointing at my letter, going: "Why aren't we doing this?" So, you know, that would give you faith that a person with so much on his mind and plate had not just an ear for the melody, but a heart for the world's poor—to be in that position and have a heart for it, and be banging the table in frustration at his own civil service's inability to work it through. So, if anyone has any doubt as to the character who sat behind that desk, which was, by the way, Irish oak . . .

How could you tell it was Irish oak?

I told you I was a carpenter. No, because he told me. It was Kennedy's desk. I just wanted to put that on the record. *[laughs]*

Let's fast-forward a few years. You're entering the Oval Office, and this time, it's George W. Bush. What are your feelings? Are you nervous?

Err . . . I'm never nervous when I go to meet heads of state. I feel they should be nervous, because they are the ones who'll be held accountable for the lives that their decisions will impact the most.

What was your gut feeling the first time you came face-to-face with President Bush?

I'm trying to remember the first time in there. I always give a gift when I have to ask or, in his case, have been asking somebody for a lot of money. *[laughs]* They can't accept expensive gifts, but I give them, you know, something small: a book of Seamus Heaney's poetry. He was much more amusing than I expected. Like, he was very funny and quick. Just quick-witted. With him, I got pretty quickly to the point, and the point was an unarguable one—that, you know, 6,500 people dying every day of a preventable and treatable disease would not be acceptable anywhere else in the world other than Africa, and that before God and history this was a kind of racism that was unacceptable. And he agreed: "Yeah, it's unacceptable." He said: "In fact, it's a kind of genocide."

Did he use that very word?

He used the word "genocide," which I took to imply our complicity in this, which I absolutely agree with. Later, his staff tried to take the edge off the word. But in the Rose Garden, there was press, and I already had used the word.

It was too late to stop you.

Right. *[laughs]* He really helped us in using that word. He knew it was hyperbole, but it was effective. You know, we had corresponded before this, and I had to get through many doors before I got to President Bush. He was very formal, and I was wearing a suit. No tie, mind you. *[laughs]* I'm just remembering now. He commented on my glasses—that's right!—and he says: "Wow! They're kind of flashy." And I said: "Are you envious? You want a pair?" It was that kind of easy banter. As I told you before, he was just about to write a check for ten billion dollars, new money to the world's poor. So he'd done the right thing. It was all very good-humored, because I wasn't pitching him on that. On the Millennium Challenge, he was delivering. He was agreeing to the pitch, so it was a different mood. I was laying the ground for the next pitch, a historic AIDS initiative, but I didn't want to be too overt. Now, getting a politician to sign a check and cash a check are two completely different things. Our organization, DATA, and other NGOs have to work very hard to make everyone keep their commitments. Every year there's a budget, and our money could end up on the cutting-room floor.

So have they come through?

Not as much as I'd like, but yes, they have. If he makes good on his promises, President Bush will have doubled foreign assistance to Africa, the single biggest increase in forty years. Because of the deficit, though, it's like pulling teeth getting to the right numbers. I have to say the person who has put the most time into all of this and the person who, if they deliver, deserves a place in the history books along with the President is Condoleezza Rice. Condi gave the keys to her office to a bunch of English activists, Jamie Drummond and Lucy Mathew from DATA—not just the rock star and the Kennedy.

When Bush went to Africa, we advised on some of the sights, organized some of the people for him to meet, made sure he got to meet some of the real stars of this struggle. There's a nurse called Agnes Nymura from Uganda. I know her testimony brought him to tears. He put his arms around her after hearing how AIDS had devastated her family. In the embrace, she whispered in his ear: "I know you've done a lot for us, but what about putting some more money in Kofi Annan's Global Health Fund for TB, AIDS, and malaria?" She's amazing, a powerful woman in such a quiet way, but . . . maybe someone whispered something in her ear.

How did he react?

I wasn't there, but I'm sure it was a groan. It's a sore subject. We're always asking for more, but we're right. United States, in the list of the twenty-two richest countries in the world, comes in at twenty-two in the percentage of national income spent on the poorest countries. And fifty percent of that goes to two countries: Egypt and Israel.

And what about private philanthropy?

Well, counting private philanthropy—and Americans are very generous privately—and adding to it the otherworldly generosity of the Bill and Melinda Gates Foundation, who are doing more on this than anybody ever, the United States still comes in at number fifteen. Now you tell that to Americans and their jaws drop open in disbelief.

So would you reckon America's about to change?

Well, I think Americans are about to re-describe themselves, re-brand themselves through some of these development problems.

How's that?

These AIDS drugs are great advertisements for what we in the West do best: our ingenuity, our science. For a small price, you can transform communities, millions of lives. I told President Bush: "Paint them red, white, and blue if you like, but where they go, they will also transform the way these communities see us."

America has been re-branding itself in Iraq. Isn't brand USA in trouble?

There is deep suspicion, not just in the Islamic world, but in the rest of the world about what we in the West stand for.

The problem is that way too often they think we don't stand for anything.

As the United States got richer in the eighties and nineties and reached unimaginable prosperity—it's the richest most powerful nation ever—it gave less and less per capita to the trouble spots in the world. The feeling was: *Our military is keeping the world safe for democracy. We paid at the office already.* But you can't talk tough on terror and not talk tough on poverty. They balance each other, they're a perfect rhyme. Colin Powell has been saying this for years, and he's a military man. Maybe we should pay attention when the military admit the war against terror cannot be won by might.

It seems to me, with perspective, that 9/11 actually revealed a phenomenon a minority was actually paying attention to: how widespread the disliking, even the hatred, for the U.S. was.

America received two shocks that week—the shock of an attack, and the second, that there was so much support for that attack in certain quarters of the Islamic world. Pictures from Palestine, Indonesia, Pakistan, of regular men and women jumping up and down, celebrating the Twin Towers turning to dust will, I believe, be seen as a turning point. After the disgust, after the anger we all felt, there was some questioning: how did it come to this? Greatest nation on Earth, the country that fought fascism and sacrificed so much for freedom was *so* despised.

Do you think war in Iraq—I mean its objectives—has a chance to make the situation any better someday?

There are those who believe in the long term that establishing a beachhead for democracy in the Middle East is the only way to bring peace in the region. I'm not one of them. I only have to look to my own country to see what the presence of a foreign military can do for swelling the ranks of terrorism. The pictures of mistreatment in Abu Ghraib will have convinced many reasonable young Arab men and women that if they take up arms, they are the ones fighting for freedom. That makes me so sad and sick to the very pit of my stomach.

So I'm asking you for the last time. Do you really like George W. Bush?

We get on very well. As I told you, I couldn't come from a more different place. We disagree on so many things. But I'm telling you he was moved by my account of what was happening in Africa. He was engaged. I think, when I'm sitting two feet from someone, I could tell if this was just politics. This was personal. I think, for all the swagger, this Texan thing, he has a religious instinct that keeps him humble.

You mean that right-wing fundamentalist neo-con scary stuff?

Actually, he's a Methodist. It has to be said that most of the people in the Cabinet are not religious extremists.

But you must have disagreed with him at some point.

He banged the table at me once, when I was ranting at him about the ARVs [AIDS drugs] not getting out quick enough. You see, I'm Irish. When we get excited, we don't pause for breath, no full stops or commas. He banged the table to ask me to let him reply. He smilingly reminded me he was the president. It was a heated debate. I was very impressed that he could get so passionate. And, let's face it, tolerating an Irish rock star is not a necessity of his office.

Many heads of state have tolerated you in their office. Let's review them while we're at it. Did Germany's Chancellor Gerhard Shröder catch on to a melody you sang to him?

I only met him a few times. We drank beer the first time. I had the impression that on another occasion he might be fun to have beer with. He was relaxed, smiling. On other occasions, he wasn't so relaxed. I suppose it's hard to relax when someone like me has their hand in your pocket. He guards Germany's wallet after all. His finance minister's a legend: Hans Eichel. He seems to have the chancellor on a very short leash. But East Germany cannot continually be blamed for lack of German leadership in development issues. The way they talk, you think it's them that needed foreign assistance. On a serious note, I implored him not to be on the wrong side of history here. There are moments when a country has to step up to the plate for people outside of their borders, and this is one of them. I think we're getting somewhere now. Fischer, the foreign minister, is an inspiring character, and I've had a lot of encouragement from the corporate sector. They think it's time for Germany to take its place in the world again.

Have you tried to put your hand in Putin's pocket? I hear he's a black belt of karate.

He did ask me to go to work for him on Russia's debt. He was joking, and I laughed, creating one of the worst moments for me ever captured in a photograph. Tony Blair had introduced me and Bob Geldof to him. It was a G8 meeting in Genoa. The city looked like a war zone. A lot of people got hurt in riots. A young man lost his life to an Italian policeman, and I was documented the other side of the riot line, laughing with the politicians. I did not know about this tragedy at the time, but it is an example of how my glad-handing and discussion approach can be badly misinterpreted and how sometimes I'm not as smart as I think. He was an expert. He was meticulously turned out, not a nose hair out of place, obviously a very big brain, and very charming. I wasn't there to talk about Chechnya. Maybe I shouldn't have been there at all.

Do you get a lot of flak from the aggressive Left? In those moments, you're a long way from the barricades.

I know it would look much better for me to be standing handkerchief over my nose and a Molotov cocktail in my hand. But, you know, my deepest conviction is that making our intellectual case rigorous and keeping our support broad by a large peaceful grassroots movement is the only way we'll get this job done. It doesn't belong to the Left or the Right.

But isn't the Left more your friend than the Right?

Not necessarily so. The Left may offer more money to fight AIDS or deal with the debt burden, but they scuttle off when we talk to them about trade reform. The CAP [Common Agricultural Policy] of Europe so supported by the Left denies African products access to our supermarket shelves while we flood them with subsidized produce.

Speaking of the CAP, I wonder what you make of my president [Chirac]. He certainly defends the French agricultural rights.

Trade is a touchy and complicated issue. French farmers enjoy a lot of protection for their way of life. French cows have more money spent on them per day than most Africans earn. But you know what? This is one issue this rock star just cannot take on.

Why is that?

Cowardice. They'll be throwing sheep over the walls of my nice villa. I don't take a fight I can't win.

So you diplomatically avoided the topic when you talked with Chirac. Or maybe he pretended not to hear you on that.

No. He acknowledged some things are going to have to change. My question was: "When?" He didn't reply to that. What he promised me was that France would continue to act as interface between Europe and Africa. He seemed to know the terrain well. He has visited Africa many more times than any other non-African head of state.

That's for obvious reasons: former colonies.

Yes, he admitted that. He seemed to genuinely have a feel for what was happening, and understanding. He rarely turned to advisers in our meetings. He was passionate. I told the assembling press corps outside that the purpose of my visit was to turn that passion into cash.

He was passionate. But was he optimistic?

Yes.

Was he serious?

Yes.

So who's your favorite politician?

It would have to be Gorbachev, a genuinely soulful man who, following the courage of his convictions, left himself so open to criticism in what was the USSR. Some people despise him for the dismantling of that old giant. But without him, the twentieth century might have had a very different end.

How often have you met him?

Lots of times, and we talk every few months, even now. He came to Ireland once, and I forgot to tell Ali he might call. It was Sunday lunch in Temple Hill. Sundays, it's like a train station in our house. People call over to sit around, eat lunch, drink wine. The front doorbell rang upstairs. Ali answered the door, not expecting to see the former head of the Soviet Bloc standing with a giant—I mean *giant*—teddy bear, his present for baby John.

She had no idea he would be visiting?

It was a loose arrangement I'd completely forgotten.

So you forgot about Gorbachev. Now I'm giving you absolution for the many times you've forgotten about me. I know Ali does a lot of work in Russia, "The Children of Chernobyl" ...

Yes, she does. She made an extraordinary documentary there, *Black Wind, White Land,* and regularly drives convoys of supplies from Ireland to Russia.

She actually drives?

Yes, ambulances. She drives all the way.

I'm glad it's not you.

[ignoring me] Her organization is led by a great woman, Adi Roche, and they bring back sick children for holidays in Ireland. The really mad thing was one of her most favorite children of Belarus, Anastasia—Ali is her godmother—was staying with us at the time.

You're joking.

No. We were all sitting around the table, with President Gorbachev nursing an Irish whiskey, some old friends—Quincy Jones, his girlfriend Lisette, Dean Ornish, the famous heart doctor, his wife, Molly, and acting as President Gorbachev's interpreter Nina Kostina—when in walked on her calipers Anastasia. She was born without legs from the knees down, part of the ongoing problem of radioactive land where she grew up in Belarus, and of course stopped everything. Gorbachev couldn't believe what was happening to him when we explained who she was. He was visibly moved. He lifted her up onto his knee, and told the table that he could divide his life into two halves: before and after Chernobyl. It was the moment he realized the Soviet Union couldn't continue as it was.

I presume you couldn't help thinking that that man had had his finger on the second-largest nuclear arsenal in the world.

I asked him about that. I asked him: did he ever come close to opening that box? He looked at me straight in the eye and said there could and never would be an occasion to use that power, and that from a very young age he had known this was madness.

Is there anything else Gorbachev said that stuck in your mind?

I asked him: did he believe in God? He said: "No, but I believe in the Universe."

14. I AM NEVER GOING TO FIT
TUTANKHAMON'S COFFIN

I was surprised when Bono's assistant, Catriona, told me that Bono wanted to talk to me on his birthday. He was in New York on business, and had brought the family along. May 10, 2004 was also the birthday of his oldest daughter, Jordan, who was turning fifteen.

When he called, it was ten A.M. in New York. He had been up for a few hours already; he said: "I get up at six-thirty. I see my kids in the morning. I love it. And if I'm in France, I get up and I swim, which is incredible. That's when my head is clear. And if I won't write, I read. And then, at nine o'clock, you start the business of the day, and open your letters, and start to read your e-mails, and all that awfulness. But those two hours, from seven to nine, that's when my imagination is most awake. Anything feels possible. In fact, it's downhill for the rest of the day."

His mood seemed jocular. He told me later that night he planned to take Jordan to the premiere of *Troy*, which she was particularly excited about. "We're quite a gang when we hang out together," he said with some pride.

[singing] Happy birthday to me, happy birthday to me / I was born in a zoo.

How pathetic it is to randomly call some number in France, and wish yourself a happy birthday. I really pity you.

You know, you're not wrong.

So has your birthday become a public holiday in Ireland already?

Well, no. I'm all for it. Like, why wait until I'm dead? *[laughs]* Do I have to die on a cross, or die at my own hand, jump out of a window? Or finally The Edge shoots me in the back of the head? Actually, with Edge, it'd be the frontal lobe. Why not get all that stuff that happens to dead people now? I could come up with a deal. Maybe we could let the tourist buses in.

I could arrange that.

Run a few tours. There's where he will die, and there's where he will be buried. What sort of funeral would you like? You'd probably like a very discreet kind of affair, would you?

I think that would be more tasteful, yeah.

No, no. Taste is the enemy of a good death.

It's very hard to argue with that.

I would like lots of weeping and wailing. The music would have to be good: Bob Dylan singing "Death Is Not the End." I think I'll have Pavarotti singing *La Traviata*. I'd like lots of Uileann pipes, a boys' choir.

Could you speak more slowly, please? I am writing down your list of demands.

Seven vestal virgins, please. I really would. I'd like to have Ali and six other girls to all dye their hair blond, including their pubic hair. And I'd like them to carry the coffin. They might have to go to the gym for a while. Prepare for this death!

But lots of crying. And then a few rows afterwards in the reception. "He was a bastard! Could nobody just get up who would say he was a *bastard*?" I'll have Gavin Friday, who finally cracks: "He never gave me back those Brian Eno albums in the seventies. And when they came back, there was jam all over the vinyl." You know, in the Maori tradition, they have a thing called a Tangi [short for Tangihanga], and I've been to one. You lie in an open casket. For three days, people sleep in the room with you, and they get up and they talk to you. They're supposed to get out any sort of bad thoughts or ill will they've had. They've to confess it to you and get it out, not to apologize, but to go through with it. If somebody has borrowed money and not given it back, get angry and shout at the corpse! Honesty, to make your passage easier into the next life. Always true, sadly.

Do you know what that reminds me of? Remember that part in *The Brothers Karamazov*? Starets Zosima, the old priest who raised Alyosha in his monastery, dies. While his body is being watched over by the monks, it gives off a horrible smell. And before that, you had only heard wonderful things about his holiness. But all of a sudden, people start saying: "He smells like a rotten fish!" I think it is a great symbol of the things that you cannot dare to say about someone who is dead—but that eventually come out anyway.

Steady on, Michka. It's my birthday. *[laughs]*

Sorry, but *you* started it.

And by the way, can I just say for the critics? This idea of only giving the plaudits to people when they're dead—you should take note. All the kindness up front . . .

Didn't you mention "those journalists who follow you into the bathroom to ask those annoying but important questions" in a speech you made recently in front of Chancellor Shröder? I don't know whether you noticed any strange sounds last night, but I was busy setting up a webcam in the bathroom and putting mikes under your mattress, Soviet-style, taking a sample of your piss for the laboratory.

Listen, they don't have equipment sophisticated enough to deal with my urine. That's a 1982 Margaux, I do believe.

In light of the fact that today is a special day, do you have any memories of birthday celebrations way back in Ballymun, when your mother was still alive?

Oh, I don't seem to remember any. I don't have very many memories of my childhood. *[Pause]* I think I can remember my eighteenth birthday, because I wrote a song on it, called "Out of Control." I remember holding the guitar, my brother's acoustic guitar. The fret action was a little out of whack, and I had to press quite hard on it. It wasn't a great lyric, but it was like: *Monday morning, eighteen years of dawning / I said "How long?," I said "How long?" / It was one dull morning / I woke the world with bawling / I was so sad, they were so glad / I had the feeling it was out of control.* It was just about realizing on your eighteenth birthday that the two big events of your life, which is your birth and your death, you don't have any say over.

Each time you discuss your childhood it seems like things only come out in a kind of haze. For obvious reasons, the strongest memory seems to be your mother's funeral . . .

Yeah. I'm just trying to think. I have some strong memories about that railway carriage my granddad had, out in a place called Rush, on a beach.

Oh yes, you told me that story.

I remember the strand and the sand dunes, and wandering around. I don't really remember being very social. I wasn't intent on making friends, so I spent a lot of time on my own.

It's hard to imagine you were so shy.

Yeah. Whereas, on Cedarwood Road, I had very good friends with Guggi, when we were kids. Although I don't remember any specific birthday, I do remember that whenever it was Guggi's birthday, which is three days after mine, he, whatever he got from his family, or whatever in cash, he would split with me fifty-fifty. And he sort of taught me one of the fundamentals, which is about sharing. He was amazing like that, because when you're kids, you don't share and you hold on to things, but he'd been taught that no, whatever you have, you give half of it to your friends. And you know, he continued that when I was in the band and I was broke. My friends continued to pay my way. Ali too. The community in Dublin has always been a bit like that. That's what I remember about birthdays; I remember Guggi's birthday. But that's it. I don't seem to remember anything else.

Do you remember the first time you heard music that really hit you hard?

Oh yeah, I can remember that. Those memories are very clear to me. I mean, very much. Now that you mention it, I'm probably getting lots of these things back now, *[laughs]* because I remember very clearly hearing the Beatles' "I Want to Hold Your Hand" on the radio. That would have been probably '63, would it? At three or four years old.

Are there any images that come to mind?

I was in the back garden. There were trees at the back, at that time, but they were cutting them down. I used to love hiding in the trees, I climbed up to the top of them and enjoyed hearing my mother shout my name when she was looking for me. I wanted to hold her hand. I just remember the transistor radio was on, and everybody was talking about this group—they were such a phenomenon. I loved the Beatles. I only recently realized, like last month, that "Beatles" was a bad pun, as in "beat." I remember Christmas, getting up with my brother, watching them on Stephen's Day, the day after Christmas. On that morning, *A Hard Day's Night* was being put on, and then *Help!*, and then *Yellow Submarine.* So their music made a real impact. And later, as I got a bit older, Elvis.

Elvis, really? But for our generation, it was the late-period, Las Vegas Elvis, and you were supposed to find him naff.

No, I loved a lot of his films. I didn't think they were naff or crap. And then, of course, there was a work of God-like genius: the '68 special.

Did you see the live program?

I didn't see the live program. I don't know when I would have seen it, but that was a pivotal moment. I dressed like him in Zoo TV. We even set up a small B stage. Yes, Elvis. And then, John Lennon, when I was eleven years old, listening to *Imagine*. That album really got under my skin, the blood of it.

Was there any music around in the house?

Yes. My father used to play opera all the time. He played it really loud. This working-class man used to stand in front of the speakers with my mother's knitting needles.

[laughs] Conducting.

Conducting, yeah. He used to do that. *[laughs]* And we kids would be saying: "Turn that down!" When he listened to it, he was completely lost in it.

It's a wonder you haven't ended up hating opera.

I don't remember liking it at the time. But at some point, it got into me. And now, with a bit of hindsight, I see that my dad was probably going through his own opera. No one has a simple life, that's what's great about opera. And he was holding on to this music very tightly. But that was what we listened to. Then my brother's music, of course, because he was seven years older than me. He would play The Who, Jimi Hendrix. Then he introduced me to this "duo": it was "David Bowie and Hunky Dory"! I thought it was a duo, like Simon and Garfunkel, and so I used to tell my brother I liked "them"! *[laughs]* And Bowie, those high notes that he hit and the way they would resonate in your skull, that made a great impression. Ziggy Stardust and the Spiders from Mars: I guess he was the first artist I became a giant fan of. Marc Bolan and T. Rex, glam-rock.

But it was after John Lennon and Bob Dylan. At eleven and twelve I was listening to them, whereas I was thirteen or fourteen when I got into dressing up.

Cross-dressing?

A woman? No. Even in a frock, I look like Fred Flintstone.

I have never read anything about your mother's taste for music. Did she ever sing?

No. My dad sang.

So she didn't sing. But did she enjoy music?

I can't remember. *[suddenly]* Oh yeah! Now, I'll tell you what. She was a fan of Engelbert Humperdinck. So she did like music, now that I think of it. She must have, because she was an Engelbert fan—and a Tom Jones fan. But between the two, there was a big rivalry. It was not Beatles and the Stones, it was Tom Jones and Engelbert. *[laughs]* I just wrote a song, by the way, Michka, for Tom Jones. It's a fun song. It's called "Sugar Daddy." I wrote it with my friend Simon Carmody. We've had such a laugh. It's great. It goes: *I've got male intuition / I've got sexual ambition / I'm the last of a great tradition / Let me state my position / The older I get, the better I was / And it's all just for show . . . bom-bom / It's all just because / The show must go on / What else can it do? / I'm gonna drop the lot on you! / Boom-boom . . . Sugar . . . dee-dee-dee / Sugar daddy / Dum . . . dee dee dee / Sugar daddy,* and it's got this really amazing bass part, which goes: "Boo-boo-bom boo-boo-boo-bom. " It's great.

Now I'm hearing Tom Jones in your voice!

Yeah. He's incredible. Again, watching him on TV, as a kid, I do remember sitting in, with my mother and father, watching Tom Jones, and the excitement of his performance. He lost himself in it. This white guy with a black voice, and the sexual charge of it. I remember, nine, ten years old, going, "Wow!"

Tom Jones was a singer for grown-ups. Actually, in the sixties, you had this very big distinction between music for adults and music for kids. He appealed to housewives.

Oh yeah, everybody. It was amazing. His performance was very physical, I mean, for white people. You didn't see that. Elvis had brought that kind of abandonment. *[breaks off abruptly]* Come over here! I've got a beautiful birthday present. The most beautiful girl jumped up on the bed beside me, my daughter. Happy birthday to Jordan! You know we share the same birthday. Here's Michka. *[hands the phone to her]*

Happy birthday, Jordan . . .

[Jordan speaking] Thank you.

How old are you?

[Jordan continuing] I'm fifteen.

It's hard to believe you, but I do.

[Jordan laughs] OK, thanks. *[Bono takes back the phone]* There you go.

Fifteen! Now she's a woman!

She is a gorgeous girl. That was the best present I ever got for my birthday— when Jojo was born.

Speaking about birthdays, which ones have been the most special for you as an adult? Is there a special memory of what you did on a birthday?

I remember one particular night. Maybe it was for my twenty-first birthday, in the Paradiso in Amsterdam. I love the Dutch. One of my best friends is the photographer Anton Corbijn. The Dutch are so progressive. I remember the most extraordinary, transcendent night on my birthday. That was at the Paradiso, a great club, and it was one of those occasions where time and space just disappear, and you are just involved in people's lives and they in yours, in a way only music can bring about. I also remember my fortieth birthday. That was pretty amazing, because Ali took me on a kind of trip with forty friends and we traveled in an old World War Two–like airplane around Europe. She wouldn't tell me where we were going. We flew to different places. It was just for a weekend, and there were very surreal things happening along the way. Ali's very good at surreality. Also, my thirty-third birthday was amazing. We were building a swimming pool in our back garden. For a guy from the North Side of Dublin, it's a big deal. It was a big swimming pool, and there was no water in it. So she made a table at the bottom of the swimming pool. We had music played, and a marquee. *[Ali's voice in the background seems to arise in protest]* Actually, she just interrupted. What are you saying? I can tell Michka! Hold on a second. *[Bono hands over to Ali, who takes over the conversation]* God! He's unbelievable.

Oh, hello, Ali.

[Ali speaking] It was a marquee, a circus, and there were cellos. Hello, Michka.

I had no idea you were in the room. I was just about to say: now, censorship is happening . . .

[Ali continuing] I know, it's very bad. There was a marquee in the bottom of the pool. It is twelve feet deeper at one end. So we put a marquee up and we put a red carpet all the way down to the center of the pool. Because the band were away, we had fixed in the garden giant heads of Adam, Larry, and Edge, very *Achtung, Baby,* and some big fires. And then we had a four-piece string quartet playing as we walked down. It was a really very interesting night, very operatic, very Bono. But I'll put you back on with him, because I don't talk to journalists.

Well, you just did. So all of you are there. First, I thought he was by himself. Then I hear Jordan, and now it's you. Next thing you're going to tell me there are fifty people in the room.

[Ali laughs, continuing] Just hang on one second. He's right here, OK? Take care. Bye. *[Bono takes back the phone]* Analyzing? Now I'm taking a pee. No, I'm not.

No need to explain. I can see everything on my monitor.

Don't you think I look well? I've lost weight.

I think you could do better with your hair color.

No. Actually, I'm gonna have a red head soon.

You mean like Annie Lennox?

No, I wish. I'll look like a traveling person from the West of Ireland. I'm closer in many ways and instincts. Yes, I'm out of my fat-Elvis period. I was just enjoying the year when we're not on tour, and just having the life with my family, drinking the wine, eating the pasta. Next thing you know, you're on stage in Vegas with the big brass band and you can't close your belt buckle.

You've just spent five minutes describing your own funeral, so I think you're up for this question. At forty-four, you probably have more years behind you than in front of you. *[Bono laughs in sardonic tones]* How do you face your own mortality? On the one hand, rock stars have this Peter Pan complex. And on the other hand, you have Keith Richards saying, "The older you get, the older you want to get." So which side are you on?

I'm with Keith.

One hundred percent?

Yeah. For all my heroes are old men, you know. And I've always sought the blessing of older men, from Frank Sinatra to Willie Nelson, to Bob Dylan, to Johnny Cash, to my friend the painter Louis Le Brocquy. In the Scriptures, the blessing of an older man is a powerful thing. Think of Jacob, who cheated his blessing out of his father Abraham, and dressed up as his brother. He wasn't the eldest, and he put the pigskin on his arm, because his brother had hairy arms. He went in to his old blind father, just before his father died. And his father was giving out the blessing to the eldest. He stole the blessing. The extraordinary thing about the story is that God honored the blessing of the blind father. I've often wondered why. It puzzled me. And Jacob continued to be a bit of a cheater, right up until he wrestled an angel, running away from his responsibilities. That finally slowed him down *[laughs]*, and he became the father of a great nation. But I was always amazed by that. For example, why would God honor this cheater, this man who stole his brother's blessing? And the only answer that I could come up with was, and it might not be unsatisfactory, that he wanted it more. *[laughs]* And I think God was moved by that. He knew that blessings were very important, and he wanted his father's blessing, and he knew that God operated through that line. Whenever there is a blessing going, I'll be out there trying to catch it. Frank Sinatra, Willie Nelson. I have shocked and surprised people by asking them for blessings.

Really? Like what?

I asked Archbishop Tutu for a blessing. I knelt down—and he gave me one. *[laughs]* He's one of the men I most admire in my life, and I've a blessing from him that's gonna get me through a lot.

Anyone else?

Loads of people. Billy Graham would have to be at the top of the list. He offered me a blessing and then laid his hands on me. A beautiful man who could turn the Scriptures to poetry with his lilting Southern accent.

Isn't it surprising that when I mention aging, the word *blessing* is the first one to cross your mind? Whereas most people cringe at the idea. Look at the way we are sold the idea of eternal youth. No wrinkles, no extra weight. I mean, most people would consider the greatest blessing in life to be eternal youth.

I just don't see it that way anymore. I think that's a hangover from the sixties, the obsession with youth. Some people die at seventeen and put their funeral off until they're seventy-seven. And I see a lot of dead young people, I see a lot of alive old people. It doesn't matter to me. I mean, voice is an amazing thing. Like Frank Sinatra, I love his voice. When I was getting ready to record "Two Shots of Happy, One Shot of Sad," I was listening to him all the time. I don't know if I spoke to you about his gift of interpretation, of re-interpreting. Have you heard "My Way" with Luciano Pavarotti? Because this song was written as a boast, and he first sang it as a boast. But you listen to his version recorded for the *Duets* album [eventually released on *Sinatra 80th: Live in Concert*], when everybody says he can't sing, and it sounds like an apology—same lyrics, same melody. No one understands singing. For instance, Pavarotti, who duets on this piece, when people say: "Oh, when he was younger, he had this extraordinary muscle, this acrobatic voice." I listen to him and I hear the same gift, but it's the life experiences in his voice that make it so rich. I hear every tear that he spilled, every row, every compromise. People just don't understand opera if they miss that. That's what it's about. And the idea that you have to sing it like some kind of Olympic sport, like ice-skating, it's missing the point that this is art, it's an interpretive art. So I love what age does to a voice. Look at how beautiful Willie Nelson looks and sings. I'm finally gonna be cool when I'm in my sixties.

You like what age does to a voice. But do you like what it does to you?

Yeah.

Definitely?

I think so. I mean, not everything.

That was my point.

By and large, I'm enjoying it. I've never been closer to my gift. I've never been closer to my friends. In so many important areas in my life, I'm finding my voice, not losing it.

You may be romantically attracted to twilight in your youth. But when it comes to your own, it is a different story. I mean, twilight, getting closer as you age. At forty-four, forty-five, you begin to think: OK, this, I won't do anymore. I don't have the strength to do certain things.

[interrupting] Maybe you, mate. *[laughs]* I'm stronger. I can run for longer. I bite harder. Maybe *you're* clapped out.

So you have a webcam set up in my house too! *[Bono laughs]*

[Without warning, sets about singing the whole lyric to a song I must admit I had no knowledge of. It started like this: "Let's put the key in the ignition / Hot and fresh from the kitchen . . ." I found out on the Internet it was R. Kelly's "Ignition," which he knew by heart and quoted without hesitation. Hearing Bono mentioning "Honeys to my left" and "Honeys to my right" sounded really weird. It seemed to me that the Prince obsessive that always lurks inside him kept defying the imaginary po-faced U2 devotee who thought his idea of fun, after a hard day's work, might be to watch a TV documentary about World War II or to browse through a book about religious architecture. Bono then put forward his own exegesis of the song] Come on! I mean, let's put the key in the ignition, start the car, and I'm just ready. I'm down the road. No driver. It's like, I'm excited about the future.

But don't tell me death is something you've never thought about. Or maybe you're just repressing it.

No. I've thought about it more than most. I've had to.

You mean your own?

My own? Yeah, I did in my thirties. I had a couple of scares, and I think my sense of my mortality, my sense of everyone's mortality, being in your thirties, I think that's the first time you feel it, because in your twenties, you're immortal. But I have so many questions to ask God. You know, there's two inches missing off the bottom of my leg, for a start. *[laughs]* I want an explanation!

Are you sure that is the first question that you're going to ask God?

I've many questions to ask God about the universe. There's some explaining too, not just by me, but by Him. *[laughs]* I'm sure He'll have a lot better answers than I will for my bad behavior.

What do you think will happen to you after you die? Do you have a vision?

You know, in this area, I don't. I close my eyes and I try to imagine Heaven. But I think, rather like Hell, Heaven is on Earth. That's my prayer. It was Christ's prayer, which was: "Thy Kingdom come / Thy will be done on Earth as it is in Heaven." I mean, that's where Heaven for me is, and we've got to start bringing Heaven down to Earth now. So what I imagine Heaven looks like is this present life without this present evil, which just scratches and bites and bullies people. So that's how I think about it. But I don't know. I can't imagine. When I try to think of, "What age would you be in Heaven?," I don't know. My brain is kind of too small for these kinds of glimpses.

But once you said to me that you heard voices when you wrote songs.

I hear melodies, yeah.

Have you ever imagined that you might be picking up words from the dead? People you knew, who come back and haunt you.

No. I never have. I think when you die, you're dead. Next up, judgment.

Do you dream about people who have died? Most people do. I mean, I dreamt about my father yesterday. He's been dead for twenty-three years.

Wow. And how did you feel when you woke up?

It's hard to explain. I think I still dream about him because I was so young when he died. I think I still want to talk to him, and I still want him to talk to me.

Yeah, you'll see him again. I mean, you see, it's just a moment. That's the thing. It's the blink of an eye, isn't it? What's the difference? Twenty, forty, sixty, eighty, a hundred? In comparison to eternity, it's only a split second. We live in a world that's obsessed about our temporal selves. We focus too much on that, and it makes us very unhappy, because the body is getting weaker, and it's difficult. But actually, the journey of the spirit is very important. We should think a little bit more about that.

Right. But you must feel a lot of pressure to stay young and fit because of your job. I mean, you need to work out more than the average Joe.

Oh, yeah. That area is one thing I've noticed. I have to fight harder for fitness. I can't drink the same amounts, I can't eat the same amounts. I can't. I don't stay on for as long as I used to. I'm not afraid of that. On death, I fear other people's. I would miss my friends.

But there are two ends of the spectrum. On one end, you have Mick Jagger, who at sixty still runs like an athlete. And on the other, you have Bob Dylan, who always was a man of his age. And you seem to be floating somewhere in between.

We'll have to see when I get there. I think my hero here is probably Johnny Cash. I've always been more mannish than boyish. The effete rock 'n' roll figure has never been mine. I've always looked more like a boxer than a singer, or a thug. *[laughs]* I've never felt that need to be of fashion. I enjoy playing with it a little bit. But the film that Mark Romanek made of Johnny Cash singing "Hurt" is one of the greatest things popular culture has ever offered. It's the end of rock 'n' roll as juvenilia. And there is a man with a dignity to let us into his death and its "empire of dirt," in Trent Reznor's line. It's the most remarkable song. And, wow! Think about India. Go to India and you'll find respect for age way above respect for youth. Respect for youth arrived at the same moment as in-built obsolescence. They discovered with this sort of production line and manufacturing in the twentieth century that if cars lasted for twenty-five years, people wouldn't buy other ones. So that's in-built obsolescence. Rock 'n' roll is the finest example of that, and the culture that came with it. We expect our rock stars to set fire to themselves. We're disappointed if they don't. If they don't die on a cross, age thirty-three, we want our money back.

I'm not so sure that rock 'n' roll invented the cult of youth. Yesterday, I was in Basel, Switzerland, where I saw an exhibition of Tutankhamon. It was the first time in my life that I could see everything that had been excavated from the tomb. So celebrating a fit, young body, and exalting youth is something that you can find in the remotest antiquity. And just look back on pre–World War Two Europe, at the Mussolinian imagery, or Hitler Youth, or even the Communist laborer as a young hero. The cult of youth wasn't born yesterday.

I think that's part of rock 'n' roll, but it's more to do with homoeroticism. The worship of boys, or girls who look like boys in fashion—that's never gonna work for me. I am never gonna fit Tutankhamon's coffin! *[laughs]* You're gonna have to dig up the Buddha.

I saw a thirty-meter Buddha in Hong Kong, a very fat one. We could take some measurements.

Me, if I wasn't so vain, I'd be living in Marlon Brando's house in Tahiti. Just me and Marlon, drinking fine wines and swimming naked in the sea.

So why don't you?

How do you know I'm not planning my exit? That's what we should be talking about. Not my actual death—my fake death, Michka. I have to set it up: airplane crash, then up to Marlon Brando. I can be Marlon Bono. I can just lie on the sand, putting flowers into the hairs of my friends and the locals.*

I wouldn't expect that from you. I thought you'd be going off to some monastery, or some cave in India.

*That, of course, was a few weeks before Brando's death in June 2004.

No, no. That's my kind of monastery. Look, I worship God at sunrise, whether I see it going to bed or getting up. I've seen some of the most extraordinary sunrises anyone's ever seen, all over the world. From the top of skyscrapers in Tokyo, or, with Liam and Noel Gallagher in San Francisco Bay, looking at the Golden Gate Bridge, or, in Africa, seeing through the mists of loss at a food station. I mean, crushing hangovers, and begging God for forgiveness. Sunrises, I love them. And as I told you, I get up early now. I don't stay up late, because I'm in a work mode rather than a carnival mode. These days, I meet the muse on her way home. *[laughs]* When I haven't been out with her, it's still nice to see her with clarity rather than with a sore head. I have an advantage.

15. FROM THE TENTS OF AMHARA TO SLEEPING IN BREZHNEV'S BED

There was something uncanny about Bono's route to Africa. Each time he had the opportunity, Bono would lay Africa on the table, whether I'd asked him about clinical depression or his impression of President Bush. My view was that since 1985, when he and Ali had spent three weeks in that refugee camp in the north of Ethiopia, Africa had more or less vanished from his field of vision. He certainly didn't set foot on that continent until the day the U2 PopMart tour stopped in Cape Town, i.e., March 16, 1998. The truth is, for twelve years, before he received a phone call from someone trying to find a worthy champion for the Jubilee 2000 campaign, Bono had very little to say or do about Africa publicly.

It's not really true in private, he said when we discussed that. *I just hadn't found an innovating or inspirational solution to some of these problems, i.e., I didn't want to be a bore. I didn't want to go on and on, be a bleeding heart without a strategy.* But what was he ready to do in private? *My definition of charity is the old idea that the right hand should not know what the left hand is doing. If it's public, it's not charity. It's PR. Unless it's taking a stand. And at that time, I hadn't a stand to take other than the sort of "Rock against bad things," which is so banal. In the end, justice is more poignant than charity, which is so patronizing.* So when did he get a strategy? *1997–98 is when I re-entered the fray. Jubilee 2000 had a great strategy for canceling the debts of the poorest countries to the richest as part of the millennium celebrations.*

In mid-2002, Bono accompanied former U.S. secretary of treasury Paul O'Neill for a tour of several African countries. I wanted to ask him how he accounted for all those "lost years" regarding Africa. Most of all, I thought I had to challenge his ideas about aid, which often contradicted some recent reports I'd read. Since I had no firsthand knowledge of any kind, I leaned on the work of Paul Theroux, whose *Dark Star Safari* I had just finished reading. The book is an account of his crossing the African continent, from Cairo to Cape Town. Rather dauntlessly, he'd traveled only either by bus or train, or on the back of a Jeep or a truck. About forty years later, he was revisiting the places and the people he knew as a young member of the U.S. Peace Corps. His conclusions were devastating: Africa is worse off at the beginning of the twenty-first century than it had been in the early sixties, when fledgling countries started to free themselves from the colonial powers, and that is the case not in spite of Western aid, but *because* of it, he stressed. Theroux's judgment on various aid organizations and representatives is a very harsh one. I wondered what Bono would make of it. The result turned out to be one of our most revealing conversations.

I'm afraid I'm going to be making some snide remarks this morning.

Oh boy!

Maybe what you said to me about your father's negative attitude encouraged me somehow.

OK. Go for it. I'm terrified.

I'm going to read out to you a few lines from a book called *Dark Star Safari*, by Paul Theroux.*

*Paul Theroux, *Dark Star Safari: Overland from Cairo to Cape Town* (Houghton Mifflin, 2003)

Yeah, yeah. I've read it.

So you've read it. Then you know the story. There is a passage I wanted to discuss with you. Maybe you remember that part where Theroux is in Ethiopia in a place called Shashemene, which serves as a sort of haven for Rastafarians. There he meets with this seventy-one-year-old bona fide Rastafarian and a young zealot called Patrick, who tells him that the millennium is about to come to Ethiopia, but it's going to be slightly behind schedule because the Ethiopian calendar runs seven years and eight months late. And this guy tells him it's not going to be water this time, but fire. And that—luckily—the Rift Valley will be spared. So Patrick invites the author to join him: that way he and his family will be saved. This is how Theroux concludes his piece: *I thanked him and walking out to the main road I reflected on how Africa, being incomplete and so empty, was a place for people to create personal myths and indulge themselves in fantasies of atonement and redemption, melodramas of suffering, of strength—binding up wounds, feeding the hungry, looking after refugees, driving expensive Land Rovers, even living out a whole cosmology of creation and destruction, rewriting the Bible as an African epic of survival.* I wonder how you reacted to that passage. You know that Theroux was very critical of the work of a lot of humanitarian workers.

Yeah. It's a beautifully written book. There are passages I will never forget. A real love for Africa comes through as well as his frustration. But some of his comments since it has been published about humanitarian relief efforts have been extremely unhelpful. He figured the debate could do with some brutal truths. He was right there, but some of his comments were not true. He wasn't really aware of the details of some of the proposals that were coming at the time. He was critical of aid propping up governments that should be let turn to dust. This has been true, and in some cases, it might still be. But to make that as an argument against aid per se is not credible. I think he's just being a crank. And I love cranks! I mean, my country is filled with them, and people should voice off. But when your lives are depending on those drugs, when the communities are depending on help to build schools, such comments are not helpful.

He gives specific examples of humanitarian projects turning to ruin, such as a school in Uganda financed by Canada or a flourmill financed by the U.S.

Such examples exist, and this is part of the reason the level of aid over the last twenty years has shrunk. We're trying to reverse that trend. It is not fair to point all the time to such exceptions. They are not the rule these days. I don't appreciate Theroux's comments, because they feed into the sort of ignorance about Africa and the continent—the "money down a rat hole" argument. I understand his frustration with corruption. Corruption is probably the biggest problem facing the continent, but it is not the only one. As I keep telling you, there are new ways to deliver aid, where it does not prop up a corrupt government, but it rewards governments that are tackling corruption and have poverty-reduction policies in place. That was the Millennium Challenge Account [MCA], which was the first major thing that we were involved in with the Bush administration [see Chapter 4]. Its concept was to reward good governance, transparency. Countries would get a special grant if they really were serious about tackling poverty, and were open to criticism, encouraging civil society, a free press, et cetera. If a government is doing the right thing by its people, they should be fast-tracked in increases in aid. *[pause]* That said, I should be fair here. It might be interesting to talk about revisiting Ethiopia, just because in a way Ethiopia is the best case for Theroux's argument—and mine.

And why is that?

Because after years and years of aid, the country is still in deep crisis. And after all that stuff, all that attention on the famine in the eighties, in the nineties, when I got back, maybe three years ago [circa 2002], I was amazed, because Addis Ababa was a very different city. It was obvious that there'd been huge migration from the countryside, and so there were new ghettos everywhere, shocking ghettos. And I met prostitutes in the ghettos—no idea about using condoms, and were HIV-positive, but not telling their customers. All the degradation that poverty can bring to a people was present in Addis. And I had visited there when the Communists had it by the balls. Now I was meeting the guerrilla leader who fought against the Communists.

Meles Zenawi.

Yes. And he's a very impressive man. He's a brilliant macroeconomist. He taught himself whilst leading a guerrilla war. He taught himself on BBC's Open University. He studied economics, apparently the brightest student they ever had. He's a brilliant man. I spent some time with him, it was very interesting to hear his stories, about how he studied economics and political science. "In Ethiopia," he said, "you learn everything by living with the farmers, because the farmers in Ethiopia are the smartest people in the country." I said: "But why is that?" And he said: "Because if you aren't smart, you starve." So you have the most innovative people. They can make something out of nothing. He'd learned an awful lot about the country from hiding out in this guerrilla war. But I could see that after the war, they really haven't recovered, and, still, though making great progress in a lot of respects, he wasn't really encouraging the civil society. He still had a little bit of a Leftist control. For a guy who fought the Communists, he was not so committed to a free and open press as we would have expected. I think, though, in essence, he is a very, very good man, maybe even a great man. It's just fear of losing control of the country. Time will tell.

So what did you think of the regression in Ethiopia?

What I'm saying to you is that there's both: regression and progression. Two steps forward, one step back. Remember, it's a war- and famine-ravaged country. Still, hundreds of thousands of lives have been saved that would have been lost. But Theroux would argue that hundreds of thousands of other lives are in danger because the Ethiopians and our NGO communities failed to put the mechanisms in place to stop that happening again. A wasted opportunity.

So he was right, there.

Yes. But recently, that's changing, and let me give you a few examples on the micro and macro levels. Take Sister Jemba, who works in Addis at a very grass-roots level with communities to improve their housing and sanitation in a sustainable way. It's a bottom-up approach, and as I say, sustainable. At the macro level, there's a group called REST: Relief Ethiopian Society of Tigre, this funded again by NGOs and donor governments in the north of Ethiopia. Their long-term integrated rural development programs working with communities and farmers try to improve the productivity of the land. For example, in Degua, stone dams have been constructed to prevent further erosion of gullies catching rainwater and building soil fertility. What was previously barren land is now producing 1,500 barrels of good quality hay for livestock every year. This is not insignificant. Save the Children have a program which will impact the lives of 150,000 people in the Amhara region. It's called Linking Relief to Development, where livestock is sold to buy food, protecting the assets of the Woredas of Sekota and Gublafto for three years till they are self-sufficient, ganging up on local problems across many different areas: soil and water conservation, micro enterprise, et cetera. I know this stuff and these extraordinary tribal names because I've been working on this this morning. This is not the old top-down type of development, where you arrive in town like a bull in a china shop, trampling all over the people you're supposed to help.

But even effective aid is not the long-run solution, is it, Bono?

No. Commerce and good government. We should look at foreign assistance as kind of start-up money. Self-sufficiency is of course the goal. The funny thing was traveling with an "entrepreneur" like Paul O'Neill, who was the United States secretary of the treasury. All the time he'd been telling me the future of Africa is in the hands of business and commerce. And I knew that to be sort of true, but not as much as I needed to, and this opened my mind to subjects like unfair trade relationships. It's a shock to discover that for all our talk of the free market, the poorest people on Earth are not allowed to put their products on our shelves in an evenhanded way. They have to negotiate all kinds of tariffs and taxes. It's not a level playing field. We can sell to them, but they can't sell to us. I started to realize that even the most friendly faces to Africa would in Congress obstruct trade reform. It was the Left that sponsored the Farm Bill in the United States, which subsidizes American agriculture and makes it impossible for African farmers to compete. Imagine the shock of walking through the markets in Accra, Ghana, where ghettos have been swollen with out-of-work rice farmers, to find cheap American and Vietnamese rice on sale to people who used to produce their own.

You say commerce is the future. Is the future happening now?

Yes, but it's slow, agonizingly slow. I want you to understand, Michka, the free market unencumbered is not the solution either. All successful economies have protected their seed industries until they were strong enough to compete. We cannot deny for others what we demand for ourselves. Successful economies in Southeast Asia had a very careful, gradual journey to competitiveness. They're the best example of how aid can work. Without it, they wouldn't be where they are.

So you're describing an increase in aid that's strategic and demanding of good government and in consultation with the people on the ground.

That's really it. As I already told you, a kind of Marshall Plan for Africa. Think back to the Second World War, think back to the United States that liberated Europe, but then rebuilt Europe, spending one percent GDP over four years. They were being strategic, it wasn't all out of the goodness of their hearts, though it was that too. The U.S. were rebuilding Europe as a bulwark against Sovietism in the Cold War. This is what we need in Africa and in some parts of the Middle East—a bulwark against the extremism of our age in what I call the Hot War. This makes sense, not just as a moral imperative, but a political and a strategic one. It's the right thing to do.

So you'd like to see the military spending into a Marshall Plan–type investment. Is it realistic?

What I'm saying is, one is bound up in the other. Might it not be cheaper to make friends of potential enemies than to defend yourself against them later? When we started the century, people were still talking about Star Wars, they were talking about building space stations with nuclear capability . . . It's a joke! Commercial airliners can be used to take down countries. On September 11, one of those airplanes was headed for the United States Congress, packed with people I know and respect and now work with. The whole of the United States Congress could have been taken out by just one of those planes, were it not for the bravery of some of the people on board. Star Wars? What were they thinking? This is a new era. We need tactical weapons in another sense. Take out hatred a different way. Destroy anti-American or anti-Western feeling by making sure they know who we are, working harder on the Middle East peace process, feeding people who are starving, bringing our pharmaceuticals to deal with the AIDS emergency. Africa is forty percent Muslim. For the price of the war in Iraq, the world could have been changed utterly, and people who now boo and hiss America and Europe would be applauding us. This is not fanciful, this is not Irish misty-eyed nonsense! This is realpolitik.

You're up to your neck in all this stuff! How did you get involved at such a level? It seems that it's only happened over the last five years. Mandela was released in 1990, but you didn't set foot in South Africa until the late nineties.

First time, I think it was on the PopMart tour. As I told you, U2 were frontline agitators for the anti-apartheid movement. We were the first artists invited to the new South Africa by the ANC [the PopMart tour stopped in Cape Town on March 16, 1998].

So it was about thirteen years later. I think you offered an explanation, albeit unconsciously. I have here the speech you just made a couple of weeks ago when you received an honorary degree at the University of Pennsylvania, trying to raise the consciousness of future American decision-makers about AIDS in Africa: "I know idealism is not playing on the radio right now," you said. "You don't see it on TV, irony is on heavy rotation, the knowingness, the smirk, the tired joke. I've tried them all out. Idealism is under siege, beset by materialism, narcissism, and all the other isms of indifference." What I'm underscoring here is: I've tried them all out. In the early nineties, U2 was very much into nihilism and irony. You and the band made a point of not being as earnest as you had been before. Does that account for your personally forgetting about Africa?

Firstly, let me say the music was not ironic in that period—it was wrapped in irony. Actually, there was real blood going through those veins. Secondly, concerning the packaging, the presentation, I think even then it was ironic in a very idealistic way. As to forgetting about Africa, all through that period, Ali and myself were quietly involved. As I told you before, it was not part of U2's agenda.

So you really don't think you lost your idealism, and to use your own kind of terminology, "surrendered to the world and its way," which is surely the smirk?

Look, we didn't want to look like the group that was too stupid to enjoy being at number one! *[laughs]* There's only so much people can take of four angry young men. We had much more dimension in our personal lives. We wanted to reflect that in our public lives. Laughter is the evidence of freedom. A sense of humor is not always defensive. It can be a great attack dog. I mean, we described *Achtung, Baby* as the sound of four men chopping down *The Joshua Tree*. We had amassed a lot of moral baggage, and we just wanted to lighten the load a little bit for those four frozen faces on the cover of that album. We had painted ourselves into a corner. We needed to circle the square. Every sort of "Right On" movement was outside our door and knocking. We couldn't let every serious issue in. We continued our work with Amnesty International and Greenpeace. That's where we met the wider world, through those organizations. We stormed Sellafield with Kraftwerk and Public Enemy, and it was amazing. But I admit the period was more inward- than outward-looking, and at a certain point, maybe the worldview suffered, I'll admit that. Compassion fatigue: I don't think we had it, but it could have been an issue for our audience if we were to take on Africa at that period. I mean, I was reading about Africa in the newspaper or in the odd specialist publication, but I wasn't anxious to stare at it for too long. I hadn't heard any new ideas at that point.

When you did Live Aid and the Conspiracy of Hope tour, humanitarian work seemed to be at the core of your music. But afterward, humanitarian work was the small print on the list of acknowledgments in your CD booklets. I was wondering if you were touched by that wave of self-disgust that was

going on in the nineties. There was Nirvana, and with grunge came the business of self-loathing. I mean it was not a business, but it was a trend . . .

[interrupting] No, it *is* a business! *[laughs]*

OK. Let me put it simply. Did you go through a crisis of faith?

Errr . . . a crisis of strategy more than a crisis of faith. I mean, taking a television station on the road, and spending a quarter of a million dollars a day wasn't just a thrill. *[laughs]* It was a bit of a worry! I mean, we were burning money, a bonfire of our vanities. But we were at least spending it on our fans. We were risking bankruptcy for an art project.

But hadn't you stopped trying to change the world in the real sense? Art projects are not something people would associate with U2.

Well you should, because it is one, and a commercial project, and a spiritual project, and a political project when it wants to be. We still had the idea in our heads that a rock star has two instincts: he wants to change the world, and he wants to have fun. If he can do both at the same time, that's the way to go. But though we had a lot of interesting and arty ideas that were flashing around on our expensive TV sets, the mainframe of Zoo TV was still pretty radical. The siege of Sarajevo was going on, and we were broadcasting it.

Yes, it's true. I'm being unfair. You were still setting up these operations. But that is my point. They were operations.

Heart wasn't enough, you had to be smart in the nineties. We were trying something new. We were looking for hard juxtapositions, the kind you'll find in conceptual art. It was uncomfortable. Because that's the thing about television—you move from a kind of McDonald's commercial to Africa in a second. And this sort of schizophrenic channel-hopping image of life that we were all leading was part of that whole thing. We needed new weapons for our arsenal. That was what Zoo TV was. We called it judo. Have we discussed that yet?

Yes, using the enemy's strength to defend yourself. What did you have to defend yourself against?

Caricaturing in the media. We were being reduced to simple lines, there was no shading. We looked naive. Yes, that's what was going on in that period. I don't think it was a crisis of faith, no. Just looking for a new way to express old idealism.

But didn't you go through a period of doubt in your personal life? I have this feeling that you were a little lost at that time.

On the contrary, I was going through a kind of glasnost. *[laughs]* The Politburo was coming out of the deep freeze.

Same years, by the way: 1989–1990.

I know. Of course I slept in Brezhnev's bed. That must have been when all this started. I told you that, didn't I? I went from the tents of Amhara to sleeping in Brezhnev's bed.

I don't remember the Brezhnev story.

When we were recording *Achtung, Baby,* the night we flew into Berlin was the last of the old divided city. And our tour manager, Dennis Sheehan, had found the old Soviet guesthouses for the old Soviet leaders. I happened to be sleeping in Brezhnev's room. What a laugh! This was a brown room. All I remember is there was brown everywhere, and very large knobs on everything, even on the stereo. If I haven't told you, I should probably. It's a complete distraction to go back to Berlin, but if you want, I will, because the most extraordinary thing happened as we were living in that house. For our very first night, there were celebrations.

Oh yeah, when you joined the wrong crowd and found yourselves with people who were demonstrating against the destruction of the wall. I'm not surprised that happened to you. *[laughs]*

How perfect is that? U2 chills out. We want to be part of the parade and the fun, and have celebrations. We're looking around, and we're going: "These people, they really don't know how to have fun, do they?" We'd heard about Bierkellers and we thought: "This is not looking like the Berliners we've heard about . . ." Then we find out: "Oops! These people are protesting the Wall coming down. They're diehard Communists." It's just a great photograph, isn't it? "U2 protests Wall coming down."

You're digressing again. In that speech at the University of Pennsylvania, you said: "I've tried them all out: the smirk, the tired joke . . ." What is it that you tried exactly?

That smirk annoys me, whenever I see it. Mostly, it's the sign that I'm uncomfortable. It's like a nervous twitch. There was an amazing moment when we played the Super Bowl recently, the finale of America's football league. It's a hyper-event in the U.S., the biggest date of the year. We had to build the stage in six minutes. Our idea was to have a music crowd on the pitch and then walk through that crowd to get up on the stage. I had on these earphones that were wireless. The band are walking through the crowd and there's a camera right in front of me, and the punters start slapping me on the back. I realize that the tiny wires of my earplugs are vulnerable. All one person has to do is pull the wire, and I'm off air. I would hear nothing. Off the air in front of a billion people! And this is going out live, and there's nothing you could do. So because this wire had been left exposed, I just started to quietly panic. But if you look at the film of that, you'll see me swaggering with the most annoying smirk ever seen. You just think: that guy is such a prat! *[laughs]* The confidence, you just hate it. I hate anyone with that much confidence. Confidence gets you not very far in this life. But for me, it's a sure sign of pure panic.

I still don't know exactly what you were trying out with that smirk. You were suggesting an intentional change of image.

I always felt like a part-time pop star, never fully comfortable with the role. For a few years, I put on rock stars' clothes and a rock star confidence to see where it would get me. I was surprised.

So where did it get you?

Everywhere.

Which means?

It was more fun than I thought.

But you seem to regret it.

No. Insecurity can take you a long way. That smirk opened doors.

You're still not answering. What did they open to?

A concept.

What?

The importance of not being earnest.

And was it painful?

Oh yeah . . . *[laughs]* Agony!

And now you're over it.

Not quite. It's fun being a rock star . . . sometimes.

In that "glasnost" period, even though you worked with Amnesty and Greenpeace, Africa was not on your agenda. But was it on your mind?

No, sadly. Not as much as it should have been. A little, yes, but not a lot. I remember Ali and myself flying back from Africa the first time. And the first few days in Europe again, it was culture shock. We had a lot more difficulty re-entering than we had landing in Africa, and figuring that out. We said to each other: "We'll never forget what we've been through." But we did. We got on with our lives. When we said grace at dinner tables, we said it a little stronger. We meant it. Food tasted a little more. But you just get on with your life, and you slowly find a place to put Africa, this beautiful, shining continent with all its ups and downs. Occasionally, you'd take it out, you'd look at it again, and then you'd put it back in that safer place called distance and time. But there was one thing I always knew. There was a structural aspect to this problem that we had witnessed. That's where I wanted to put my energy the next time round.

So Jubilee 2000 and DATA led you back to that continent for the first time in more than ten years. But had you met Nelson Mandela when U2 played in Cape Town for the PopMart tour?

No, I hadn't, but we met Archbishop Tutu. Nelson Mandela's story is one of the great stories of the twentieth century. But Archbishop Tutu's is one of the great stories of the twenty-first century.

And why is that?

Because the lessons of his Commission for Truth and Reconciliation can be applied to the Middle East, can be applied to Ireland, can be applied to Kosovo, can be applied to so many places. This is the most important story of the last fifty years. Somehow, they realized, this new African leadership, that truth sometimes is more important than justice. So on the grounds of not being prosecuted, they offer people a chance to come forward and confess to their crimes under apartheid, be they police, be they from black to brown, from brown to black, whatever crimes were committed. You remember the awful "burning necklace." Those were horrific crimes. But they didn't set up law courts. They began a new kind of convention where you will see a policeman standing in front of the family he has abused, and the man of the house, the tin hut, is saying to the policeman: "Did you see a woman wearing an olive green dress that day?" And the policeman says: "I can't remember the colors."—"Her name was Melinda, and she was wearing a green dress.

Did you see her? Do you remember shooting her? She was my wife." And the policeman, with tears rolling down his face, is going: "I don't remember her. I just remember shooting into the crowd." I mean, it's devastating. But Archbishop Tutu felt that the country needed to come clean if it was to go forward, that it needed to repent, and that maybe prosecution was not as important as that. It's an amazing thing, you must find and write about. U2 went to visit that center on that trip, my first trip to Africa in ten years. And the four of us arrived. It was overwhelming. He brought us in to this place of Truth and Reconciliation. We were dumbstruck, but it was not without comedy. I remember this great man rebuking me . . . *[laughs]* It was really a turning point.

How did he rebuke you?

I was making polite conversation with him. He's known by his people as "The Arch." So it was like: "The Arch, this is The Edge." He was laughing all the time, big-hearted, big-brained smiling man. Then I said: "You're so busy with all these things. Do you get any time for prayer and meditation?" He stopped at me and said: "What are you talking about? Do you think we'd be able to do this stuff if we didn't?" I felt it was like a rebuke to my own life, because I get so busy, and I have so many things on. At that time, I'm not sure I was spending as much time as I would like in reflection, in prayer and meditation. Not that I'm a monk, but I do like to spend some of the time in quietness, and I hadn't been. I remember it felt like a rebuke.

That's what you felt, but he probably didn't mean it that way.

Yeah, maybe. He is a comedian. When he laughs, the sky, the trees, the room change shape. For a saint, he's quite wily. He said: "I've some people that I'd like you to meet, who work in this Truth and Reconciliation program. Would you be up for meeting them?" So we said: "OK. Yeah, sure . . ." We walked up, and there was a room with six hundred people. And he ushered us in. *[impersonating]* "Ladies and gentlemen, I have brought to you the group from Ireland, they're going to play for you . . . U2!" We just looked at each other. It was like:

there's not even an acoustic guitar, what are we gonna play? We thought it was a photo op, you know, pressing the flesh, shaking hands.

So what did you do?

We sang a cappella.

What did you sing?

Err . . . "Amazing Grace."

The four of you? Even Adam?

[laughs] I wouldn't call it singing! They joined in, they've got much better voices. But his is a story of Grace in action. It's Grace interrupting Karma again, that's what Truth and Reconciliation's about. So actually it felt like the right song. And then I think we sang "I Still Haven't Found What I'm Looking For."

Did the crowd know the words?

To "I Still Haven't Found What I'm Looking For"? They knew the chorus, though, pop life being what it is. Elevators, Holiday Inn bands, they probably never heard us singing it. Actually, the band is pretty popular in South Africa. I hope they'll figure it out.

What kind of feeling did you get from the crowd in South Africa? Did they react in the same way a crowd in Europe or America would react, or was it something completely different?

Well, you know, whenever you're playing big events in South Africa, you're excited about integration and what they've been through and survived—apartheid. But now having survived that, they have to face the AIDS emergency. You just think: these people are so resilient and so amazing. You go and you play a gig, it's like "Spot the black people." *[laughs]* You're looking out at a sort of Irish audience. They look Irish . . . OK, maybe it's ten percent, but it's just that culturally they're not into rock music. That's no big deal, but it's funny. The end of apartheid is everywhere but in music. *[laughs]*

What was it like when you met Nelson Mandela for the first time?

We didn't see him on the first trip. I met him in his house outside Cape Town. One of the houses, I'm not sure where. It was a beautiful house on a sunny day. He was sitting with some of his family near him. Big beautiful trees outside the window. He's just a very beautiful man in his demeanor as well as his spirit. He says to me *[impersonating]:* "What would you be coming to see an old man like me for?" Immediately turning it right around . . . It makes you burst out laughing! He always does that.

Was it easy for you to make a connection? I mean, he's such a monument.

Well, he doesn't behave like one. He's a lesson in humility. If Tutu is "grace in action," he's "forgiveness in action," bears no malice. Within six months of leaving prison after twenty-three years, he had befriended a lot of his one-time enemies. His re-entry into the real world of politics and compromise was supersonic. Having once proclaimed he would nationalize the diamond industry, he quickly copped on that maybe they were not the best people to be in charge of South Africa's great national resources and employment centers. He made friends with commerce. Diamonds, as it turns out, are more to do with show business than you think. There are far more diamonds in the ground than any jeweler would like you to know. It's by very careful manipulation of the market that they keep their value. It's not a cartel, but the diamond industry is very shrewd: one false move, and a happy couple's wedding ring would not be such a family treasure. Things like that say a lot about him and his Cabinet when they took power. How they avoided bloodshed and bile in the transition is one of the great miracles of the age.

What makes Mandela so different?

His imagination. His ability to see, taste, and almost touch a future that wasn't yet there. Most people in his situation would have focused on what they had lost—the past. He's only thinking about the future. I read an article about his amateur painting. He was eighty years old at the time, telling the journalist that this love of painting would come in handy when he retires. That's hardcore.

You've appeared onstage with Mandela. When was the first time?

I went to an event with him we both agreed to in Barcelona. The event had not a great name, but memorably so—it was called "Frock and Roll"! It was fashion and music coming to the aid of the Nelson Mandela Fund. My friend Naomi Campbell was organizing it. We had agreed to go, but there had been all kinds of confusion with the promoter, and the city had turned on the event, and nobody knew whether it was happening or not happening. People, right up to the last day, were just pulling out. In the end, I think it was myself, Wyclef Jean, Alexander McQueen, Galliano, and a couple of other people. But at seven o'clock, there were about 500 people in the 20,000-seater arena. At eight o'clock there was about 2,000. Mandela was supposed to walk on at eight o'clock. So they held him back. There had been confusion. People thought the gig was canceled or whatever. And we waited until eight-thirty. There were about 4,000. People must have gone home to get their sisters and brothers. The organizers didn't want to worry him, so they turned the lights down.

You mean they tried to fool him into thinking that there were lots of people at the event.

Yeah, in a nice way. But this is a man who can't be fooled very easily. And I walked out with him, me on the left and Naomi on the other side. We stood there, the small crowd clapped and cheered him as they should, and he just took the microphone and he said, looking out with his wise eyes *[impersonating]*: "It is a dangerous thing to have high expectations. And I'll admit to you I had high expectations coming to Barcelona." The crowd grew a little restless.

Not to mention you, I suppose.

I start staring at my shoes. He leaves a long pause that has everyone sweating, and with perfect dramatic timing continues: "I want you people to know this is a welcome I could never ever deserve or expect. Thank you for coming out to see me and for supporting the Nelson Mandela Foundation. It is a matter of great honor and pride that you have all come!" I looked out at the crowd . . . and suddenly it looks full! It is the same amount of people, it just didn't look empty anymore. Because that's the way he sees the world. If you spent twenty-odd years in the slammer, every day you're out is a good day. As I say, his modesty is overpowering. He taught me a real lesson there about our way of seeing the world. I remember when we were kids, looking out, asking our manager: "How many people are in the hall?" He'd say: "Well, there's 120. Capacity is 500, but it looks fine, it looks OK . . ." I remember feeling sick, or playing to eleven people in Bristol. It was just wonderful. We always tried to play our best, whoever turns up. But, Nelson Mandela teaching, it was a just a great way of seeing the world—that what you have in your hands is more than enough sometimes.

You just brought up the topic of performance. Something just crossed my mind. Haven't you ever had a weird feeling while onstage in front of adoring people, worshipping you whatever you do?

[interrupting] But they're not worshipping us . . .

OK, they're not worshipping you. But I mean, they're ready to have the time of their life whatever you do, even if you're on a bad day, even if the sound is shit, and I've certainly experienced this kind of night. Isn't that weird for you?

Well, you see, I don't think they will. As I've told you before, I think the screaming and those deep roars are for themselves. That's the thing that's going on in a U2 show, in fact a lot of rock shows. People are screaming their souls out, they're screaming for themselves, because their lives are wrapped up in those songs. So one starts, and then they go off. You see, it's not about us—it's about them. If we weren't great, they wouldn't be there the next time. That's just the way it is. People are discerning, and tickets cost money. The reason people are there is because we really give a lot of ourselves in our live shows. So I don't see it as that sort of adoring crowd thing. I think that's almost a Hollywood idea. What's going on is much more complex than that. They're not really adoring.

Really? Are you serious?

An amazing thing happened in Chile—it has happened more than a few times. I think you might call it dissent. Whatever you call it, I think it disproves your theory of adoration.

I'm all ears.

In Chile, we played our song "Mothers of the Disappeared," a very controversial song in that country. Lots of families had children "disappeared" while in the custody of "government police." We asked for the show to be televised that night. Most of the population couldn't afford tickets and be able to see it. I brought the *madres* out on to the stage, and they said the names of the missing children into the microphone. Then I spoke to Pinochet as if he was there, as if he was watching television, which I'm sure he wasn't. I just said: "Mister Pinochet, God will be your judge, but at the very least, tell these women where the bones of their children are buried, because years later they still don't know where their loved ones are, you see . . ." They reckon that he does, or some general does. And this crowd divided quickly into two halves. One half cheered, and one half booed, because there are still mixed feelings about what went on. I thought: "Wow! This is not all just people who are on our side. They don't agree with us, they're letting us know, here . . ." Two songs later, they were back cheering again. People are smart. They don't have to agree with you all the time. The rock audience, the U2 audience, does tend to be smarter than your average bear. They're not like a bunch of arty-farty types, they're not intellectuals, but they're thinking people.

I guess music isn't about what you think. It's much more about what you feel. And U2's music is no exception.

That's absolutely right. A feeling is much stronger than a thought.

But U2 has always been about ideas as well. Maybe there's a contradiction here.

Well, I don't see it is a contradiction. I think they work side by side. Anyway, I'm gonna have to run.

16. FAITH VERSUS LUCK

In June 2004, I went back to Killiney for the first time in eighteen months. My ambition to "sit down together and read through the manuscript" with Bono had been conjured up several times, but always postponed. So it was looking good. After a quick cup of coffee in the kitchen, Ali left and the house seemed deserted. Before we got started, Bono was anxious for me to listen to a few songs the band had just completed. One of them was "Sometimes You Can't Make It on Your Own," which he'd previously sung at his father's funeral. Neither CD system, either in the kitchen or in the study, seemed to work. So we eventually listened to the unfinished studio CD through his daughter Eve's ghetto blaster. I made the predictable joke about the shoemaker's children who always go barefoot. It had been the same at Elton John's place, Bono revealed.

I remember Bono telling me that U2 fans knew him better than his best friends, because he sings through his fans' headphones directly into their ears. Well, may I contradict him? He *does* sing in the ears of his friends. As the song was playing and I was sitting next to him, he kept on interrupting, singing over his own lines like an annoying passenger in a car. Except, it was not annoying—it was moving. The three songs I heard made a huge impression, especially "City of Blinding Lights": here was the original sadness and

pounding melancholy of old U2, shot through with the same desperate crav-
ing. The band sounded twenty-five years old but at the same time reborn.

Anyway, things—and that didn't exactly come as a surprise—didn't go
according to the plan. Sure, Bono was available for a couple of hours, but the
idea of "reading through" the manuscript was out of the question. I was the
only one to bring a text all scribbled through with question marks and inci-
dental questions. Bono had no idea where his copy was and did not seem to
really care. I found one of the chapters lying next to the phone, one of his answers covered with a cryptic circle in the middle (no, not a coffee-cup ring).
I needed him to talk more about his father and his childhood. It felt like he'd
been a bit reticent about it. You already know the result; it found its way inside chapters 1, 2, and 4 of this book.

I remember that just as the gates opened to let his new Maserati get
through ("We shouldn't leave everything to the Germans," he pronounced),
he sang along to "Vertigo," the new U2 single, which sounded like an undis-
covered punk-rock stroke of genius from 1979. I noticed an unexpected pair
standing there by the gates, waiting to get a glimpse of Bono: a dignified
father and his young son, waving with a kind of humble pride at King Bono
driving his own coach. It seemed to me they were paying their respects to a
nineteenth-century poet and national hero, not a rock star.

Just a couple of weeks later, we talked again on the phone. It turned out
we had the same topic in mind. The news had just been announced in the *Wall
Street Journal* that Bono was joining the board of Elevation Partners, a new
venture capital firm. This is how Robert A. Guth's report read:

> *Bono, lead singer for rock band U2 and antipoverty activist, is starting*
> *a new gig: media and entertainment investing. The 44-year-old rock*
> *star is joining Elevation Partners, a new Silicon Valley fund set up ear-*
> *lier this year by veteran technology investor Roger McNamee and John*
> *Riccitiello, who in April left his post as president of videogame maker*
> *Electronic Arts Inc. for Elevation. Fred Anderson, 60, who retired ear-*
> *lier this month as Apple Computer Inc.'s finance chief, also will join*
> *Elevation. The participation of Bono should sharply raise the profile of*
> *Elevation, which people familiar with the fund say initially will raise*

*$1 billion for buyouts and investments in media and entertainment
companies, seeking to profit from turmoil in those sectors. Elevation is
expected to look for investment opportunities in media and entertainment companies disrupted by the advent of the Internet and other digital technologies. Music, movies, publishing and other traditional media
industries are grappling with how to exploit new distribution means—
including the Internet or cellular phones—while stemming piracy that
such technologies enable.*

Once again, Bono found a way to bring up the subject of Africa as he was answering my third question. But I guess I found a deft way too to maneuver
that devil.

I think I'm going to address the businessperson today.

Sure. Have you seen the *Wall Street Journal* piece this week?

**Yes, I'll be getting to that. But I was wondering how I should address you now
that you are a co-chairman of that board: "Mister President," maybe? That
reminds me of a silly yet funny story that my father used to tell me. He was
raised in Milan. You're aware that Italians love grand-sounding titles, to such
a degree that calling someone "Sir"—"*Signore*"—may be close to insulting
him. There is a man crossing some street in Milan, quite absentmindedly,
and a car is just ten seconds away from hitting him. Someone is desperately
trying to call for his attention: "*Attenzione, dottore!*" No reaction. Then he
calls out louder: "*Avvocato, attenzione!*" Still no reaction. Then, he goes at the
top of his voice, wringing his hands: "*Commendatore! Attenzione!*" But the
man wouldn't turn round. And nobody in that street dares to say *Signore!* So
bang, the car crashes into the unfortunate man, and he's lying dead on the
road, surrounded by a crowd of onlookers with their mouths wide open. So
after I read about this *Wall Street Journal* thing, I was thinking: Now, how
shall I address Bono in his new capacity? I mean, it might be dangerous for
you if people dare not address you as Bono anymore. How about: "You dirty
capitalist pig"? Will that do the trick? [Bono laughs heartily]**

Guilty, your honor! Yeah, that's a high compliment, pretty good for me. Pigs are useful. They're the cleanest animal in the farmyard, and they bring home the bacon.

I'd like to get into the details of your glorious life as a pig. Did you really want to be that pig in the first place? In U2, are you the born businessman of the group?

Well, the first time we went to get a record deal, I went as the band's manager *[laughs],* which was interesting, because Paul [McGuinness] had, rather wisely perhaps, said: "You're not ready for a record deal." He didn't want to go around the record labels until we had better songs. But I thought our songs had something. So I went to London with Ali. We were eighteen and seventeen years old in 1978. I'd never been before. It was a very special trip for us. We stayed in a guesthouse. I brought the demo tape around to record companies, and then to the *NME, Sounds,* and *The Record Mirror.* So I remember I would drop in with the tape, I'd give it to a journalist I had read and wanted to meet, and ask them to listen. Usually they would say: "Look, if I like it, I'll give you a call back." And I would interrupt: "Well, then I'll call you in an hour." *[laughs]* And they were going: "What?"

It's true. That's the way it happened, in those days. You'd push the door open into the editorial office of a rock mag. It wasn't guarded, or anything, and you'd propose your stuff, be it a tape or an article.

They were all so very kind to me, those writers. After hawking the music around, two record companies were interested in offering us a deal. Now this was before we'd had a management contract with Paul. So he got a bit of a fright when I came home. We had two record companies wanting to make a deal, and he wasn't even signed up as a manager. He quickly signed us up. Look, we never did close those deals. But the point is I always felt that with the gift comes the urge to bodyguard it. I never bought into the cliché "I'm the artist. Keep me away from the filthy lucre and the tawdry music-business world." It's just complete horseshit. It's horseshit! It's been going on for years.

I just want to say: "Stop that!" Because I know I've grown up with a lot of these bands. Some of them are the most awful, selfish, darkest individuals you could find. And some of the people in the record company who go home to their wives at night might be people you'd rather go on vacation with. I know some incredibly inspired business people, and ethical, and I know some real assholes with a golden voice. So I just don't have that picture of the world.

So what was the first important business decision that you made?

Within our band, we started a kind of cooperative where we published everything equally amongst us. That quickly got all those arguments that normally happen in bands about whose song is going on the album and whose song isn't. This was at the behest of Paul, and established a pattern of extraordinarily smart advice over the years. It was Paul who felt that it would be a great thing if we could keep ownership of our songs and our copyrights, and even our master tapes. So at one point, I think it was, like, 1985, we renegotiated our deal with Island Records, took lower royalties, but at the end of the day, meaning after the contracts concluded, as I think I already told you, all the master tapes and the copyright would return to us. Another thing I will be forever grateful to Chris Blackwell for.

So very soon, U2 was tainted by the filthy lucre and the tawdry music-business world.

U2 were never dumb in business. We just had a strong sense of survival in us. We essentially became our own record company, living in Dublin, not in London, or New York, or Los Angeles. We don't sit around wondering about world peace all day long. We're not sitting around like a bunch of hippies. We're from punk rock, and we're on top of it. I wish we were more on top of it, but that's an important part of that story. I've just been out, speaking to various people in business. They are completely bewildered when I tell them my story. I mean, they have no idea. They think that the record company came up with the name U2! Or they think that our manager was the person who planned our pathway to success. It couldn't be further from the truth. Paul

McGuinness mentored us in principles that proved to be the best there were, and the record company helped us in our journey. But we are very much in charge of our own destiny, and have been always. I think that's really important.

I remember you described yourself as a "traveling salesman." *[Bono laughs]* I mean, many artists would rather hide their business-savvy side.

Yeah. No! Particularly, I've had an epiphany in recent years about commerce, for my work in Africa. It has upended everything for me. You start to see that Africans are looking for a commercial way out. One of Africa's big problems is trying to foster an entrepreneurial culture. And so you start to see that they get the thin end of the capitalist wedge. But there is a wide end. Globalization has become a pejorative term, but it's meaningless. Globalization is like saying communication. Globalization has happened formally since deregulating international flow of money, going back to the eighties. But before that, you could say that globalization started with the sail and trade. And it turns out that the sail has done more good . . .

. . . than evil . . .

. . . than evil. Africa needs more globalization now than less. I think it's really funny. "Globalization! What's it doing to Africa?" And Africans are saying: "What do you mean? We can't get any!" What critics mean is the abuse of globalization.

I think that you're dodging the topic.

What I'm saying is: I've started to set up a few companies. I started to see commerce—conscious commerce—as the way forward for Africa. As an example, I've set up a company with my wife and the designer Rogun, called Edun. It's a clothing line. We're launching this in the spring of this year [2005]. We've invested a lot of time, energy, and capital in it. It's an amazing thing. I want it to work as a business, I want it to make profit, but I also want it to contribute something to all the people in the chain. We have this concept of "four respects" at the heart of our company: One, respect for where the clothes are made. We want them eventually to be all made in Africa, but certainly the developing world. Two, respect for who makes them. Three, respect for the materials that they are made of. We're trying to use organic cotton when we can. Four, respect for the people who are going to buy them—the consumer. We want to do business with Africa, because that's what they want. I want to facilitate that. And I want to say: you can make profit without ripping people off, consumer or manufacturer. We want our clothes to tell their story, and the story to be a great one. Because when you buy a pair of jeans, the story of those jeans, where the cotton was grown, who grew it, how the sewers in the factory were treated, those stories are all woven into your jeans, like it or not. If there is a happy beginning, middle, and end, I mean if everyone in the process was treated fairly, well, then [laughs] when you put on those clothes, you're going to feel better about them and yourself. There's going to be some good Karma. But not if they were made by children. Ali said to me: "I want to buy children's clothes that aren't made by children." So I am getting very excited by these ideas of commerce now.

Is Edun anything like your other company, Nude?

"Edun" is "Nude" in reverse. Nude, my brother and I started as a good-for-you fast-food chain. At the moment, it's turning into a line of body-conscious products that will be made, like chocolate and coffee, in Africa, and makeup products from India. It's just exciting, creating a product range, where again, the story of the products, and how they got there, is something you want to buy into as well as the product itself.

But, Bono, you are a performer in a band. That's your first job. You've turned into a part-time humanitarian crusader. And now you're on the verge of becoming an almost full-time businessman. Aren't you afraid that this is all going to carry you farther away from the U2 mystique? Or, to quote a word that you used in Bologna, from the "sexiness" of being in a rock band?

But it's never gonna be. I do all my business one day a week. And if I can't do it in one day, I don't want to do it. That's it. I'm doing this with my wife. So Ali does this. And the same with the Elevation Partners fund. I told them I've got one day a week for this.

Sorry for the cliché, but it's not very rock 'n' roll, is it?

I think there's a lot of baggage carried over from the sixties, that says a musician shouldn't be a businessman, because—hey, man!—you're supposed to be out there, man, just smoking the weed, putting your toes in the river, surrounded by a bunch of beautiful girls combing your hair as you watch the sun come up.

Don't tell me that stuff never happened to you.

I have to say it sounds better and better now that I think about it . . . *[laughs]*

You're describing that with lots of gusto.

I did a lot of things when the sun came up in the mid-nineties. I can't think of anything better right now than having my hair washed. I loved the sixties. It was the renaissance of pop. But these are different times demanding different strategies. Look at hip-hop culture, those old biases against commerce just don't apply. It's sexy that Jay-Z has his clothing line, or Sean "P. Diddy" Combs. People like it. People want to see an entrepreneurial spirit. They don't want their stars to be out of it.

It seems like there's a kind of unconscious apartheid in music. On one side, you have urban black music, which tackles materialistic concerns head-on, and on the other, white music, which is not supposed to address money and business.

That's right. There are unwritten rules about what a rock band can do. And the rules, I am breaking them. We started dismantling them from Zoo TV, right away on. We want to take some of the good ideas of the sixties, but hopefully, we're gonna leave out some of the less rigorous ones. We're just saying: "No, not taking it." What's wrong with wanting to play arenas instead of clubs? What's wrong with selling records? What's wrong with wanting to make music that communicates on a grand scale? What's wrong with writing operas? Operas were popular . . . At the time, they were looked down upon by serious musicians. The scene of the time was: "This is just a piece of fun. Let's not take it seriously. This is not real music." So we've thrown out a lot of these ideas. They're antiquated. We can move into business, and let's bring our idealism into whatever piece of the world we happen to be standing in.

I'm still trying to see how it was born and fostered in your mind. Can you think of fellow musicians who did great things with their money?

Well, there are very few examples in music, that's my point. But one of the people who's had the most impact on my life is Bob Geldof. Firstly, just through Live Aid, I ended up in Africa. I have followed on his coattails through that journey. He encouraged me, being there for me all the way. But he also gave me confidence to be . . . who I am. You don't have to be a politician to hang out with them. You don't have to wear a suit to be a businessman. You can be yourself at all times. And you can be as bohemian as you want to be. It's about the quality of ideas. That's really what Bob's all about. Bob's great hero is Samuel Pepys, a seventeenth-century English naval administrator and businessman.* In the end, it's ideas that turn us on, whether they are philosophical, commercial, or political. What I would call them is melodies. I think we talked about this. I need to hear a great melody even if it's not in a song.

Lots of people come up with brilliant ideas. But life teaches you that most of the time many obstacles prevent those ideas from turning into realities. I mean, we discussed the discrepancies between great ideas and not so great realities in Africa. Sometimes you can't find your way around an obstacle.

Yeah, I do have a blind spot. I mean, I have a few blind spots. *[laughs]* But one of them is: I don't sometimes see obstacles.

*Samuel Pepys (1633–1703) is most renowned for his *Diaries*.

Sure, but you must bump into them at some point.

Yeah, I've had a few black eyes. I mean, I know I have to climb them all the time. But it's usually been very fortunate for me. If I'd seen the obstacles, I might have just left the idea lie. But fortunately, U2 has usually been able to overcome those obstacles by finding brilliant people. We always knew that if we didn't know, we'd find somebody who did. And so, in U2, we've surrounded ourselves with the best people in business. Lawyers and accountants, and record company, and people who run our companies are the best at their job, and I think that makes overcoming the obstacles a lot easier. Look, we're gonna find out. I mean, this clothing line, Edun, this is a whole new way of doing business. I'm told that the rag trade makes the music business look like a church fête. *[laughs]* And the sharks will circle, and I'm about to become shark soup. So we'll see. But I've found some people in the business at the top end who are guiding myself and Ali. I think that they'll help us negotiate these dangerous waters.

Speaking of sharks, have you ever gotten bitten in your career as a businessman? And did it leave a scar?

Yeah, we've made mistakes in our business.

What was the biggest one?

We made a lot of money from the sale of Island Records, because we owned a piece of it. And we put it in the hands of some people whom we liked personally, but weren't as expert as they thought in the areas that they were investing in. And we lost a lot of money.

What sort of business did they handle?

It was a portfolio of investments. There were some great ones, and some, they just were really not great ideas, and we gave them a lot of money. As this one particular ship started to sink, rather than us jumping out, the man in charge of the fund kept spending more of our money to keep it afloat. I know it's with hindsight, but I think anyone would have known that the ship, actually, when we bought it, had a hole in it. *[bursts out laughing]* So we learnt a lot. I don't want to be too flip here. Losing money was not a nice feeling, and you've got to be careful because nothing begins the love of money more than the loss of money. But on the positive side it made us take more charge and interest in our business. This was, I guess, very early nineties. We had to take our financial matters very seriously, which means, when you're involved with dealing this kind of money, you do need to take extra care not just that the cash can warp the people around you, but that it can get to you too. *[laughs]* Because money is a big thing, especially if you don't have it. You have to give it respect, but you don't want to give it too much of your love. So it means we have to sit the band in rooms, when we'd rather be making music, going through boring shit. But if you do it right, it means you only have to do that once a month, or, in my case, once a week.

But does plotting business strategy give you a thrill, the way it would to a chess player figuring out a couple of moves in advance?

Perhaps in some sort of odd way. I do love watching people work together, and build something together. When we're making music, I'd say it's like making a chair. Björk used to say that to me *[impersonates accent]:* "I'm a ploom-errrr ... and we make ploo-ming." *[laughs]* The idea that artists are different from everybody else is a dangerous idea, an arrogant one.

I also feel like you're a manipulator sometimes. There's a part of you that might be called ... I don't know, "perverse" might be going a little too far ...

[interrupting] No, not a lot. *[laughs]*

But it's something that I find really funny about you. Lots of people perceive you as very candid, full of Irish exaltation ...

Irish whiskey, more like.

Probably. But, I feel, at the same time, you're a gambler, or a chess player . . .

I really don't feel like a gambler. And the reason I like the game of chess is because each move has countless repercussions, but you're in charge of them. And it's your ability to see into the future and the effects of the decisions you've made that makes you either a good or not a good chess player. It's not luck. By the way, I'm no longer a good chess player, as it happens. But I think . . . gambling, you don't know what's going to happen. And I never want to be in that situation. I think in business, you have to rule out as much accident as possible.

Have you ever gambled in Vegas or Monte Carlo, just for the adrenaline rush?

Very occasionally.

Did you win or lose?

I've been very lucky, and very unlucky. Funny, that. But I don't do it very often. I'm fascinated by casinos for other reasons. Faith versus Luck. It's a favorite subject.

Funny. I thought you were one hundred percent on the side of Faith.

Yeah, but I like to know what I'm up against. Luck is the opposite, if not opponent, of Faith. But let me illustrate by a complete contradiction. I had a very strange experience many years ago. A friend of mine was getting married, and he was broke. So was I. And I knew somewhere that somehow, some way, I was going to be able to help pay for his wedding. I didn't know how, but I knew I would be. I was like a child that believed that every prayer would be answered. I haven't really changed in that. I think every prayer is answered, but unfortunately, "No" happens much more than we'd like. *[laughs]* I didn't know that then. So I thought to myself in my naiveté, in my childish way: "Oh, you know, at the back of a corn flakes box, they have these competitions and you can win a car. Maybe I should send away one of those. I bet I will win and I'll give him the car." Anyway, I never did send the back of the corn flakes box, and his wedding was getting closer and closer. I thought in my daftness: "I'll win it on a horse..." So the Grand National, which is the biggest race in Ireland, was coming up on the weekend. I said: "That's it. OK, I just need to get a tip." Anyway, I'm just getting to know Ali's parents. We were still kids, we were like eighteen or nineteen, actually. So when they asked us to go away for the weekend with them to County Cork, it was a big deal. Ali was excited; I was nervous: one, because they were sussing me out, and two, because we might miss the race. So we were both nervous. I was thinking: "Oh, damn! The Grand National. I won't be able to go." But on the afternoon of the race, we found ourselves in a pub called the Swan and Signet, in Cork. So I was sitting there, thinking: "What am I to do? There's only fifteen minutes to go. I haven't a clue about horses," when—I'm not kidding—this kind of tramp, some odd character, walked out of the gents with a dog, and gave me a tip. I can't remember, unfortunately, the name of the horse. Something like Rolled Gold: "Rolled Gold for the National!" he whispered under his breath. So I went: "There it is. OK, I've got the tip." I turned around, swallowed hard, and said to Ali, her father and mother: "Look, I know this sounds mad, but I'd really like to make a bet in the Grand National." And they said: "Really? But aren't you broke?" I said: "I'd just like to put a pound on it."—"All right, OK. If you really want to." They were kind of disapproving, but we went to the bookies, and I sneakily put twenty pounds on Rolled Gold. So we went in, and I had twenty pounds. There was, I think, two pounds tax. I put eighteen on the horse. It was ten to one, this horse. After we left the bookies, I told them the story: I have a friend, he's getting married, he's broke. I want to give him the money, and I've had this feeling I'd be able to help him. I was so sure of the tip. And they said: "What?" And I said: "Yeah." And they just looked at me with the kind of half smile parents have when their daughter brings home the wrong boyfriend. I told them I didn't even want to watch the race. I was so sure of myself. Is this Faith? I don't know. You tell me. Then we went off for a walk. Two hours later, Ali's father, Terry, said: "Do you want to go back and see who won the National?" I said: "No, I'm not in any rush. I know who's going to win." And so, three hours later, we went back. I can't remember how much it was—nearly five hundred pounds. I gave it to my friend, and he got married. It was a funny one. Ali's father gets a laugh out of telling that story. I'm not sure what to make of it myself. Proof God has a sense of humor . . . A fluke? A cautionary tale about blind faith? Or, if you do—somewhere in the back of your subconsciousness—know some funny stuff . . .

So was it Faith or Luck?

I like to think Faith.

So, back to the Elevation Fund. I'm really curious to learn about your strategy with the music industry. There is a part of the *Wall Street Journal* piece that really puzzled me: "Elevation's expected to look for investment opportunities in media and entertainment companies disrupted by the advent of the Internet and other digital technologies. Music, movies, publishing, and other traditional media industries are grappling with how to exploit new distribution means—including the Internet and cellular phones—while stemming piracy that such technologies enable." Stemming piracy? How will you pull that off?

[laughs in slow motion like a Frenchman] Just for once, Michka, could you not ask the hard question? The "how" is not clear, but I can answer the "why." Look, there's a moment when you can feel a tremor in the ground underneath your feet. And then there's another moment when there is no ground underneath your feet. We are about to enter a phase with music and film, where everything is changing, where things like the way music is bought and sold will change the kind of music that is bought and sold. As an example, in the downloading of music, pop kids are not buying the whole album. They're just cherry-picking the best songs off the Internet. With pop music, they made the money on the album, not on the single. The single just lured the young kids to buy the album, half of which would be of no interest.

But kids aren't buying these albums anymore. I mean, mine don't. My son, who's fourteen now, is quite content with Nirvana's back catalog. And my daughter, who's eleven, developed a passion for an old Bangles album. I don't know about yours, but my kids don't seem to be great consumers for the music industry, yet they're big fans of music technology.

Madonna didn't want to sell her songs individually online because she felt that she'd made albums, and she didn't want people to be able to just break in and take a few songs, which I understand. But it's a little like King Canute, the king who sat with his chair in front of the waves and told the tide not to come in. Because people are cherry-picking your songs, whether you like it or not. Like Madonna, U2 will be very, very anxious that people buy our whole album rather than cherry-pick the songs, but we still feel a commitment to let people make that decision for themselves.

What's been happening since *How to Dismantle an Atomic Bomb* was released? Have people mainly been cherry-picking or buying the album?*

I should find out the exact percentage, but I'm happy to report from this most downloaded band, most people want the album.

Even though "Vertigo" has been the most downloaded song in the world in 2004, your point is that it affects rock music less than pop. I would say you and Madonna don't exactly play in the same field.

I would give Madonna more credit than that, but it is less of a problem in rock music than it is in pop. Rock fans have historically been more interested in an album format. So there is an example of how investment in pop will change if there's no way to sell that audience the album anymore. That was where the music industry got its return. The amount of money that's spent on promoting these kinds of pop stars will drop or be redirected to different genres where the album format is still alive. Take Norah Jones. She comes from jazz, she's the most gifted interpretive singer around. She couldn't be further from what they look for on *Pop Idol;* but she's a sales phenomenon, because people over thirty are buying her records.

Sure. They must be people like me. I've never figured out how to burn CDs.

*That question obviously was a last-minute addition.

That's exactly right. A lot of them don't know how to download. There's a huge audience there, that's been ignored for years, whilst eighty percent of energy and cash is spent on marketing music to people under twenty-five. New distribution models are going to make the face of the music industry unrecognizable from what it is today. Another phenomenon is telephony. Telephony is changing the way we communicate: texting. The very syntax and design of sentences have been changed. Wait till you see what this will do to music: not just ring tones or true tones! You will be able to dial up any song at any time, watch the video if you want, find out where the band is playing near you and buy tickets. What I'm really trying to say is: I'm excited about the future. It's coming fast, and I don't want to be run over by it. I want U2 to be a part of the future and a part in shaping the future. This opportunity with Elevation Partners is for me a chance to involve myself in the business that runs my life. I don't want to be a casualty. I don't want to be bullied by the business in the future. I heard a story. Jack Lemmon is in a meeting with a major Hollywood bigwig at the peak of his powers. He's pitching something he's been working on for years. This great genius of American cinema is halfway through his pitch, and the phone rings. Bigwig picks up the phone, goes: "OK, OK, I'll be right with you. So, listen, Jack, project sounds great, we're gonna have to get back to this. I've gotta go . . ." Jack is unceremoniously shuffled out of the building, because . . . [pauses for dramatic effect] Tom Cruise is coming in. Now, Tom Cruise would never want Jack Lemmon out of the building. He's not that kind of person. But the story really stuck with me. And I thought, you can do all the best work in the world, but there's a moment where some guy can just sit there and write you in or out. I don't want to give that power to somebody.

But don't these people already have that kind of power over U2?

No, not really. We're in control now. But there may be a moment, in five or six years, I don't know. We've got great people in the music company now, and we've got great relationships with them. Jimmy Iovine, who runs Interscope, the smartest and most successful music man of the last ten years, is like a blood relation. His commitment to us is way beyond business, and ours to him. But what if he wasn't there? What if relations weren't good with whoever was? U2 doesn't want to be in that position. The last record before *All That You Can't Leave Behind* was called *Pop*. Now, it sold, I think, 7 million albums or something, which is a huge success. But compared to what people were expecting, they were disappointed. Someone could have said: "Well, now, you know, it's the end of the nineties. You guys have had your run. We're not prepared to invest any more money in this."

Did you actually hear that?

No, no. I'm just saying it could have happened. And then *All That You Can't Leave Behind* would never have.

So your point is, given what's going on in the music business now, even the biggest sellers are in danger.

I think the music business is really traumatized. On the one hand, I don't think the music companies are making the best of their relationship with the audience. I think artist and fan have lost out in the music business. Neither benefited as they should have from the CD boom. The price of music went up because the price of production was at first high, but then it stayed there even when CDs were much more cheaply made. I think in the future there can be more for all three parties: more for the record company, more for the fan, and more for the artist, but only if we cooperate better together. Never has more music been listened to than today, in more locations. Instead of having one record player like they had in the seventies, in every American house, there is an average eight CD players. There is the car. People are listening to music when they're moving. With iPods we have the most beautiful design icon for years. I'm very proud to say that U2 has its own black iPod. It is an embarrassment to me that it took a technology person, Steve Jobs at Apple, to sort out the biggest problem in the music industry—downloading music. Apple's iTunes have proved the point that people are prepared to pay for music online as long as it's made easy and fun and reasonably priced. So I think the music business can prosper, but it's going to have to rethink itself before it does so.

But what makes you think it's going to survive anyway? Look at what Prince did. He said: "We don't need the record companies anymore. We just have to produce the music, and then we will distribute it through the Internet, so we won't be feeding any parasites in the record industry anymore."

But he didn't sell any records or CDs. Not enough anyway for an artist of his stature. That was a brave and bold move, but he underestimated how important all those people are in the process. They're not parasites. They're important. He used to have somebody going into NRJ* or Radio One and saying: "This new Prince single is great!" And they go: "How long hasn't he been around? I haven't heard anything from him . . ." And that guy goes: "No, it's great. Listen to it." And then, there's somebody going into Virgin, Tower, or the FNAC† and saying: "Prince's new album is amazing. I want to have a whole special shelf just for him. And I want to have a cardboard cutout of him." And they go: "Well, I don't know, we got Britney Spears coming through"—"No, no, Prince! He's a great artist. We need him. Please." They have a relationship. In Nice, or Paris, or Santiago, these are people working for you, working with you. These are important people representing us. The music business is necessary.

But how will it survive in the world you're describing?

People will pay for downloads. What will happen is the download will be the paperback, and the CD will become like the hardback. But the CD, the object, will have to become a more interesting object. Instead of this little jewel box with twenty pages, this U2 album, we have a book to go with it—things you can't download. We wanted to create the art object again. *Sgt. Pepper's,* when it was released by the Beatles, wasn't just a listening experience. It was an art experience of looking and owning this incredible Peter Blake artwork. So I think that will open a few new formats, different formats. Cynics say: why would they buy a thing you can get free by stealing it? Think about bottled water. You can get water out of a tap, without risking prosecution.

*French pop radio station
†French chain of multimedia stores

Fewer people buy hardcover books than paperbacks, don't they?

Yeah, but a million people buy a twenty-five-dollar item. That's a lot of money.

How many will U2 sell?

A million.

But why are you investing in the business now? What's the urgency?

[vehemently] Because I want to understand it better! I don't understand it as well as I can. I don't like when I don't know what's coming round the corner. Some people are saying, when you turn that corner, someone's going to mug you, right? I've worked for twenty years. And we own our master tapes, we own our copyrights. I don't want that not to be worth anything. That's for our children.

So what's your vision of the future? How far do you see? We were talking about chess. How many moves in advance can you come up with?

Well, *[clears throat]* in music, the thing that I'm excited about now is how the iPod will turn into a phone. You will be able to carry your entire collection with you wherever you go on your phone. If the Internet is the freeway, your phone is the car. For the very first time, U2 is considering technology partners. We have to understand the way our music is going to be bought and sold, and the sort of systems of distribution. So now we're on to meet phone companies. We want to meet the people in Vodaphone. We like the people at Apple. Jonathan Ive, the genius who designs for Apple, if he had a fan club, I'd be in it. As I told you, Steve Jobs made the downloading of music sexy with iTunes, while the music business argued amongst themselves. He has created these beautiful objects that are Apple Macs. Even their commercials are great. We want to be in them, turn them into music videos.

I guess I see what you're getting at. But I'm not quite sure about a world where artists are becoming businessmen, and businessmen are becoming artists.

The world would certainly look different. I mean, why aren't people like this designing cars? The roads are filled with bad ideas, ugly objects with no femininity, no humor, no sex. If the job of art is to chase ugliness away, let's start with the roads and the automobiles. Let's get people like the Apple people on the case. I want to form relationships that are mutually beneficial rather than disadvantageous for U2.

Are the other members of U2 following you on that?

I think the band are getting extremely interested in this. These are people who've refused huge sums of money for relationships with commercial companies, just because they didn't feel it was a real relationship. So a car company comes to us, offers us 23 million dollars for an old song. That's a lot of money to turn down. We could have given the money away. As it happens, if it was another song, we might have said yes. But the song that they wanted, we just didn't want to see it in a car commercial. We turned down another incredible sum of money from a computer firm for "Beautiful Day." Worse than that, we liked the people involved. But we didn't, at that point, want to be working for someone. We want to work *with* someone if they give us creative control. We can collaborate if you let us into your company to play with your scientists. We're talking to various people. That was our manager's first question to Carly Fiorina of Hewlett-Packard when they approached us: "Can Edge get into the lab?" And she said: "Yes." I appreciate that all of this can look like megalomania. But what's the alternative? Just to let the world go by? To be left behind, or worse: run over, lie down in the middle of the information freeway and get hit by a truck? And you know, the truck has a "For Sale" sign on it. Why? Because it used to be delivering CDs in the old model. *[laughs]*

Aren't you also involved in video games?

Video games are now where the movies were in 1920, but they're a much less passive medium. Fathers can play with their children. Dating will never be the same again, and with giant screens and Sensurround sound, it's total immersion. It's a new global art form. Language is a barrier in movies, not in video games.

I hear in China, it's the biggest thing.

Well, you see, if the world doesn't go into recession in year 2005, it will be because of two things: because of India and China. If 200 million people in India and 200 million people in China now have disposable incomes, think about it. There's still great poverty to be overcome, but nevertheless, there's a new middle class of 400 million people in the world economy. They like our cars, our movies, and our music, especially in India, but they prefer theirs. *[laughs]* They have Bollywood there outside Delhi. In China, actually, they love video games online, so there's not even a piracy problem. If you create a great new video game, you won't just be selling it to the United States and Europe, Australia. You'll be selling it to China, to India, to everywhere. The world is a completely different size for that creative act. So what's going to happen is the same thing that's happened with movies at the turn of the century. These interactive games, because they will be so popular, will start to draw all the most creative and talented people, even away from movies and music. You should meet my friend John Riccitiello, who is the smartest guy in that business. I'm working with him in Elevation. He's a partner. I remember asking him: "How can we make video games emotional?" And he said: "Wow! Now that's a project that everyone wants to be a partner of." Am I as excited about this as I am for an AIDS vaccine? No. But there it is. It's still very important to me.

17. TIDYING MY ROOM

This last conversation happened in August 2004, in the villa owned by Bono near Nice. After nearly two years, we had to draw a line somewhere. As I am writing this, I don't seem to remember exactly what happened there, or in what order. Disconnected images flash through my head. Bono orders his sons Elijah and John to attack me in the pool . . . It's 8:15 A.M., the sun's already scorching, the house is silent, Bono and I are reading through the manuscript on my computer screen, bursting into laughter from time to time . . . Invisible Italian fans lying on the narrow beach down below are giving out a surreally sparse applause between numbers of the new U2 album played on the house CD system as the sun sets . . . White wine again . . . Ali closing the doors, not to hear the album again . . . More wine . . . A reading session ending way past midnight, Bono hardly raising an eyebrow when I say we have to go through one more chapter . . . The endless rattle of cicadas threatening to drown Bono's voice on my MiniDisc recorder . . . The two of us, at dawn, sitting side by side across the street in a nondescript café, in the midst of indifferent regulars, reading through more chapters, trying to get the language right, adding new lines . . . Bono pedaling and sweating in the gym downstairs, sitting on a machine thought up by the Devil himself . . . and finally waving good-bye with a broad smile.

I think there is something we need to make clear for this last time. Last year, you wrote and delivered long speeches in front of German bigwigs, students at the University of Pennsylvania, and not least the U.S. Congress. You turned your hand to writing a few screenplays, and your friend Wim Wenders even filmed one of them, *The Million Dollar Hotel*. Bob Dylan is about to publish the first volume of his *Chronicles*.* So, I mean, you would not be the least qualified person to write a memoir. I'm sure a lot of people will see this book and say: "Why the hell did he need that French guy with a strange name *[Bono laughs]* to tell us what matters the most to him in his life? Why didn't he do it by himself?"

It's like playing handball. I need a good hard head to be the wall. The speed of the ball is going to set the mood of the game. You're really slow.

Thank you very much.

Of course, I could have written this book, but it wouldn't have been this book. And it would have taken a year.

Or ten ... Anyway, I presume the results would not have been the same.

That's right. The results would not have been the same. It would be more interesting in some ways, because it would be even more personal. But it would be less interesting in the sense that it would not have an argument up against it. I like to be pushed, I'm familiar with being pushed. And I think, at this point in time, I have some explaining to do.

Explaining? But who's asking?

I suppose I'm talking about our audience, the ones who gave me this incredible life. The nature of magazine interviews is such that they often have to condense things into some easy quotes and explanations.

Chronicles: Volume One was published in October 2004. The book actually mentions Dylan's own conversations with Bono: "Spending time with Bono was like eating dinner on a train—feels like you're moving, going somewhere. Bono's got the soul of an ancient poet and you have to be careful around him. He can roar 'til the earth shakes."

I still don't know why you need to explain yourself to anyone.

Maybe I'm trying to explain myself to myself.

So that's what you need my hard head for.

I told you, at the beginning of this, the past is not a place I like to visit. This project is forcing me to go there, to tidy up a few things in my mind before I can move forward. I normally wouldn't give time to such thoughts. I'm not normally a navel-gazer. I've always thought you find yourself in other people. I'm visiting here. I don't want to set up house.

That's why you never thought of psychoanalysis. Or maybe I'm completely wrong. Maybe you actually did.

As I told you, this is as close as I'm going to get to introspection.

So I've become a part-time celebrity shrink. I should be ashamed.

Shrink or priest—you choose.

A cross-examining cop, while you're at it. How about bartender? I mean, I supply the booze [which I actually do each time I visit], you tell me the stories.

Perfect. Though wine can be cloudy. What we need here is probably plain ol' still water, cold and clear.

I guess a head can get too full. Maybe yours was about to burst.

I have a room, which is my brain, and it's very, very, very . . . untidy! There is stuff fallen everywhere. There are some very important ideas next to some very silly ones. There is a bottle of wine that was opened five years ago, and there is a lunch I haven't eaten from last summer. There are faces of children who are going to die but don't have to. There's my father's face telling me to tidy up my room. So that's what I'm doing—tidying my room.

And you really think talking helps you do that?

I could write it, I could paint it. I usually sing it. I usually talk my way out of things—not into them.

I know that the painter Louis Le Brocquy is an important figure for you. Also, the presence of that big Basquiat canvas in your house in Dublin makes a statement. Your best friend Guggi went on to become a painter. You do sketches yourself. You told me once that one of the most important people you've met in your life was Balthus. It seems to me that he was as important to you, in a way, as Johnny Cash.

Very similar.

Do you regret not becoming a painter?

They are two very different actions that you can do completely at the same time. You can paint and listen to music, and be in complete discipline, which is interesting. Painting strikes me as just a way of getting to those feelings that are from somewhere way off. And rather like writing songs, rather like talking to you, painting helps me clarify my mind, which is an untidy mind, and pick up the stuff off the floor. I feel better after I painted.

Would you go so far as to use the word *remorse*?

You mean a sadness that I'm not doing it? No. As I get older, I'm doing it more and more.

I didn't expect you to surrender unconditionally when I compared the importance of Louis Le Brocquy to the importance of Johnny Cash in your life.

They're both men that left me with the most important clues on how we should live. Both had incredible dignity, incredible honesty. Louis's still alive. I'm always looking for clues. Some people have them, and some people don't have any. When people don't have any clues, I'm less likely to stick around. I don't in any way consider myself to be above anybody else, but I'm just excited when I'm in the company of older people, because they have so much more to offer. Sitting there with some punk rocker who's just figured how to look good in the mirror is not really on to keep me up, nowadays. *[laughs]*

I don't know much about that relationship with Balthus.

We had a very unusual relationship. It was very intense. He lived very privately, some would say reclusively, in a place called Rossinière, in Switzerland, in this extraordinary-looking "grand chalet." I had met him through Louis Le Brocquy, who was very aware of Balthus when he was the head for the Villa Medicis [from 1961 to 1976]. He was just in his eighties then. Louis told me to bring a bottle of Irish whiskey. With his wife, Setsuko, they lived a formal nineteenth-century life, really. I just adore this woman. When I first met her, she was in traditional Japanese garb. Harumi, their daughter, has become a very good friend—she's a jewelery-maker, a very gifted girl. I also knew Stash and Theo, who were from an earlier marriage. I think I just got on with the whole family. I remember Balthus showing me a room that he had in honor of Harumi, called "the room full of toys." He made this room full of all her toys as a child, collected as art objects. Then they had another room full of birds, with these beautiful birds just flying around. It was a magical place. So whenever I was there, he wanted to say hello, and so did I. We would meet up and talk about everything: God, death, sex, painting, music. And it became ongoing, this discussion. He asked me to his eighty-fifth birthday [i.e., 1993]*. I arrived, and the room was full of friends and family, some famous faces, some down-to-earth locals, some of what you might call . . . the noble rot. *[laughs]* Old European families. It was very interesting. I felt honored to be there. There was a moment when Setsuko explained this was a costume ball. I said: "I didn't know. I don't

Balthus, born in 1908, died in 2001.

do costume balls." She came to my room and said: "Balthus has chosen something for you. He's the only other person that's going to be wearing this." And it was a ... samurai costume! *[laughs]* So, OK. So I put on the samurai costume. In the end, myself and Balthus ate together on our own, dressed as samurais. Because he wanted to talk. I don't know what it was with Ireland, or what it was with musicians, but I think he wanted to talk more about art and music. So we just spent a lot of time together. At one point, he took me into his studio. He was staring at what must have been one of his last paintings. I asked him if he was finding it difficult to paint. He said: "No, I can paint." He said: "The thing that I miss the most is drawing. I was a very good draftsman, he said, now I can't draw. It makes me feel afraid for the future." And in that moment the great man looked bereft, abandoned by the future. This man, accused of arrogance all his life, humbled himself in front of a musician. I asked him: did he pray? He looked around at all the unfinished work in the studio: "These are my prayers." And he wept. I have no words to describe to you how that moment changed me as an artist. This old dignified painter—the only painter Picasso ever spoke enviously of, however much he loved Matisse—one of the great masters of the twentieth century, wept in front of me, about how he could only paint now and couldn't draw.

I guess you didn't dare to mention your own drawing or painting to him.

No, it wasn't the right moment to hit him with my demos. *[laughs]* Mind you, I've been drawing a lot recently.

Which one do you prefer, by the way, drawing or painting?

I guess, drawing would be my answer. It's where you make the breakthroughs. Painting is where you execute what you learned in the breakthroughs. The thing about Balthus that struck me was his attempt to turn his life into art as well as his work . . . even his death. His funeral was extraordinary. Most incredible thing.

What was extraordinary about it?

It was in Rossinière, with those twenty-foot Alphorns being blown, and a horse-drawn hearse driven by an undertaker in a black top hat. The night before, his gorgeous daughter Harumi picked me up at the train station. We went to the "grand chalet." He was lying in his bed, windows open, snow blowing through. We spent some quiet time with him, and I thought: I haven't spent a lot of time with him. Why do I feel so close to this man, to this family? Then Balthus's wife Setsuko came in, and asked me the most disarming and unexpected question. She explained to me that she was a Buddhist, but wanted to become a Catholic. She said: "The cardinal's coming down from Rome. I want to be made a Catholic. Will you be my godfather?," which is really one of the most moving moments for me. Now I have a Japanese godchild in her sixties who, I might add, is getting younger by the year. I'm not a great godparent. I forget to send the Christmas cards, but she always remembers to send me. She is the angel at the top of my tree.

Did he ever say anything about music to you: your own, or music in general?

[pause] He didn't really. He didn't speak a lot about music. He didn't know our music. He knew my conversation. That's all that he knew.

He knew you were a musician.

Conversation to him was music. I don't think he had ever listened to a U2 song as well. It was the conversation we were having. Somebody told me that at one particular event he was eating with twenty or thirty of the "litterati glitterati." He banged the table and just said: "Has anyone here got anything at all interesting to say?" [laughs] Look, I'm not sure if I had. But maybe it was just a different accent, a different point of view. His work was obsessed with the concept of youth . . . and innocence, and the moment of losing it.

Rotting innocence. That's the subject of the Beach Boys' *Pet Sounds*. And of course U2's *Boy* as well. Even on *How to Dismantle an Atomic Bomb*, you've been back there again.

Yeah, exactly. I hadn't thought of that, but that is exactly right. I think he had what some of us share—a certain Tourette's syndrome. The Tourette's syndrome is where you say the words you're not supposed to say. The best example of it I know was in a church in Dublin. The vicar's wife, as people were leaving the church in the morning, would be saying: "Good-bye, Mrs. Andrews! *Fuck you, Bitch!*," "Hello! What a nice little *fucker bastard cow!*" And it's the most amazing syndrome. I think myself and Balthus had it in terms of subject matter. In his era, the only subject you couldn't approach with any curiosity was puberty. You weren't allowed to go there, so he had to go there. For me and rock 'n' roll, it was spirituality. You just can't go there, so I went there. There's a little bit of Tourette's syndrome involved, I think.

So what did Balthus leave you with?

He left me with the idea, best said by the Dalai Lama, which is: "If you want to meditate on life, you start with death." That's what the beginning is. I've always held older people to be more interesting, as I say, right through from Frank Sinatra to Willie Nelson, to Johnny Cash, to Balthus. In this sense, I have more in common with Hindu societies than with Judeo-Christian, where we are obsessed with youth.

You quoted your late friend Michael Hutchence, who said: "Stars are the worst starfuckers." But it seems to me—and it's a good thing you'd mention your relationship with Balthus—that you are a bigger fan than a star. I think of you as a superfan as much as a superstar.

Great!

Among all the stars you've met in your life, what do you think all the greatest ones had in common? I'm talking about stars in the sense of people who went on to achieve extraordinary things. It may be Frank Sinatra or it may be Balthus.

[*ponders*] Well, the older stars in the firmament, the more ancient stars in the firmament, I look at them sometimes just to understand how they're still in the sky, OK? Wisdom. My fascination is warranted just by that. But the ones whose light will remain with me long after they have burnt out are the ones that had grace. Because it's rare that the gift comes with grace. You get the gift—you don't get the grace. Some of the biggest assholes I've ever met are the most gifted. So when you're getting both together, like Louis Le Brocquy, like Nelson Mandela, like Johnny Cash, like Willie Nelson, they leave an indelible impression. Because it's "pretty girl" syndrome. Being gifted is like being born beautiful. You don't have to work a day in a year in your life for it. You were born with it. In one sense, it's like blue blood, money, gift, or beauty. They are the things that should make you the most humble, because they are not things you have earned. They are things you were given. Yet, it is my experience that they make people the most spoiled. And the people who work the hardest, and who have overcome the most obstacles in their life, who have a reason to be arrogant, who have a reason to beat their breasts are the most humble, sometimes. I can't get over that. If it's maddening to me, how mad must God be, who's giving these gifts out. I don't quite know how He dishes out those gifts, whether it's DNA or favor, but it's bewildering to me. So to make it through success and still have manners, to still have curiosity, intellectual curiosity, to still have some grace, to keep your dignity, that is really . . . rare.

You mean there are very few examples.

We'll, I'm not one, but I'd like to be. I think there are very few. In music, the hardest thing seems to be to make it through with your marbles, your mentality intact. *[laughs]* You might even be a nice person, but . . . the drugs! You're looking at people and they've one eye. You're thinking: was it really worth it? Why did you give yourself to this? And they look at you like they're Van Gogh who had to cut off his ear. I think: "You know what? I didn't need you to cut off your ear. I liked your paintings before you cut your ear off." I don't want people to climb up on a cross and die aged thirty-three to be a great musician. My heroes are survivors, the ones that lived: Bob Dylan, who kept his privacy by creating disinformation by a series of elaborate masks, by avoiding the mainstream and creating his own path through the thicket. So I love these people. I'm much more interested in them than in some new star or starlet.

I was wondering: were you ever fascinated by cult figures such as Syd Barrett. The ones who died or disappeared into seclusion when they were young?

Death cults.

Yeah.

No. Never.

I mean, it's quite widespread in rock culture, that mythology of the shooting star.

I'd rather be the North Star. As Bob says, you can navigate by it.

Speaking of stardom and fame, you know that you're a cult figure. I mean, a massive one. Right?

Is that better than celebrity?

I mean, there are so many Bono obsessives out there.

Mmh . . . hmm . . .

Isn't there a secret part of you that wonders: "Sure, I'm proud of what U2 and I have achieved. But what the hell do they see in me?" or "No, they got it all wrong. I never wanted to be a cult figure"?

I understand the mechanism . . . They say the worst fans, the most obsessive fans of magic . . . are magicians. They know they put the rabbit in the hat earlier but are still amazed when they pull it out later. *[laughs]* I have no illusions at all about myself as to why people care about me. I know why they care about me. I'm in a great band that has stuck together. I'm being open and vulnerable in my music, and I've gotten away with it. End of story. That explains it all, OK? So I swear to God I do not even consider it. These days, I sometimes forget that I'm in a band. That's the strangest thing. I've gotten used to the extra leg. I don't see it anymore. Actually, I've got to the stage now where I'm almost a civilian again.

So you're saying that whether you're a cult figure or not, it's all the same to you.

Somebody said: "Do not judge your fans by the people you meet." I think it was me. *[laughs]* I don't know, because it's not true in my case, because U2 fans are kind of easygoing. Generally we have very good relationships with our fans, but sometimes they go too far. I know the fringe people who deny you your privacy and are sort of rooting through your dustbins—and we had somebody taking our dustbins just recently—are not our audience. I do not judge our audience by them.

Bob Dylan had a guy called A. J. Weberman, who hailed himself as a "Dylanologist." He actually went through his dustbin once. May I reassure you? I'm not ready to screw a plaque reading "Bonologist" on my wall yet.

When I went to Los Angeles the first time, in 1980, I wanted to go to the house of Bob Dylan and Brian Wilson. Did I tell you that? The first thing I wanted to do. These two people's music touched my life. I could not give them back what they gave me. I wanted to pay homage, to just go and say thanks. Then, of course, I caught myself and thought: "Maybe they don't want me to say thanks." And I stopped. So I have tolerance. When people arrive at my house, I explain to them: "I can't talk to you now, because, if I do, I will be divorced." The Italians go: "It's Mamma!" And I say: "Yeah, that's exactly right. *[articulating in kind of baby talk, putting on an Italian accent]* Mamma will kill Bono! *[laughs]* It's not like I look at them and go *[imitates heavy sigh of exasperation]*. I'm not fuming like some sulking movie star, you know.

And what's your reaction to sycophants?

Sycophants? I'd like some. Thank you, please! *[laughs]* I am in a band. All my life, I'm surrounded by arguments. All my friends I've grown up with are brutally truthful. Sycophants? Where are they? Do I meet them? Of course. But not in my life as a general rule.

So what do you do?

When I meet them?

Yeah.

Yawn. *[laughs]* I mean, you will notice this. It hasn't happened here because you keep me on my toes, but I have a very low concentration span. If it's not the case, I go to sleep, because I usually haven't slept very much. So I'm not likely to spend much time with people where there is not an equal relationship.

***[looking at list]* Err, this is a good one. An early nineteenth-century French woman writer, Mme. de Staël, said: "Fame is the shining bereavement of happiness." Would you agree?**

[pause, then low voice] Oooh, wow! Myself and Simon [his friend the screen-writer Simon Carmody], we've spent two hours on such semantics last night. You should talk with him. There's a line in a song called "Mercy" that we left off this album: "Happiness is for those who don't really need it." So I can live without happiness. If that's the price of fame, good riddance! Joy, on the other hand, is not up for sale. And my joy comes from a completely different place. But you're not wrong, Michka. Somewhere there does seem a deal with the devil, concerning celebrity.

Which is?

Which is: you can have the seat at the table, but you can't leave with your sense of humor. *[laughs]* And I'm not running with it. I'm just not. In U2, it was our sense of humor that's negotiated our way through this whole jamboree. We nearly lost it in the eighties.

Really?

Yeah. We thought too much about it.

About what, exactly?

Fame, that is. What it was to be stared at, what it was to be photographed, what it was to be muttered about in a restaurant. We thought a lot about it.

And what did these thoughts bring you to?

Self-consciousness. These thoughts can bend you out of shape. You walk differently. You carry yourself differently. Ask any photographer. Ask Anton [Corbijn]. You see, a photographer understands that a face once beautiful can become ugly because of self-consciousness. The great gifts of models are not that they're more beautiful than the next person, it's that they're able to be photographed and not be self-conscious. And so the distorting lens that is fame makes people ugly and self-conscious. The lips drain of blood, the face is suddenly harrowed. The photograph is being taken, but the reason why you wanted to take the photograph has gone. In the eighties, I was that. I thought about it too much.

I would see you occasionally in the early eighties. I didn't think you were then the person that you are describing.

I wasn't like that with you, because I felt a kindred spirit, I felt relaxed, there were things we had in common. But I would feel, when I was going out, that I didn't want to let people down who looked up to me. I was trying to live up to their expectations. *[puts on angry, self-righteous voice]* "I'm not a rock star, I'm a real person!" Now, I just go: "I'm a fucking rock star. Get over it." *[laughs]* It took me a long time, but I eventually got there. If rock 'n' roll means anything: it's liberation, it's freedom.

You weren't feeling that freedom in the eighties.

The eighties were a prison of self-consciousness. "Oh, my Lord, I'm making money!" *[caricaturing cry of terror, then adopting voice of a person followed by a vampire in a horror film]* "Oh, I must be selling out. But hold on a second, I haven't screwed anyone over today. Oh, I must have!" *[laughs]* Now, I don't feel I have to prove myself to anyone. It's like: Are your songs any good? Is your band any good? That's it, mate. I can't live up to the songs. These songs are better than me. Don't fence me in as a good person, because I'm going to let you down. Hey, I'm complex, I'm an artist! I can be a jerk. I'm over it. Now I'm very happy to let people down. Now, if somebody sees me crawling out of a nightclub on all fours, they can't go *[caricaturing cry of a shocked person]*: "But YOU said!!!"—"WHAT did I say? I want you to take your fucking flashbulb out of my face, pal. *[putting on drunken voice]* And by the way, this is a friend of my wife." *[laughs]* Now I'm over it. Our family doesn't live by the media. We don't read those newspapers. Occasionally, they get under our door. Everyone's got to get their teeth filled, you know.

So how did you get your sense of humor back? What happened?

Interestingly enough, in terms of this discussion that you started out, it began in 1986, when I made up the ground I had lost in my relationship with my friends Guggi and Gavin, and we started to paint together. We used to go out on Thursday nights, painting and playacting. I found the beginnings of freedom there, that later kicked in.

Funny. You make celebrity sound like a disease you had to recover from.

The people who really revere the cult of celebrity are the ones who spend all their energy trying to avoid it. People who . . . *[suspends sentence, caricaturing sigh of someone who's tired of it all]*. Somebody told me of this character, I won't tell you who he is. He once was a completely regarded and respected figure in music. It's twenty years later. He still leaves his house *[imitates gaze of a Cold War spy in a Hitchcock film]* and shuffles into the taxi, lest the fans spot him. No one's there, no one's interested! Look, no one is a star by accident. To reach that place and cry foul is churlish. The ones that hide do that so they can be discovered. They give it too much energy.

Who or what helped you chill out?

Chrissie Hynde was a real gift to me at a time when I was thinking about it too much. She had humor and attitude: grace for the right people, and abuse for the ones who put her on too high a pedestal. Here's a mad tangent for you, Michka. I heard a story about a church, and in the congregation, there are demons, devils. The preacher keeps trying to cast out devils, but he keeps being thrown on the ground. They keep making a fool of him. So they bring on another priest. He speaks to the congregation: "You must rid your life of these devils. Who is it here?" He calls them out. They knock him down. They run amok, the organ starts playing, and all the ladies end up with their dresses over their heads. Eventually, after three or four or five exorcists, the Big Cahuna arrives. And he speaks to the devil. He says: "In the name of Jesus, I command you to identify yourself." And they all identify themselves. They're afraid. He goes: "Why are you terrorizing this place?" And the answer comes back *[putting on shy voice]*, "Because we get so much attention." *[laughs]* You know what I'm getting at? The people who run away from stardom, like me in the eighties, must be the ones who are thinking too much about it. Who do the paparazzi chase? The ones who avoid them or punch them.

Were there moments when fame made your friendships more difficult?

In the very early eighties—'82, '83.

Did you ever regain them?

Yeah, I had to go after them. I don't let go of people very easily. I still have all the people I love in my life—and some of the people I don't. *[laughs]* I'm very stubborn about people.

Do you ever wake up and forget completely about being Bono and in U2?

It's true. Most mornings, now, I really don't think about being in a band. I think about being a father, I think about being a husband, I think about being a friend.

But what else do you think about when you open your eyes in the morning and you're still lying in your bed?

Err . . . I do think about what I have, not usually in the mornings, but in the night. I do take time out to thank God. I think to myself sometimes: "What if this was gone?" I'm working as a journalist—I have a smaller house. Nothing else would have changed, because the people who are sleeping in the house or in the garden from the night before would be the same people. The newer ones, because I have developed several new friends over the years, maybe we would not have met up. But should my world change shape, all of the ones that I hold close would still be there. So I do think about it, occasionally, because it's an incredible lifestyle, not to have to worry about the things most people have to worry about, but usually in the nights. In the mornings, I'm just thinking about how I'm going to fit my life into the day, which is tricky.

Do you have what they call recurring dreams? I have one. I'm always passing an exam, and I'm failing.

Wow! Do you understand what it's about?

I think there is a word: illegitimacy. It's like I bluffed my way into my life.

Very good. You feel a fraud . . .

Yeah. A usurper.

I have a recurring dream. I've had it for all my life. It concerns two houses. One of them is boarded up, and one of them is not. They're both on the water. Not unlike these two houses in France. I've had this dream years and years before Edge and I bought this place. And oddly, for the first ten years, this house we're sitting outside now was boarded up, and that house over there was not. And we lived there. They didn't look like this in the dream, but they must have something to do with this place.

It's amazing. And what do you make of it?

I have no idea, because when we bought them, they were both boarded up. But then very quickly one wasn't.

So it's a premonition.

But they didn't look like this. They would change locations. I could even draw them. But it's the same concept. And I've had the dream recently.

Do you have a clue?

No. One is a ruin and one is a nice house.

Hard to divine that one. The forked stick doesn't seem to be going in any direction. *[laughs]* But I guess the interesting thing is that we're actually here.

This place has brought me the closest to . . . feeling free. When it was even just two ruins and we were kind of camping here, it really did teach me a way to live that I didn't know before. How do you call it in French? *Savoir-vivre?*

***Savoir-vivre* means how to behave, being polite and civilized.**

OK, no. That is the opposite. *[laughs]*

But in a way, you're right. In the broader sense, it means the art of directing one's life. So maybe you mean you've learned to taste the good things in life and savor them in style.

This is more in an unstylish, uncivilized way; but certainly how to taste them. And I've learnt it here, listening to music with my friends. The big thaw happened for me here. The ice age came to an end in 1992.

You are a different person here.

Yeah.

You have so many different personas. The one I meet in Dublin, the one who speaks on the phone, who's much looser.

On the phone? Much more. On the phone, it's about as intimate as it can get. The person's right in your ear. You got to be careful on the phone. You can leave yourself wide open.

There are a few other Bonos: the one who writes in the morning, the one who performs in front of crowds.

[low voice] Hmm . . . hmm . . .

The one who addresses U.S. congressmen, and of course the one who now sits on the board of Elevation Partners.

Hmm . . . hmm . . .

Of course the same person shelters all those different roles. But don't you ever feel like a comedian?

You mean a chameleon . . .

Well, both do the same job, don't they? I think that maybe Bono is just a trademark, and no one actually knows the person behind it, starting with you.

[laughs up his sleeve] You're a tough guy. *[long pause]* All art is an attempt to identify yourself. You try out many characters on the way to finding the one that most fits you, and therefore is you. I mean, all children do. In adolescence, you see them trying out different sides of their personality. So I'm just ex-

ploring and trying to find out what I'm capable of. What's useful for me to con-tribute to my family, my friends, and . . . the world.

You mean you're too busy doing things to understand who you really are.

I will say this: there's a noise that you see on the surface, a kind of certain frenetic hyperactive person doing lots of things, with lots of interests and ideas that I'm chasing. But below that, really, at the very bottom of that, there is . . . peace. I feel, when I'm on my own, a peace that's hard to describe, a peace that passes all understanding. Some people look really calm on the outside and serene, but deep down, they are cauldrons. They're boiling with nervous energy. All my nervous energy's on the outside. On the inside, there is a calm. If I'm left on my own, I'm not panicking to find those different peo-ple that you've described. Whoever that person is, that's the closest to who I am.

But does that calm you're describing get close to indifference sometimes?

No. It has a lot of concern for my friends. It's a very warm feeling. And it's where I go, actually. When things are really upside-down in my life, I do go there. And I'm always restored, and I'm always refreshed. That person is the closest, I sup-pose, I'm going to find, to who I am, what I'd like to be.

How do you find that person? Reading, praying?

Reading, praying, meditating. It might just be walking around. People often say to me: "How do you do all that stuff? You're doing this, you're doing that." I guess that's probably how. It doesn't take me very long to go there. You can call it a Sabbath moment, if you want, because the Sabbath Day was a day of rest. Human beings are not just what they do, but who they are. A lot of my life is about what I'm doing.

Perhaps you don't have much time to be who you really are.

That's why I really do need that seventh day. But I don't necessarily have that Sabbath on the seventh day or on a Sunday, or on a Saturday, or whatever. I just take it in moments. In those moments, I'm incredibly still, and I'm incredibly myself. *[laughs]* I can't describe it, but I don't seem to need to describe it when I'm in that moment. Negotiating a route through the world can be difficult for me. But when you take the world out of the picture and you just leave me on my own, I don't seem to feel the same need to prove myself. In the outside world, it might be as simple as: I don't like losing. I don't like wasting opportunities. There are so many! I get excited. I don't even mind the obstacle course. It's fun to run it, jumping, leaping as fast as I can. What's that? Don't wanna miss that. Can I help here? I can fix that. Gosh, I'll take that. What does that taste like? Hmmmm! What is that? Oooh, that's beautiful. What year is that? Thank you!

There are very few questions left. Who'd you give the first call to when you feel down? Or would you rather keep it to yourself?

I think it would be . . . my family . . .

You mean your wife?

"E.T. phone home!" *[laughs]*

And what do you fear the most inside yourself?

[long pause] Hmmm . . . Losing perspective . . .

Has that ever happened to you before?

I think.

How would you define losing perspective?

Well, the first signs are depression . . .

Have you ever gone through that?

Yes. It just means I'm losing perspective. I'm not seeing things in their proper shape.

Would it last for weeks? Months?

No. It might take a day out of my life, it might take a couple of days. *[pause]* It's the only real lesson I remember from my mother, which is: you stood on a piece of glass, and you were complaining too much about the cut and the blood. And she would say: "I'll take you up to Cappagh hospital—which was close by—and I'll show you people who'll never walk again." So, in a very folksy way, perspective's very important. I also think it's one of the first casualties of stardom. You think that because you're good at acting, at writing songs, at whatever, that you are a somehow more important person than somebody who, say, is a nurse, or a doctor or a fireman. This is simply not true. And in God's order of things, people like me are . . . very spoiled. I still find it confounding that the world turns people like rock stars or movie stars, artists of any kind, into heroes.

So what do you know about depression? It sure is not easy to have you opening up on that subject. I already tried it once.

Well, occasionally, I feel depression nudging its way into my life. I think that in all our conversations, you have to admit I'm not a whinging rock star, and God spare us from whinging rock stars! But, yes, you screw up, you make mistakes, you beat yourself up. But I have my faith to turn to. If I can be intimate for a second, when you asked me earlier about what happens when I wake up in the morning . . . When I wake up in the morning, I sort of put my hand out—spiritually—and I reach for what you might call God. Sometimes I don't feel God, and I feel lonely. I feel on my own, and I wonder where God is. And then *[pause]*—again, I don't want to be melodramatic about this—I ask God: "Where have You gone?" God usually replies in a way that is hard to describe: "I haven't gone anywhere. *[laughs]* Where have *you* gone? I haven't moved." Then I have to check, and I realize that I have somewhere sold myself out. It usually happens incrementally, in tiny steps. You never betray yourself—at least I never betray myself—in big dramatic bold moves, like: OK, this morning, I'm going to rob the bank, and find out where my enemy lives and tie him to his bed. You slowly move away from that person that is most like you . . .

Aren't you afraid of losing your way for more than a couple of days?

Well, especially if you are intellectually curious, of an experimental nature, you're going to pick up stones, look what's under them, and occasionally pick up the creepy crawlies, and occasionally they're gonna bite. You're going to go: "Oooh!" So that's what I do, and yeah, I'm surprised at my ability to trick myself. I find myself then waking up in a place you might call despair.

And you'd say God takes you out of there. That sounds pretty exotic to me, though.

[bursts out laughing] Great word! Yeah, right. *[keeps laughing then resumes seriousness]* You know, I have to find God. You have to put it right. That's what the problem is. You have to put it right.

So I guess you're not expecting to be speechless when you meet God? What do you expect Him to say to you?

I'm glad you said that in the affirmative. Err . . . *[laughs]* "Looking good." Thank you for your faith in me, Michka. I hope that's what God might say to me if He can get a word in edgeways: "Come on in, but please stop explaining yourself!" *[laughs]* And by the way, you asked earlier about why I didn't write this as a book. Do you think I would be writing about this in a book? No chance!

You said about your father: "He would disappear into silence and wit." I think that in your case, you do disappear into volubility and wit. *[Bono bursts out laughing]* **What do you make of that?**

Guilty, your honor.

No further comment?

"Be silent, and know that I am God." That's a favorite line from the Scriptures. "Shut Up and Let Me Love You" would be the pop song. *[laughs]* It's really what it means. If ever I needed to hear a comment, it might be that.

Ultimate question, then you're rid of me. What leaves you speechless?

[sighs . . . twenty-second pause, continuous sound of cicadas] Does singing count?

I'm afraid not. Songs have words.

But not when I start. Usually, it's just a melody and nonsense words. Hmm . . . Songs are about as succinct as I get. I'm just sparing you. *[laughs, then ponders for a moment]* "Forgiveness" is my answer.

You mean "being forgiven."

Yeah.

Sometimes you answer a question by quoting a song you've written. But would you say a subject becomes over and done with once you and U2 have written a song about it?

No, no. Again, one of the more interesting aspects of agreeing to this dialogue is you ask questions I haven't asked myself. But when you ask a question that I have asked myself, I probably already answered it.

You mean in a song? Does that mean that a few of the questions I've asked you might turn into songs someday?

Hmm, probably. They're nagging questions.

It's tough to bring this to an end. But tell me sincerely: do you genuinely think that there are things that have been revealed to you for the first time in our conversations?

[ponders for a moment, then smiles] A life unquestioned is not one you should envy.

Michka Assayas is a music journalist and novelist who lives and works in Paris. He met Bono in London in 1980, and was the first journalist to champion U2 outside Ireland and the United Kingdom. He and Bono have spent the last two years putting this book together in Dublin, Paris, and Bologna, and on the French Riviera.

WHAT YOU CAN DO TO HELP

For more information about DATA (Debit, AIDS, Trade, Africa): www.data.org
To donate to the fight against global AIDS: www.theglobalfund.org